D0119899

PRAGMATICS AND DISCOURSE

'This is an ideal book for anyone beginning the study of discourse and pragmatics; it is transparently written without being simplistic or patronising, and is thorough and detailed without being obscure or mystifying'.
Michael McCarthy, University of Nottingham.

'Joan Cutting's book provides an excellent introduction to one of the most intensively researched areas in linguistics and communication studies – pragmatics and discourse analysis. It offers the novice in the field exciting, creative and accessible ways in which to gain an understanding of the most important issues, and it also gives us old hands stimulating new food for thought.'
Richard Watts, University of Berne, Switzerland

Routledge English Language Introductions cover core areas of language study and are one-stop resources for students.

Assuming no prior knowledge, books in the series offer an accessible overview of the subject, with activities, study questions, sample analyses, commentaries and key readings – all in the same volume. The innovative and flexible 'two-dimensional' structure is built around four sections – introduction, development, exploration and extension – which offer self-contained stages for study. Each topic can also be read across these sections, enabling the reader to build gradually on the knowledge gained.

Pragmatics and Discourse:

- ❑ is a comprehensive introduction to pragmatics and discourse
- ❑ covers the core areas of the subject: context, co-text, speech acts, conversation structure, the cooperative principle, and politeness
- ❑ draws on a wealth of real texts, from *Pride and Prejudice* and *Winnie the Pooh* to *Who Wants to be a Millionaire* and mobile text messages
- ❑ provides classic readings from the key names in the discipline, from Sperber and Wilson to Fairclough, Wodak and Gumperz.

The accompanying website providing weblinks and extra resources for lecturers, teachers and students, can be found at: http://www.routledge.com/textbooks/pragmatics

Joan Cutting is Reader in Applied Linguistics at the University of Sunderland.

Series Editor: Peter Stockwell
Series Consultant: Ronald Carter

ROUTLEDGE ENGLISH LANGUAGE INTRODUCTIONS

SERIES EDITOR: PETER STOCKWELL

Peter Stockwell is Senior Lecturer in the School of English Studies at the University of Nottingham, UK, where his interests include sociolinguistics, stylistics and cognitive poetics. His recent publications include Cognitive Poetics: An Introduction (Routledge, 2002), The Poetics of Science Fiction, Investigating English Language (with Howard Jackson), and Contextualized Stylistics (edited with Tony Bex and Michael Burke).

SERIES CONSULTANT: RONALD CARTER

Ronald Carter is Professor of Modern English Language in the School of English Studies at the University of Nottingham, UK. He is the co-series editor of the forthcoming *Routledge Applied Linguistics* series, series editor of *Interface*, and was co-founder of the Routledge *Intertext* series.

OTHER TITLES IN THE SERIES:

Sociolinguistics
Peter Stockwell

Grammar and Vocabulary
Howard Jackson

FORTHCOMING:

Pragmatics and Discourse
Joan Cutting

World Englishes
Jennifer Jenkins

Phonetics and Phonology
Beverley Collins & Inger Mees

Psycholinguistics
John Field

Child Language
Jean Stilwell Peccei

Stylistics
Paul Simpson

PRAGMATICS AND DISCOURSE

A resource book for students

JOAN CUTTING

ROUTLEDGE

Taylor & Francis Group

London and New York

First published 2002 by Routledge
2 Park Square, Milton Park, Abingdon, Oxon, OX14 4RN

Simultaneously published in the USA and Canada
by Routledge
270 Madison Ave, New York NY 10016

Routledge is an imprint of the Taylor & Francis Group

Transferred to Digital Printing 2005

© 2002 Joan Cutting

Typeset in 10/12.5pt Minion by Graphicraft Limited, Hong Kong

British Library Cataloguing in Publication Data
A catalogue record for this book is available from the British Library

Library of Congress Cataloging in Publication Data

ISBN 0-415-25357-8 (hbk)
ISBN 0-415-25358-6 (pbk)

HOW TO USE THIS BOOK

The Routledge English Language Introductions are 'flexi-texts' that you can use to suit your own style of study. The books are divided into four sections:

A Introduction – sets out the key concepts for the area of study. The units of this section take you step-by-step through the foundational terms and ideas, carefully providing you with an initial toolkit for your own study. By the end of the section, you will have a good overview of the whole field.

B Development – adds to your knowledge and builds on the key ideas already introduced. Units in this section might also draw together several areas of interest. By the end of this section, you will already have a good and fairly detailed grasp of the field, and will be ready to undertake your own exploration and thinking.

C Exploration – provides examples of language data and guides you through your own investigation of the field. The units in this section will be more open-ended and exploratory, and you will be encouraged to try out your ideas and think for yourself, using your newly acquired knowledge.

D Extension – offers you the chance to compare your expertise with key readings in the area. These are taken from the work of important writers, and are provided with guidance and questions for your further thought.

You can read this book like a traditional textbook, 'vertically' straight through from beginning to end. This will take you comprehensively through the broad field of study. However, the Routledge English Language Introductions have been carefully designed so that you can read them in another dimension, 'horizontally' across the numbered units. For example, Units A1, A2, A3 and so on correspond with Units B1, B2, B3, and with Units C1, C2, C3 and D1, D2, D3, and so on. Reading A5, B5, C5, D5 will take you rapidly from the key concepts of a specific area, to a level of expertise in that precise area, all with a very close focus. You can match your way of reading with the best way that you work.

The glossarial index at the end, together with the suggestions for further reading, will help to keep you orientated. Each textbook has a supporting website with extra commentary, suggestions, additional material and support for teachers and students.

PRAGMATICS AND DISCOURSE

In this book, six numbered sub-sections in Section A introduce you to the key concepts in pragmatics and discourse study. Terms and ideas are introduced quickly and clearly, so that if you read this section as a whole, you can rapidly start to link together the different approaches to the study of language. Then you can use the numbers for each area to follow a theme through the book. For example, Unit A4 sets out key ideas in the study of the structure of conversation. In Section B, you will find that Unit 4 presents a real conversation, together with my commentary. The idea behind this is to show you in as practical a way as possible that you can develop an understanding of the approach and the skills needed to undertake a study of language using pragmatics and discourse analysis in a fairly short space of time.

The best way to learn about language in use is to investigate the area for yourself and think about your own place in it. Section C gives you a chance to do this, and following on from A4 and B4, for example, Unit C4 provides you with some genuine data of conversations and some questions to consider. Finally, in Section D, Unit 4 offers some published reading and suggestions for further study, to complete your thorough understanding of the strand.

The same pattern applies for every numbered section throughout the book. In general, I have tried to increase the cumulative difficulty through each section, and giving you guidance at the beginning and then helping you to work more independently as the book advances. My hope is that you will become enthused by the study of language in use. If, by the end, I have encouraged you to discover more about pragmatics and discourse, and if you are encouraged to take issue critically with existing studies in the area, and want to continue to explore more, then this book will have served its purpose. I hope you will find your study stimulating, enlightening, and enjoyable.

Transcription conventions:

=	Interruption
//	Overlap
/.../	Lines from original omitted to make example quoted simpler
(0.5)	Pause (number of seconds in brackets)

CONTENTS

CONTENTS **CROSS-REFERENCED**

CONTENTS **CROSS-REFERENCED**

LIST OF TABLES

ACKNOWLEDGEMENTS

I should like to thank Mr Jo Reed of the University of Birmingham and Marjory Moore of the Higher Institute of Medical Sciences of Havana for introducing me to linguistics and in particular, to pragmatics and discourse analysis. I am indebted to Professor Alan Davies and Dr Hugh Trappes-Lomax of the University of Edinburgh for training me in my research. In writing this book, I have been inspired by Mike McCarthy, and guided and encouraged by Ron Carter, Hilary Nesi, Louisa Semlyen and Peter Stockwell. I would like to say thanks to my students and colleagues in the University of Sunderland for the good times spent talking about language, and also thanks to my family and friends for their understanding and tolerance.

This book is dedicated to Meimi Sanchez Cutting, without whom I would be just a linguist.

Further acknowledgements:

R. Wardaugh, *How Conversation Words* © Blackwell Publishers Ltd, 1985

M. Hoey, *Patterns of Lexis* © Oxford University Press, 1991

R. Wodak, *Disorders of Discourse* © Pearson, 1996, reprinted by permission of Pearson Education Ltd

N. Fairclough, *Language and Power* © Pearson, 1989, reprinted by permission of Pearson Education Ltd

John Gumperz, *Discourse Strategies* © Cambridge University Press, 1982

Sperber and Wilson, *Relevance* © Blackwell Publishers Ltd, 1995

D. Tannen, *Gender and Discourse* © Oxford University Press, Inc., 1994

Nelson, Al-Batal and Echols, 'Arabic and English compliment responses: potential for pragmatic failure' © Oxford University Press, 1996

Delia Smith, *How to Cook*, courtesy of Deborah Owen Literary Ltd

INTRODUCTION

CONCEPTS IN PRAGMATICS AND DISCOURSE

CONTEXT

Understanding concepts

- ❏ introduction
- ❏ situational context
- ❏ cultural and interpersonal background context
- ❏ exophora, deixis and intertextuality

Introduction to pragmatics and discourse

Some of the approaches to language description that are described in this book involve both pragmatics and discourse analysis, others involve either one or the other. The first section of this unit defines them, and should serve as a reference guide to all the units of this book.

First, let us look at what they are *not*, by using an example. In Queen Victoria's famous words 'We are not amused', if we analyse the grammar and say that 'we' is the noun phrase subject of the sentence containing a first person plural pronoun, 'are' is the main verb agreeing with 'we', 'not' is a negative marker, and 'amused' is an adjectival complement, we are doing an analysis of the **syntax**. Syntax is the way that words relate to each other, without taking into account the world outside; it includes grammar, and does not consider who said it to whom, where, when or why.

Returning to the Queen Victoria example, if we analyse the meaning of her words in isolation, and say that 'we' indicates the person speaking, 'are' identifies a state rather than an action, and 'amused' has a sense synonymous with 'entertained' or 'distracted', we are looking at the **semantics**. Semantics is the study of what the words mean by themselves, out of context, as they are in a dictionary. Semanticists would not consider, here, the contextual background features about Queen Victoria and her courtiers, or why she said this.

Moving on to what **pragmatics** and **discourse analysis** are, we can start by saying that they are approaches to studying language's relation to the contextual background features. They would take into account the fact that, in the example, Victoria had been in a prolonged depression, caused by the death of her husband Albert, and her courtiers knew this, and that her words were a response to a joke which they had just made. Analysts would infer that the Queen's intention was to stop them trying to make her laugh and lift her out of the depression, and that her statement implies a reminder that she has to be respected as Queen. Pragmatics and discourse analysis have much in common: they both study context, text and function.

First, let us look at **context**. Both pragmatics and discourse analysis study the meaning of words in context, analysing the parts of meaning that can be explained by knowledge of the physical and social world, and the socio-psychological factors influencing communication, as well as the knowledge of the time and place in which the words are uttered or written (Stilwell Peccei 1999; Yule 1996). Both approaches focus on the meaning of words in interaction and how interactors communicate more information than the words they use. The speaker's meaning is dependent on assumptions of knowledge that are shared by both speaker and hearer: the speaker constructs the linguistic message and intends or implies a meaning, and the hearer interprets the message and infers the meaning (Brown and Yule 1983; Thomas 1995). This aspect is first explored in this book in this unit, and is followed up in Units B1, C1, and D1 Context.

The second feature that pragmatics and discourse analysis have in common is that they both look at **discourse**, or the use of language, and **text**, or pieces of spoken or written discourse, concentrating on how stretches of language become meaningful and unified for their users (Cook 1989). Discourse analysis calls the quality of being 'meaningful and unified' **coherence**; pragmatics calls it **relevance**. Both approaches would take into account the fact that Victoria's words were intended to be seen as relevant to the courtiers' joke and to anything that they should say afterwards. Units A2, B2, C2 and D2 Co-text, concerned more with the discourse analysis, focus on **cohesion**, how words relate to each other within the text, referring backwards or forwards to other words in the text. Units A5, B5, C5 and D5, dealing with the cooperative principle, an area of pragmatics, also examines **relevance theory**, which is the study of how the assumption of relevance holds texts together meaningfully.

Finally, pragmatics and discourse analysis have in common the fact that they are both concerned with **function**: the speakers' short-term purposes in speaking, and long-term goals in interacting verbally. In the example, the Queen's purpose was to stop the courtiers trying to make her laugh and to make them respect her. Units covering function are A3, B3, C3 and D3 Speech Acts. **Speech act theory** describes what utterances are intended to do, such as promise, apologise and threaten. These units also introduce **critical discourse analysis**, an ideological approach that examines the purpose of language in the social context, and reveals how discourse reflects and determines power structures.

Where discourse analysis differs from pragmatics is in its emphasis on the **structure** of text. Discourse analysis studies how large chunks of language beyond the sentence level are organised, how the social transaction imposes a framework on discourse (Coulthard 1986). It has traditionally covered the topics of **exchange structure**, or how certain situations have fixed sequences in the overall framework of the exchange, and conversation structure or how what one speaker says can influence the next speaker's response. **Conversation analysis**, which examines conversation structure, would show that Victoria's response to the joke was not the preferred response: someone telling a joke expects a response containing laughter. Similarly, it would show that her reprimand predicts an apology in response: something like 'I'm sorry Your Majesty'.

The units concerned with these two ways of approaching the structure of discourse are A4, B4, C4 and D4 Conversation. They also discuss **interactional sociolinguistics**, which combines the conversation analysis approach, in that it studies the structural patterns of conversation, with a pragmatics approach, studying social interaction, and giving importance to context, function, and social norms, conventions and principles.

Pragmatics differs from discourse analysis in the importance given to the **social principles** of discourse. Pragmatics can explain the example thus: the Queen complied with the social maxims of being relevant, precise, clear and sincere, and her courtiers expected her to do so, and she obeyed the social principles of politeness in that her request for the courtiers to stop is indirect, which aims to avoid offence. Pragmatics takes a socio-cultural perspective on language usage, examining the way that the principles of social behaviour are expressed is determined by the social distance between speakers. It describes the unwritten maxims of conversation that speakers follow in order to cooperate and be socially acceptable to each other. In this book, units dealing with these issues of pragmatics are: A3–D3 Speech acts, A5–D5 Cooperative principle, and A6–D6 Politeness principle.

Context outside text

A1.2

We said that Units A1 to D1 deal with the meaning of words in context (the physical and social world) and assumptions of knowledge that speaker and hearer share. Take a look at this excerpt from a conversation between MSc students in the common room of the Applied Linguistics department of the University of Edinburgh. DM, an Englishman, had planned to go to Spain for Easter but could not afford the tickets; he tells AF, a Scottish woman, that he ended up going hill walking in Arran, an island off the west coast of Scotland. What knowledge do they assume that they share?

AF (2) So you went to Arran. A bit of a come-down isn't it! ((laughing))
DM It was nice actually. Have you been to Arran?
AF No I've not. (1) Like to go.
DM Did a lot of climbing.
AF // (heh)
DM // I went with Francesca (0.5) and David.
AF Uhuh?
DM Francesca's room-mate. (2) And Alice's – a friend of Alice's from London (1).
    There were six of us. Yeah we did a lot of hill walking. (0.5) We got back (1) er
    (2) Michelle and I got home she looked at her knees. (0.5) They were like this.
    Swollen up like this. Cos we did this enormous eight hour stretch.
AF Uhm.

(Students on hill walking 1996)

Typically, there are three sorts of context to observe here:

❑ the **situational context**, what speakers know about what they can see around them
❑ the **background knowledge context**, what they know about each other and the world
❑ the **co-textual context**, what they know about what they have been saying. We will come to this last sort in Units A2–D2 Co-text.

Situational context

In the excerpt about hill walking in Arran, there is an example of words taking on meaning in the situational context: 'They were like this. Swollen up like this.' DM must be making a gesture that he knows AF can see, holding his hands open and rounded to show what Michelle's knees looked like. You may have seen people talking on the telephone and making gestures with their hands or face; what is funny about this is that hearer and speaker do not share the situational context, so the gestures do not add meaning to the words. The situational context is the immediate physical co-presence, the situation where the interaction is taking place at the moment of speaking. It is not by chance that DM uses the words 'like this'. 'This' is a demonstrative pronoun, used for pointing to something, an entity, that speaker and hearer can see. Any overhearer who cannot see DM's hands would not know how badly his wife's knees were swollen.

Let us look at another example, this time from the classroom, (taken from the British National Corpus, a database of 100 million words of naturally occurring written and spoken text). A male lecturer from London is explaining a mathematical problem to a male pupil from London, named Berkam:

Lecturer   Forty-nine? Why do you say forty-nine?
Pupil   Cos there's another one here.
Lecturer   Right, we've got forty-nine there, haven't we? But here there's two, okay? Now, what is it that we've got two of? Well, let me give you a clue. Erm, this here is forty, that's four tens, four tens are forty.

(BNC: jjs Bacons College lesson, date unknown)

The situational context is obviously the classroom, and presumably the lecturer and the pupil are pointing to either the blackboard or an exercise book. Their 'here' and 'there' are demonstrative adverbs indicating a figure in an equation, and the 'this here' is a demonstrative pronoun and adverb together emphatically indicating what is being puzzled over. Without the surrounding situation, the exchange makes little sense.

Let us take an example from written language, now. You may be familiar with *The English Struwwelpeter*, a book from the beginning of the twentieth century that contains moralistic, humorous tales about naughty children who are punished for their bad behaviour. There is one such tale called *The story of Augustus who would not have any soup*. The tale begins with Augustus as 'a chubby lad who ate and drank as he was told, and never let his soup grow cold'. Then one day he screams 'I won't have any soup today.' Here is verse two:

> *Next day, now look, the picture shows*
> *How lank and lean Augustus grows!*
> *Yet, though he feels so weak and ill,*
> *The naughty fellow cries out still –*
> *'Not any soup for me, I say:*
> *O take the nasty soup away!*
> *I won't have any soup today.'*

Needless to say, by the fifth day, he was dead. The poem is meant to be read to a child who can look at the book in front of them: the words 'the picture' refer to the one in the book, and the name 'Augustus' refers to the boy in the picture. The child who does not look at the picture will not know exactly 'how lank and lean' the boy is. The picture adds a visible situational context.

Background knowledge context   A1.4
The second type of context is that of assumed background knowledge. This can be either

- ❑ **cultural** general knowledge that most people carry with them in their minds, about areas of life
- ❑ **interpersonal** knowledge, specific and possibly private knowledge about the history of the speakers themselves

Cultural
In the hill-walking-in-Arran excerpt, AF and DM share cultural background knowledge about the low mountains on the island: AF does not appear surprised that DM and his friends went 'hill walking', that they could walk for eight hours there, or that the walk was strenuous enough to make somebody's knees swell. If interlocutors establish that they are part of the same group, they can assume mutual knowledge of everything normally known by group members (Sperber and Wilson 1995). Here, the community of people who could be assumed to know about the mountains are British people, or people who have visited or studied the British Isles.

Groups with mutual knowledge vary in size. The community of people who share knowledge of the cultural background context can be much larger than the one in the hill-walking excerpt. For example, most nationalities of the world would understand a conversation assuming knowledge of the fact that stars come out at night, the sun is high at midday or the world is round. The community can also be relatively small: in the hill-walking example, out of all the forty or so students on the course, maybe only AF and DM know that 'Francesca' is David's girlfriend, and that 'Alice' is from London. Take the next example, from Sawyer's book *B. B. King*:

> Rock music was born twins: there were two sibling styles, one derived from country and western, one from rhythm and blues. These two sources were distinct and separate corners of the music industry, one white, stemming from Nashville, Tennessee, and Wheeling, West Virginia, the other black, stemming from Chicago, Memphis, Houston, St. Louis, and Kansas City. But of course, there was an overlap between the two styles and their locations, especially both had wide national followings.
>
> (Sawyer 1992: 82)

The community who could fully appreciate the meaning of these words would be people with an interest in North American popular music. Within that community there will be a smaller group of people who know all about rhythm and blues, its singers and bands, its history and geography. Within that community, there will be an even smaller group of people who know every song that a particular rhythm and blues band has recorded, as well as the life histories of each of the band members. These smaller groups may form what Swales (1990) calls **discourse communities**, if they have the broadly agreed common public goals, special mechanisms for communication and they have a special lexis or vocabulary.

Going back to the hill-walking excerpt, AF and DM think that they share the cultural background knowledge about 'Arran' itself, but in any conversation the participants will have different kinds of knowledge about almost anything that is mentioned (Wardhaugh 1985: 18). AF assumes that DM shares her knowledge of it as 'a bit of a come-down after Spain'. Arran is portrayed in books as beautiful but cold, rainy and mosquito-ridden. None of this context is mentioned; something negative is assumed. AF is wrong; DM finds that 'It was nice actually.' DM then wonders if they do in fact share experience of Arran or if AF just knows about Arran from books. It emerges that she has not been there.

Talk assuming shared knowledge of cultural context often shows an assumption of shared attitude towards that cultural context. Once AF knows that DM found Arran 'nice', she modifies her attitude to make it less hostile to Arran, saying that she would 'Like to go.' When speakers modify their expressions to reflect that of their interlocutors, they can be seen as accommodating their attitudes in order to be accepted and be seen as belonging to the same group. In this case, it is the group of people who can overlook the mosquitoes and see the beauty of the island.

It is this cultural context and shared attitude of a group that can make the humour of one country difficult to understand for people of another country, and the humour of one generation incomprehensible to another generation. There is a cartoon from *Punch*, the humorous London magazine, dated 1894, that depicts a young girl in a grocer's shop; the caption reads: 'Arf a pound er margarine, please, an' mother says will yer put the cow on it, 'cos she's got company!' The context seems to be that the grocer had barrels of margarine and butter, and when he made up a packet of butter, he would put a stamp with the shape of a cow on it. The grocer and the mother would have known that margarine was cheaper, that the mother could not afford butter, and that she wanted to impress her guests by making them think that she could afford it. Today, we might not find this funny. This 1894 humour reflects a middle-class attitude of the time, that it is amusing that the poor try to hide their poverty, in vain.

Interpersonal

In the hill-walking excerpt, we see that AF and DM know who 'Michelle' is. This is the interpersonal context. DM will have told AF in a previous conversation that his wife's name is 'Michelle'; he might also have told her where 'home' is – AF might have actually been to DM's home and learnt quite a lot about Michelle. Shared interpersonal knowledge is knowledge acquired through previous verbal interactions or joint activities and experiences, and it includes privileged personal knowledge about the interlocutor.

There was a US television advertisement that featured a telephone dialogue like this:

Her How are you?
Him OK.
Her Did you have friends in and get a video last night?

Him Oh, I had friends in, but we just watched a little TV.
Her Ah right.
Him That was great. How do you feel?
Her OK.

It is only when she says 'OK' at the end that there is a flashback and we see that she won a gold medal in an Olympics event. At this point, we understand that 'Oh, I had friends in, but we just watched a little TV' means 'I had friends in to watch you playing on TV and I know you won.' The interpersonal knowledge shared by a husband and wife is obviously enormous: this is why reference to any part of it can be so vague, implicit and minimal.

Referring to context

A1.5

The act of using language to refer to entities in the context is known as **reference**: an act in which a speaker uses linguistic forms to enable the hearer to identify something. The speaker uses linguistic forms, known as **referring expressions**, to enable the hearer to identify the entity being referred to, which is in turn known as the **referent**. For example, in the words 'I went with *Francesca* (0.5) and *David*', the first person singular personal pronoun 'I' is a referring expression which refers to the person speaking, who is the referent. Similarly, the proper nouns 'Francesca' and 'David' are the referring expressions that refer to the two people whose names are Francesca and David, the latter being the referents.

When this is the first mention of the referent, in the sense that there is no previous mention of the reference in the preceding text, we call it **exophoric** reference. Exophora is dependent on the context outside the text. Thus, in

DM // I went with Francesca (0.5) and David.
AF Uhuh?
DM Francesca's room-mate. (2) And Alice's – a friend of Alice's from London (1).
      There were six of **us**. Yeah **we** did a lot of hill walking.

the 'us' and the 'we' are not exophoric because they refer back to DM, Francesca, David, Francesca's room-mate, the friend of Alice's, and Michelle, who are all mentioned elsewhere in the text. The nouns 'Francesca' and 'David' are used as exophoric reference because they point to people who are in the cultural context and are not referred to previously in the text.

In this unit, we have said that some words actually point to the entity that they refer to. If the referring expression points to the referent in the context (whether interlocutors can see it or not), it is known as **deixis**. There are three types of deixis: person, place and time. When we talk of **person deixis** we mean the use of expressions to point to a person, with the personal pronouns 'I', 'you', 'he', 'she', 'it', 'we' and 'they':

– **We** are not amused
– So **you** went to Arran.
– **We** got back (1) er (2) Michelle and **I** got home **she** looked at her knees. (0.5)
– **They** were like this.
– Yet, though **he** feels so weak and ill.

Spatial or **place deixis** is words used to point to a location, the place where an entity is in the context, as in the demonstrative adverbs 'there', 'here', the demonstrative adjectives and pronouns 'this', 'that', 'these', 'those':

- They were like **this**.
- **That** was great.
- Cos there's another one **here**.
- Right, we've got forty-nine **there**, haven't we?

Time deixis is expressions used to point to a time, as in 'next day', 'then' and 'now':

Next day, now look, the picture shows

All of these take part of their meaning from the context of utterance.

Finally, when a referring item refers to entities in the background knowledge, whether cultural or interpersonal, that have obviously been mentioned in a previous conversation or text, or have occurred in a previously shared situation or activity, we call this **intertextuality** (de Beaugrand and Dressler 1981). In the telephone call about the Olympic medal, the 'that' of 'That was great' is an example of intertextuality because it refers back to the wife's performance in the Olympic event which she won. The previous text becomes part of background knowledge. Since 'That was great' refers to an event that millions of viewers around the world would have seen, it is in the cultural context. If the husband had been referring to a romantic evening beside the fire with his wife, the intertextuality would have been interpersonal. Intertextuality is more often interpersonal than cultural, since it usually refers to knowledge gained in previous conversations between the people who are speaking. Common ground is a result of the interpenetrating biographies of the participants, of which the conversation of the moment is only a part (Coulthard 1986).

A2   CO-TEXT

Understanding concepts

❑ grammatical cohesion
   – endophoric reference
   – substitution and ellipsis
❑ lexical cohesion

A2.1   Co-textual context

We saw in Unit A1 that there are three sorts of context: the situational, the cultural and interpersonal background one, and the co-textual. This unit deals with the co-textual context, the context of the text itself, known as the **co-text**. If we go back to the hill walking excerpt:

DM   // I went with Francesca (0.5) and David.
AF   Uhuh?

DM Francesca's room-mate. (2) And Alice's – a friend of Alice's from London (1).
There were six of us. Yeah we did a lot of hill walking.

/.../ **AF** Uhm.

We can see that the personal pronouns 'us' and the 'we' refer back to Francesca, David, the room-mate and the friend, who are all mentioned elsewhere in the text. The inter-locutors assume that everyone in the conversation has enough knowledge of what they have been saying, to be able to infer who the 'us' and the 'we' include.

Grammatical cohesion

A2.2

Reference

We can look at how the co-text hangs together from the point of view of reference, which, as you will remember from Unit A1, is the act of using referring expressions to refer to referents in the context. We saw then that when there is no previous men-tion of the referent in the text, we call it exophoric reference, dependent on the con-text outside the text for its meaning. In the excerpt above, the example was the proper nouns 'Francesca' and 'David' pointing to people not already mentioned in the con-versation but in the common cultural background. The reference of the 'us' and 'we', on the other hand, is not exophoric because the pronouns refer to items within the same text; it is **endophoric** reference.

When a referring expression links with another referring expression within the co-text, we say that it is cohesive with the previous mention of the referent in the text. This is part of what is known as **grammatical cohesion**; it is what meshes the text together. Let us take another example:

> We have been established by an Act of Parliament as an independent body to elimi-nate discrimination against disabled people and to secure equal opportunities for them. To achieve this, we have set ourselves the goal of: 'A society where all disabled people can participate fully as equal citizens'.
>
> (The Disability Rights Commission leaflet 2000)

Here, the personal pronoun 'them' refers to the same referent as the noun 'disabled people' did. There is also grammatical cohesion through the phrase 'To achieve this', in which the demonstrative pronoun 'this' is cohesive with the aim of eliminating 'dis-crimination against disabled people' and 'securing equal opportunities for them'. Endophora avoids unnecessary repetition. This is how the example would have sounded without it:

> We have been established by an Act of Parliament as an independent body to elimi-nate discrimination against disabled people and to secure equal opportunities for disabled people. To achieve the aim of eliminating discrimination against disabled people and securing equal opportunities for disabled people, we have set ourselves the goal of: 'A society where all disabled people can participate fully as equal citizens'.

Notice how the repetition makes the text now seem over-explicit; it sounds as if the writer is assuming that readers will not understand unless it is all spelt out. It gives more information than is needed, as all readers would be able to make the connection between the pronoun and the phrase that it links with, if their short-term memory is functioning normally.

There are two types of endophora. In the example above, the pronouns 'them' and 'this' link back to something that went before in the preceding text. This is called **anaphora**, and it is the most frequent of the two types. The other, **cataphora**, is the opposite – pronouns link forward to a referent in the text that follows. This is in evidence in the next example, which is typical of the opening sentences of books:

> Students (not unlike yourselves) compelled to buy paperback copies of his novels – notably the first, *Travel Light*, though there has lately been some academic interest in his more surreal and 'existential' and perhaps even 'anarchistic' second novel, *Brother Pig* – or encountering some essay from *When the Saints* in a shiny heavy anthology of mid-century literature costing $12.50, imagine that Henry Bech, like thousands less famous than he, is rich. He is not.
>
> (Updike 1970: 11)

Here, we meet 'copies of his novels' before we know who 'he' is. It is only several lines later that we learn that the possessive adjective 'his' links forward to the proper nouns 'Henry Bech' in the text that comes after. As you can see, whereas anaphora refers back, cataphora refers forward. Here, it is a stylistic choice, to keep the reader in suspense as to who is being talked about. More usually, the noun that the pronoun links forward to follows soon after:

> An actor with whom she was rehearsing caught Coral Browne's fancy. Informed by a colleague that she was *most* unlikely to get anywhere with that particular man, she bet the colleague a pound that she would. Next morning, the colleague who had accepted her bet asked her, loudly and meaningfully, in the presence of the actor, 'Well, dear, do you owe me anything?' Browne replied, disappointedly: 'Seven and six'.
>
> (Rees 1999: 30)

Here, the 'she' links cataphorically with 'Coral Browne'. Since seven shillings and six pence was much less than a pound, we must suppose that she was not very successful.

We can summarise reference with a diagram to make it easier to grasp:

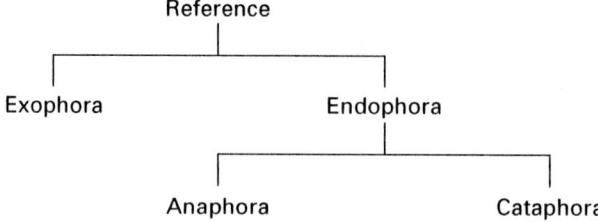

There are occasions when the noun phrases (these can be nouns or pronouns) are not linked explicitly to each other, but one noun phrase is linked to entities simply associated with the other noun phrase. This is called **associative endophora**. Here is an example from an article entitled 'Pay attention, please' from the British national newspaper the *Guardian*:

> Students are almost twice as likely to get top degree grades if they are taught by good university teachers, new research shows. The study suggests that the wide differences in numbers of firsts and upper second class degree awarded at universities comes down in large part to the work of inspirational lecturers, not just extra spending on students for books, libraries or computers.
>
> (Major and Plomin, the *Guardian*: 14 April 2001)

Here, readers can infer what 'lecturers', 'students', 'books, libraries or computers' are being talked about, by drawing from their knowledge of the **presuppositional pool** of 'universities'. Associative endophora is half way between endophora and exophora, because it depends partly on knowledge of what went before or after within the same text, and partly on background knowledge of the cultural or interpersonal context, in this case what is associated with 'universities'.

Substitution

Endophoric reference, with personal and demonstrative pronouns and possessives, is only one form of grammatical cohesion. There are two other forms: substitution and ellipsis. Let us start with **substitution**. Many of you will be familiar with the song about the characterless little houses of the pretentious lower-middle class:

> *Little boxes on the hillside,*
> *Little boxes made of ticky-tacky,*
> *Little boxes, little boxes,*
> *Little boxes, all the same.*
> *There's a green one and a pink one*
> *And a blue one and a yellow one*
> *And they're all made out of ticky-tacky*
> *And they all look just the same.*
>
> (Reynolds 1963)

The lines 'There's a green one and a pink one / And a blue one and a yellow one' contain the substitute 'one'. As with endophoric reference, substitution holds the text together and avoids repetition: 'a green one' replaces 'a green box', the 'one' 'substituting' for the 'box'. The plural substitute is 'ones'. We could have substituted 'boxes' in line 2 of the song with 'ones', and said 'Little ones made of ticky-tacky', but then the song would have lost some of its cynicism. Substitution tends to be endophoric: the noun phrase being substituted is usually in the text. Take this children's poem:

> *The Polar Bear is unaware*
> *Of cold that cuts me through:*
> *For why? He has a coat of hair.*
> *I wish I had one too.*
>
> (Belloc 1896)

Here, readers know from the co-text that, in 'I wish I had one too', the 'one' 'replaces a coat of hair'. In the next example, the substitute 'so' coheres with an adjectival phrase. It is from a *Guardian* women's page article entitled 'Does length matter?':

> Self-confidence should not be a gender issue. Boys are not born more confident than girls. Society makes them so because it traditionally values their skills and aptitudes above those of women.

(Winterson, the Guardian: 14 April 2001)

We understand 'makes them so' to mean 'makes them more confident than girls'.

Ellipsis

The other form of grammatical cohesion is **ellipsis**. Take a look at this snatch from *Catch 22*, the famous World War II novel:

> "He's afraid of you," Yossarian said. "He's afraid you're going to die of pneumonia."
> "He'd better be afraid," Chief White Halfoat said. A deep low laugh rumbled through his massive chest. "I will, too, the first chance I get. You just wait and see."

(Heller 1962)

'I will, too' is an example of ellipsis: Chief White Halfoat misses out a piece of text. He means 'I will die of pneumonia' but he omits 'die of pneumonia' because it is not necessary. Just like substitution, ellipsis avoids repetition and depends on the hearer or reader's being able to retrieve the missing words from the surrounding co-text. The same happens in the next snippet of a conversation between two 16-year-old female students:

Catriona	What was he doing? Tell me, make me cringe.
Jess	Oh nothing to make you cringe or anything. He was just, he was just like . . . saying you know just stuff that was really pretty well sick.
Catriona	Oh last night, last night he was as well with Romeo and Juliet.

(BNC: kp6 Catriona, 1993.)

Catriona uses ellipsis in her 'he was as well', and thus avoids saying 'he was saying stuff that was really pretty well sick as well'. Ellipsis is a typical feature of both spoken and written text, although it occurs more often in conversation because conversation tends to be less explicit. Even in literature, when conversation is included, it is often full of ellipsis. In the Graham Greene novel, *The Human Factor* (1978), one character asks, 'How are things with you, if I may ask, sir?' and another replies, 'My boy's sick. Measles. Oh, nothing to worry about. No complications.' Here, the informal utterances 'Measles. Oh, nothing to worry about. No complications' would have read less naturally as 'He's got measles. Oh, there's nothing to worry about. He has no complications.'

Both substitution and ellipsis can only be used when there is no ambiguity as to what is being substituted or ellipted. If there is more than one possibility, the result can be confusion. Take this advertisement, quoted by Richard Lederer in his *More Anguished English* (1987): 'FOR SALE: Very unique home in downtown Craigsville. Large lot. Many trees. One you will enjoy living in.' The advertisement reads strangely because of the fact that, since 'One you will enjoy living in' comes straight after 'Many trees', it sounds as if the 'One' contains ellipsis of 'tree' and means 'One tree you will enjoy living in.' Of course 'One' is a substitute for 'a home', but because 'Very unique home in downtown Craigsville' is far away from 'One you will enjoy living in' and the phrases have become separated by other nouns, the idea would have been more clearly expressed by repeating the noun, as in 'A home you will enjoy living in.'

Finally, it should be noted that the use of grammatical cohesion varies from genre to genre. It is much less likely to occur in texts which strive to be completely unambiguous, such as legal texts, or some kinds of instruction texts.

Lexical cohesion

A2.3

We began this unit by saying that grammatical cohesion (reference, substitution and ellipsis) holds texts together. Cohesion is also maintained by lexical cohesion. The following diagram summarises what both types of cohesion consist of, and points to what the rest of this unit will discuss, in terms of lexical cohesion.

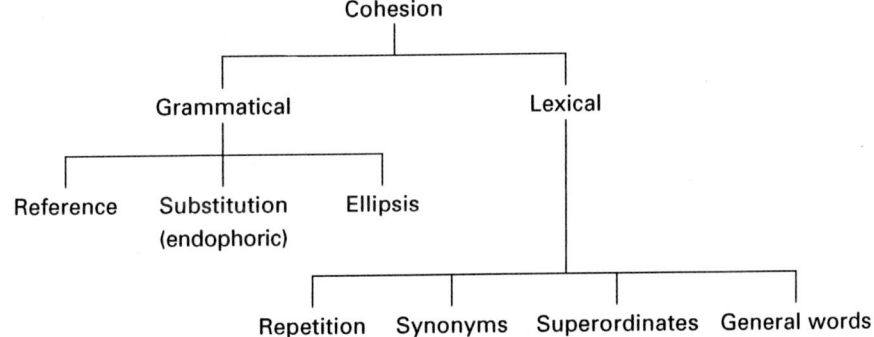

Repetition

Of all the lexical cohesion devices, the most common form is **repetition**, which is simply repeated words or word-phrases, threading through the text. Take this example from D. H. Lawrence's short story *Odour of Chrysanthemums*:

> The child put the pale chrysanthemums to her lips, murmuring:
> 'Don't they smell beautiful!'
> Her mother gave a short laugh.
> 'No,' she said, 'not to me. It was chrysanthemums when I married him, and chrysanthemums when you were born, and the first time they ever brought him home drunk, he'd got brown chrysanthemums in his button-hole.'
>
> (Lawrence 1981)

Here, the repeated 'chrysanthemums' have the effect of pounding through the text and showing how they have been a repeated and unwelcome feature of the mother's life. We saw a similar repetition in the song 'Little boxes on the hillside' above, where the repetition contributed to the cynicism. Substitution and ellipsis avoid repetition; lexical repetition exploits it for stylistic effect.

Synonyms

Instead of repeating the exact same word, a speaker or writer can use another word that means the same or almost the same. This is a **synonym**. Here, we are back to avoiding repetition. Take this little excerpt from the *Times Higher Education Supplement*

> At some 75 cm across and capable of cracking open a coconut shell with its formidable claws, the land-dwelling coconut crab is your beach lounger's worst nightmare. Fortunately for the sunbather, the world's largest terrestrial arthropod has seemingly always been confined to tropical islands across the Pacific and Indian oceans.
>
> (*THES*: 17 November 2000)

Here you will see that 'the land-dwelling coconut crab' and 'the world's largest terrestrial arthropod' are two ways of referring to the same animal, just as 'your beach lounger' and 'the sunbather' are the same person. As the saying goes, 'variety is the spice of life': using different ways of referring to an entity makes for more interesting prose or conversation.

Superordinates

In order to observe the lexical cohesion device of **superordinates**, let us go back to *Odour of Chrysanthemums* and continue with the story:

> The candle-light glittered on the lustre-glasses, on the two vases that held some of the pink chrysanthemums, and on the dark mahogany. There was a cold, deathly smell of chrysanthemums in the room. Elizabeth stood looking at the flowers.
>
> (Lawrence 1981)

Here again there is repetition of 'chrysanthemums', but then they are referred to with the words 'the flowers'. This not a synonym of 'chrysanthemums'; it is a more general term known as a superordinate, an umbrella term that includes 'pansies', 'tulips', 'roses' and so on. This is another way of avoiding repetition and still referring to the referent with a noun. Lawrence could have used a personal pronoun in endophoric reference instead, and said 'Elizabeth stood looking at them', although this might have given them less prominence, and he does want them at the centre of his story.

We can use what we know about superordinates to help explain the absurdity of the rhyme:

> *The elephant is a bonny bird*
> *It flits from bough to bough*
> *It makes its nest in a rhubarb tree*
> *And whistles like a cow*

Of course, 'bird' is the wrong superordinate for 'elephant', because 'bird' includes 'seagull', 'blackbird', 'hummingbird' and so on, and 'elephant' comes under the superordinate 'animal', which includes 'giraffe', 'cow', 'dog' and so on. Even these can be superordinates on a lower level, for example 'dog' is the overall term including 'labrador', 'poodle', 'Irish wolfhound' and so on.

General words

The last form of lexical cohesion that we are going to cover here is the **general word**. These can be general nouns, as in 'thing', 'stuff', 'place', 'person', 'woman' and 'man', or general verbs, as in 'do' and 'happen'. In a way, the general word is a higher level superordinate: it is the umbrella term that can cover almost everything. In the following, Peter, a 49-year-old chemist, uses the general noun 'place' to refer back either to the 'poly' or to the city:

> and so he went off to Wolverhampton Poly which he selected for, you know, all the usual reasons, reasonable **place**, reasonable course, a reasonable this a reasonable that t-term to do computer science which of course all the kids want to do now erm twentieth centu – no it isn't it's a sort of nineteen eighties version of wanting to be an engine driver.
>
> (BNC: kc3 Frederick, 1992)

General nouns and verbs do not carry much information, in themselves; they mostly depend on the co-text for their meaning, so are used when hearers and readers can identify what is being referred to from the rest of the text. Like pronouns, substitutes, ellipsis, synonyms and superordinates, they avoid repetition, and give just the amount of information as is necessary.

Once again, just as with grammatical cohesion, it should be noted that lexical cohesion varies from genre to genre. Synonyms and superordinates are unsuitable for some types of text, such as technical or scientific ones where key words cannot be substituted for other more general terms without precise meaning being lost.

SPEECH ACTS

A3

Understanding concepts

A3.1

- ❏ direct speech acts
- ❏ felicity conditions
- ❏ indirect speech acts
- ❏ interactional / transactional function

Introduction

A3.2

> To a hostess who had sent an invitation stating that on a certain day she would be 'At home', George Bernard Shaw succinctly replied: 'So will G. Bernard Shaw'.
>
> (Rees 1999)

At the risk of killing a funny tale, we can explain what happened here in terms of speech acts. The hostess's invitation will have read something like 'Mrs Eleanor Higgins will be at home 10 April 7–9 pm', which are words usually taken as performing the speech act of 'inviting'. Shaw pretended to read it literally as a statement of where she would be and responded in kind; his answer consisted of words to be taken as performing the speech act of 'declining'.

Speech acts

Austin (1962) defined speech acts as the actions performed in saying something. **Speech act theory** said that the action performed when an utterance is produced can be analysed on three different levels. Let us look at the action in the conversation below. Three students are sitting together at the 'bun lunch', the social occasion at which the university lays on filled rolls and fruit juice on the first day of the course, to welcome the students and help them to get to know each other.

MM   I think I might go and have another bun.
AM   I was going to get another one.
BM   Could you get me a tuna and sweetcorn one please?
AM   Me as well?

(Students at bun lunch 1996)

The first level of analysis is the words themselves: 'I think I might go and have another bun', 'I was going to get another one', and so on. This is the **locution**, 'what is said', the form of the words uttered; the act of saying something is known as the **locutionary act**. The second level is what the speakers are doing with their words: AM and MM are 'asserting' and 'expressing intentions about their own action', and BM and AM are 'requesting action on the part of the hearer'. This is the **illocutionary force**, 'what is done in uttering the words', the function of the words, the specific purpose that the speakers have in mind. Other examples are the speech acts 'inviting', 'advising', 'promising', 'ordering', 'excusing' and 'apologising'. The last level of analysis is the result of the words: MM gets up and brings AM and BM a tuna and sweetcorn bun each. This is known as the **perlocutionary effect**, 'what is done by uttering the words'; it is the effect on the hearer, the hearer's reaction.

Austin developed, but soon abandoned, the **performative hypothesis** that behind every utterance there is a **performative verb**, such as 'to order', 'to warn', 'to admit' and 'to promise' that make the illocutionary force explicit. The example above could be reformulated:

MM   I express my intention to go and have another bun.
AM   I inform you that I was going to get another one.
BM   I request you to get me a tuna and sweetcorn one.
AM   I request you to get me one as well.

Austin realised that often the implicit performatives, ones without the performative verbs, as in the original version of this dialogue, sound more natural. He also realised that implicit performatives do not always have an obvious explicit performative understood. Take the expression, 'I'll be back!' It can mean either '*I promise* that I'll be back' or '*I warn you* that I'll be back.' Searle's (1976) solution to classifying speech acts was to group them in the following macro-classes:

Declarations

These are words and expressions that change the world by their very utterance, such as 'I bet', 'I declare', 'I resign.' Others can be seen in: 'I baptise this boy John Smith', which changes a nameless baby into one with a name, 'I hereby pronounce you man and wife', which turns two singles into a married couple, and 'This court sentences you to ten years' imprisonment', which puts the person into prison.

Representatives

These are acts in which the words state what the speaker believes to be the case, such as 'describing', 'claiming', 'hypothesising', 'insisting' and 'predicting'.

The fact that girls have been outstripping boys academically has been acknowledged for the past 12 years or so   (*Glasgow Herald*: 28 November 2000)

I came; I saw; I conquered   (Julius Caesar)

Macbeth shall never vanquished be until / Great Birnam wood to high Dunsinane hill / Shall come against him   (Shakespeare: *Macbeth*)

Commissives

This includes acts in which the words commit the speaker to future action, such as 'promising', 'offering', 'threatening', 'refusing', 'vowing' and 'volunteering'.

'Ready when you are.'
'I'll make him an offer he can't refuse'   (Mario Puzo, The Godfather)

I'll love you, dear, I'll love you / Till China and Africa meet, / And the river jumps over the mountain / And the salmon sing in the street   (Auden)

Directives

This category covers acts in which the words are aimed at making the hearer do something, such as 'commanding', 'requesting', 'inviting', 'forbidding', 'suggesting' and so on.

From ghoulies and ghosties and long-leggety beasties / And things that go bump in the night, / Good Lord, deliver us.   (Scottish prayer)

Better remain silent and be thought a fool, than open your mouth and remove all possible doubt.   (Ancient Chinese proverb)

Do not do unto others as you would they should do unto you. Their tastes may not be the same   (Shaw)

Expressives

This last group includes acts in which the words state what the speaker feels, such as 'apologising', 'praising', 'congratulating', 'deploring' and 'regretting'.

A woman without a man is like a fish without a bicycle.   (Steinem)

I've been poor and I've been rich – rich is better.   (Tucker)

If I'd known I was gonna live this long, I'd have taken better care of myself.   (Blake)

Felicity conditions

In order for speech acts to be appropriately and successfully performed, certain **felicity conditions** have to be met. For Austin, the felicity conditions are that the context and roles of participants must be recognised by all parties; the action must be carried out completely, and the persons must have the right intentions. For Searle, there is a general condition for all speech acts, that the hearer must hear and understand the language, and that the speaker must not be pretending or play acting. For declarations and directives, the rules are that the speaker must believe that it is possible to carry out the action: they are performing the act in the hearer's best interests; they are sincere about wanting to do it, and the words count as the act.

To understand the need for felicity conditions, let us return to the students in their bun lunch:

MM   I think I might go and have another bun.
AM   I was going to get another one.
BM   Could you get me a tuna and sweetcorn one please?
AM   Me as well?

Here, we have a directive speech act of 'requesting' ('Could you get me a tuna and sweetcorn one please?') which can be explained using Austin's model. The context of the bun lunch is recognised by all parties: it is an appropriate place to talk about the buns and about wanting another one. The roles of participants are recognised: the students are equals and it is not a great imposition therefore for one to ask another to get a bun. The persons have the right intentions: BM and AM must trust that MM is indeed going to get a bun and they presumably intend to eat the buns that they ask for.

The situation can also be explained using Searle's model. AM and BM seem to believe that it is possible for MM to get them buns: he has functioning legs and the buns are not too far away. They genuinely want the buns to eat; they are sincere. Their words count as a request. It cannot be said that BM and AM are performing the act in MM's best interests, however, as they are performing it in their own interests. On the other hand they are not asking for the buns in order to burden MM and make it difficult for him to bring all the buns back, and if MM wants to appear sociable and obliging, he is being offered an occasion to demonstrate it.

Let us look at an example of a declarative speech act. There was a situation reported, in the local press, of a man and woman who discovered, a month before their wedding, that they had not completed all the necessary paperwork and that it would not be ready in time. They decided to go ahead with the wedding ceremony as if nothing were wrong, and sign the papers later, because all the preparations had been made and they wanted to save face. Thus, the priest's words 'I now pronounce you man and wife' did not marry them, legally because the papers were missing, and pragmatically because not all the felicity conditions were met. Although the context and roles of participants were recognised by all parties, and the priest was saying the words in the couple's best interests, the speech act was not successfully performed since they were 'putting on a show' for the benefit of the guests: the action was not carried out completely, and the priest did not believe that it was possible to carry out the action, did not have the intention to carry it out, and was not sincere about wanting to do it.

Indirect speech acts

Much of the time, what we mean is actually not in the words themselves but in the meaning implied. In the bun lunch example, we said that AM's words 'I was going to get another one' had the illocutionary force of 'expressing intentions about his own action'. It should be noted however, that he says this straight after MM's 'I think I might go and have another bun.' It is possible that in fact he was implying that he would like MM to get him one while he was there and save him the bother of getting up. If this is so, he is expressing a directive, 'requesting' indirectly, with the force of the imperative 'Get me one'; this what we call an indirect speech act.

Searle said that a speaker using a **direct speech act** wants to communicate the literal meaning that the words conventionally express; there is a direct relationship between the form and the function. Thus, a declarative form (not to be confused with declaration speech acts) such as 'I was going to get another one' has the function of a statement or assertion; an interrogative form such as 'Do you like the tuna and sweetcorn ones?' has the function of a question; and an imperative form such as 'Get me one' has the function of a request or order.

On the other hand, Searle explained that someone using an **indirect speech act** wants to communicate a different meaning from the apparent surface meaning; the form and function are not directly related. There is an underlying pragmatic meaning, and one speech act is performed through another speech act. Thus a declarative form such as 'I was going to get another one', or 'You could get me a tuna and sweetcorn one' might have the function of a request or order, meaning 'Get me one.' Similarly, an interrogative form such as 'Could you get me a tuna and sweetcorn one please?' or 'Would you mind getting me one?' has the function of a request or order, and 'Can I get you one while I'm there?' can be taken as an offer. Finally, an imperative form such as 'Enjoy your bun' functions as a statement meaning 'I hope you enjoy your bun'; 'Here, take this one' can have the function of an offer, and 'Come for a walk with me after the lunch' serves as an invitation.

Indirect speech acts are part of everyday life. The classification of utterances in categories of indirect and direct speech acts is not an easy task, because much of what we say operates on both levels, and utterances often have more than one of the macrofunctions ('representative', 'commissive', 'directive', 'expressive' and so on). A few examples will illustrate this.

The following excerpt from the novel *Regeneration* demonstrates that in indirect speech acts, it is the underlying meaning that the speaker intends the hearer to understand. Graves arrives after Sassoon at the convalescent home and asks:

> 'I don't suppose you've seen anybody yet?'
>   'I've seen Rivers. Which reminds me, he wants to see *you*, but I imagine it'll be
> all right if you dump your bag first.'
>
> (Barker 1991)

On the surface, Sassoon's reply 'he wants to see you' is a declarative with the function of a statement and a direct representative describing Rivers' wishes. However, it appears to be intended as an order or a suggestion to Graves, meaning the same as the imperative 'Go and see him', and therefore an indirect directive, and the suggestion is reinforced by the 'but I imagine it'll be all right if you dump your bag first', which is uttered as if he had actually said 'Go and see him.'

Let us take another example, this time from the thriller *Tooth and Nail*. Inspector Rebus and Inspector Flight come out of an autopsy:

> 'Come on,' he said, 'I'll give you a lift.'
>
> In his fragile state, Rebus felt this to be the nicest kindest thing anyone had said to him in weeks. 'Are you sure you have room?' he said, 'I mean, with the teddy bear and all?'
>
> Flight paused. 'Or if you'd prefer to walk, Inspector?'
>
> Rebus threw up his hands in surrender, then, when the door unlocked, slipped into the passenger seat of Flight's red Sierra. The seat seemed to wrap itself around him.
>
> 'Here', said Flight, handing a hip flask to Rebus. Rebus unscrewed the top of the flask and sniffed. 'It won't kill you,' Flight called. This was probably true. The aroma was of whisky.
>
> (Rankin 1992)

Here again, there is a declarative that is more than a statement: 'I'll give you a lift' is a direct commissive offering a lift to the inspector, and committing himself to future action, although it could be classed as an indirect directive, carrying the meaning of an imperative such as 'Get in the car.' More complex is 'Or if you'd prefer to walk.' It is not half a declarative, and yet it is not just a direct directive suggesting alternative action either, since it implies 'If you're going to be cheeky, I won't give you a lift', which is an indirect commissive making a threat. Similarly, 'It won't kill you' looks, on the surface, like a representative, describing the contents of the flask, but in fact the implication is 'Drink it', an indirect directive commanding.

Film lovers will be familiar with the film star Mae West, who once said to an admirer, 'Why don't you come up and see me some time?' She did not actually say 'Come up and see me some time.' The hearer will, however, have understood the indirect directive inviting, and ignored the direct representative asking why.

A3.6   Speech acts and society

Social dimension

Indirect speech acts constitute one of many forms of politeness, and we will look at this in more detail in Units A6–D6 when we look at all the linguistic features of politeness. Indirectness is so much associated with politeness that directives are more often expressed as interrogatives than imperatives. This is especially the case with people with whom one is not familiar. An interesting case here is the sign to the general public in many British restaurants, book shops and petrol stations, that says, 'Thank you for not smoking.' The expressive 'thanking' speech act is presumably used because it sounds more polite and friendly to all the strangers who read the sign, than the impersonal directive prohibiting 'No Smoking.'

Other factors that can make speakers use indirect directives, in addition to lack of familiarity, are the reasonableness of the task, the formality of the context and social distance (differences of status, roles, age, gender, education, class, occupation and ethnicity). Social distance can give speakers power and authority, and it is generally those of the less dominant role and so on who tend to use indirectness. Thus, in the short story *Dealer's Choice*, a young woman walks into the office of a private detective, older, male and in a position of authority:

> She got to her feet. Perched on top of her boxy four-inch heels she just about cleared my armpit.
>
> 'I've been hoping to see you, Mr Marlowe. Hoping to interest you in taking a case for me. If you have time, that is.'
>
> She made it sound as though her problem, whatever it was, was just a bit on the dull side, and that if I didn't have time for it the two of us could forget it and move onto something more interesting.
>
> (Paretsky 1995)

She expresses her request indirectly, 'hidden' under a representative describing herself 'I've been hoping to see you, Mr Marlowe. Hoping to interest you in taking a case for me.'

Cultural dimension

Speech acts and their linguistic realisations are culturally bound. The ways of expressing speech acts vary from country to country, from culture to culture. In India, for example, the expressive speech act of 'praising' and 'congratulating' a person on their appearance can be realised by the words 'How fat you are!', because weight is an indicator of prosperity and health, in a country where there is malnutrition. In Britain, these words express a speech act of 'deploring' or 'criticising', since the fashion and diet foods industries, and possibly health education, have conditioned many into thinking that 'slim is beautiful'.

Differences in speech act conventions can cause difficulties cross-culturally. The following example comes from Cuba: person A, a British woman, telephoned the work-centre of Mr Perez. B, a Cuban who worked with Mr Perez, picked up the phone:

A   Is Mr Perez there?
B   Yes, he is.
A   Em . . . can I speak to him, please?
B   Yes, wait a minute.

A's question, 'Is Mr Perez there?' is intended as an indirect request for the hearer to bring Mr Perez to the phone. B only hears an interrogative with the function of direct representative checking whether Mr Perez is at his place of work.

Limitations of speech act theory

A3.7

When we try to categorise utterances in terms of speech acts, we often find that there is an **overlap**, that one utterance can fall into more than one macro-class. Take the following example from the novel *Lord of the Flies*:

> "They're all dead," said Piggy, "an' this is an island. Nobody don't know we're here. Your dad don't know, nobody don't know –"
>
> His lips quivered and the spectacles were dimmed with mist. "We may stay here till we die."
>
> (Golding 1954)

On the face of it, this is a representative, a description of the present state of affairs, when the boy realises that they are all alone on the island, and yet it is a very emotive little outburst – the boy is obviously crying, so it could also be classified as an expressive.

Another problem with the speech act model is that it has no provision for the 'messiness' of everyday spoken language. Utterances such as 'So there you go' and 'You know' amount to fillers that say very little; this lack of semantic content makes it difficult to put in any of the classifications, as they are neither representatives nor expressives. This type of utterance has an interactional, socially cohesive function of avoiding silence, so that all speakers feel comfortable, and it intensifies the relevance of surrounding utterances. There is not a neat speech act category for it, however. Likewise, **backchannels** and feedback, the responses that show that the hearer is listening and encourage a speaker to continue talking, such as 'Was it?' and 'Oh really?', do not fit neatly into the speech act model either. They too have a social function, but do not constitute a speech act. The same goes for **incomplete sentences,** as in: 'But she didn't do the – er – no' does not fit neatly into any category. A lot of what we say in everyday speech is left unfinished either because we have no need to complete the sentence or because we are interrupted.

The following excerpt, from a law seminar on the topic of accomplice liability, taken from the British Academic Spoken English (BASE) corpus has instances of fillers, backchannels and incomplete sentences. The lecturer is L, and the students S1 and S2:

S2　// isn't that implied, surely that /.../ implied, that you're driving a car, you have duties that are implied, not necessarily don't have to only be statutory um possibility they also have to be implied sort of . . .

L　well umm, that's an argument although it is slightly odd isn't to base criminal liability on a duty that's merely implied //

S1　　　　　　　　　　　　　　　　　// yeh

S2　when I say impli . . .

L　you may not realise you have outset

(Listening to lectures, BASE 2000)

S2 has difficulty formulating his thoughts and on two occasions leaves his sentences incomplete: 'to be implied sort of . . .' and 'when I say impli . . .'. The lecturer opens his comment with a filler 'well umm'. S1 just contributes a 'yeh' backchannel. All of this is perfectly normal in real-life spontaneous talk, yet it is difficult to categorise each utterance in terms of speech acts. Units A4, B4, C4 and D4 take another approach to the analysis of real-life spontaneous talk, this one designed to take into account speech acts and also handle casual conversations.

A3.8　Macro-functions

Finally, it should be noted that over and above speech acts, there are two main macro-functions of talk. Brown and Yule (1983) describe them as the **transactional** function and the **interactional** function of language. The transactional is the function which language serves in the expression of content and the transmission of factual information.

The interactional is that function involved in expressing social relations and personal attitudes, showing solidarity and maintaining social cohesion. Speakers establishing common ground, sharing a common point of view, and negotiating role-relationships are speaking with an interactional purpose.

In fact, most talk has a mixture of the two functions: there seems to be a cline from the purely transactional to the purely interactional. At the extreme end of the transactional end is the language used when a policeman is giving directions to a traveller, and a doctor is telling a nurse how to administer medicine to a patient. At the extreme end of the interactional is what is known as 'phatic communion', language with no information content used purely to keep channels of communication open. Brown and Yule give the following example:

> When two strangers are standing shivering at a bus-stop in an icy wind and one turns to the other and says 'My goodness, it's cold', it is difficult to suppose that the primary intention of the speaker is to convey information. It seems much more reasonable to suggest that the speaker is indicating a readiness to be friendly and to talk.
>
> (Brown and Yule 1983: 3)

Brown and Yule point out that much of everyday human interaction is characterised by the primarily interpersonal rather than the primarily transactional use of language.

CONVERSATION

A4

Understanding concepts

A4.1

❑   exchange moves and IRF
❑   conversation analysis
❑   interactional sociolinguistics

Introduction

A4.2

So far, we have described language as if it existed in isolated sentences and speech acts, first one speaker talking and then another in an unrelated manner. Although we studied the way that words are grammatically and lexically cohesive with each other, we did not focus on the fact that complete utterances are linked to other complete utterances through their function, and indeed that whole chunks of conversation are related to the surrounding chunks by the structure of conversation.

Look at how the following excerpt hangs together. BM and DM, have finished their core courses, which all students did together, and moved on to options (e.g.: second language acquisition). They are in different classes and have not seen each other as much as before.

BM   You do you do Language Planning don't you?
DM   Yeah. I've stopped doing that though. I did stop doing that last week. SLA?
BM   I'm not doing that.
DM   Ah. We haven't got many things in common then.

BM Wow. We've parted ways.
DM That's right. That's right. Yes. (2)
BM We'll have to go out sometime.
DM Yeah.
BM Before we forget each other's faces. // (heh heh) It's true.
DM   // (heh heh heh)

(Students on parting ways 1996)

BM and DM are not just talking: they are talking *to each other*. Each speaker is affected by what the previous speaker said, and what each speaker says affects what the next speaker says. Thus, BM asks a question, 'You do you do Language Planning don't you?' and DM gives him an answer, 'Yeah. I've stopped doing that though.' DM's expresses regret with his 'We haven't got many things in common then', and BM agrees with him: 'We've parted ways.' BM makes a suggestion, 'We'll have to go out sometime', and DM takes him up on it with 'Yeah.' Conversations tend to occur in strings of related and combined utterances.

In this unit, we examine two approaches to looking at the structure of discourse. One analyses the **exchange structure** or the conventional overall patterns that occur when people are talking. The other is **conversation analysis**, studying the way that what speakers say dictates the type of answer expected, and that speakers take turns when they interact. The two approaches are radically different in that exchange structure starts with a model and sees how real data fits it, whereas conversation analysis starts by observing real data and describes what patterns emerge. Let us begin with exchange structure.

| A4.3 |

Exchange structure

This is the approach taken by Sinclair and Coulthard (1975) and the Birmingham School of Discourse Analysis. They studied primary school lessons and found a regular structure. Take a look at the excerpt below (from the Scottish Council for Research in Education database) from a secondary school lesson. The teacher is guiding a pupil in colouring in a map on the computer, using information from an atlas:

1	T	The mountain ranges brown. How will you know the mountain ranges?
2	C	They are brown.
3	T	How can you spot the mountain ranges? What's the clue from the key?
4	C	The mountain ranges are brown.
5	T	Only brown? Any other colours?
6	C	Purple.
7	T	Why do you think some are purple?
8	C	Because some are smaller than the others.
9	T	And the purple ones are what?
10	C	*Inaudible.*
11	T	Are they going to be the taller mountains or the shorter mountains?

12	C	Shorter.
13	T	They're actually *inaudible*. The purple ones are the taller ones. These
14		are very tall ones called the Alps, and they're purple. You've got to put
15		them on this map. Now, are you sure you know what to do here? I'll
16		leave you to get on with it.

(McPake 2000)

This is not a real conversation, in the sense of people having a casual chat. There is an unequal power balance: the teacher does all the asking and Christine does all the answering, and it is the teacher who expresses the directive (see Unit A3), ordering with 'You've got to put them on this map', and the commissive, expressing intention with 'I'll leave you to get on with it.' It is quite typical of the structure of a lesson, however, according to the Birmingham School. They said that the lesson can be broken down into five levels of structure, or ranks.

The **act** is the lowest rank. Sinclair and Coulthard build on Austin and Searle's speech act categories (see Unit A3), but Sinclair and Coulthard's acts are more general and they are defined by their interactive function. They cover the 'messiness' of spoken discourse such as fillers, as in 'you know' and 'I mean', and backchannels, as in 'Was it?' and 'Oh really?' Their categories include, for example, 'Marker', as in 'Well', 'OK' and 'Right' that mark a boundary between ideas or topics, and 'Acknowledge' which is what we have called 'backchannel'. Importantly, their categories also include acts such as 'Cue', as in 'Hands up' and 'Don't call out' which encourage a hearer to contribute, and 'Evaluate' as in 'Good' and 'Interesting' evaluating a hearer's answer. As you will appreciate, these are acts that occur more typically in a classroom than anywhere else.

Sinclair and Coulthard said that these acts tend to be carried out in a fixed order of **moves**, as they call the next rank up. They found that there are three basic moves: the **initiation** from the teacher, the **response** from the student, and the **follow-up**, which is the teacher's comment on the pupil's answer, the three moves being abbreviated to **IRF**. Lines 1–12 in the geography lesson above come in pairs of 'interrogative representative' and 'statement representative'; they would say that the structure is I–R–I–R–I–R with, in this case, no follow-up.

Each part of the IRF has characteristic acts that occur in it. What follows below is just a sample of the sort of acts:

Move acts	Function	Example
Initiation		
Inform	gives information	'The purple ones are the taller ones'
Direct	gives orders	'You've got to put them on this map'
Elicit	requests response	'Any other colours?'
Cue	encourages hearer to contribute	'Hands up', 'Don't call out'
Nominate	names responder	'Christine?' 'Johnny'
Check	checks progress	'Finished?' 'Ready?'
Prompt	reinforces directives and elicitation	'Go on', 'Hurry up'

Response

| React | non-linguistic reply to a directive | [nod], [raise hand] |
| Reply | to an elicitation | 'Purple' |

Follow-up

| Accept | shows heard correct information | 'Yes', 'Good', 'Fine' |
| Evaluate | evaluates hearer's answer | 'Good', 'Interesting' |

The combination of moves in the IRF structure is known as the **exchange**. The exchange is the series or chain of moves in the interaction. In the geography lesson, we have one exchange in lines 1–2, another in lines 3–4, another in lines 5–6, and so on. Exchanges then combine to make the **transaction**, the next rank up. Thus lines 1–2, 3–4, 5–6 combine to make the whole transaction, which is lines 1–16. The **lesson** is the highest rank; it is the speech event that consists of combinations of transactions.

The diagram below shows the rank structure for classroom interaction. Obviously a lesson contains many transactions, not just two as the diagram appears to suggest.

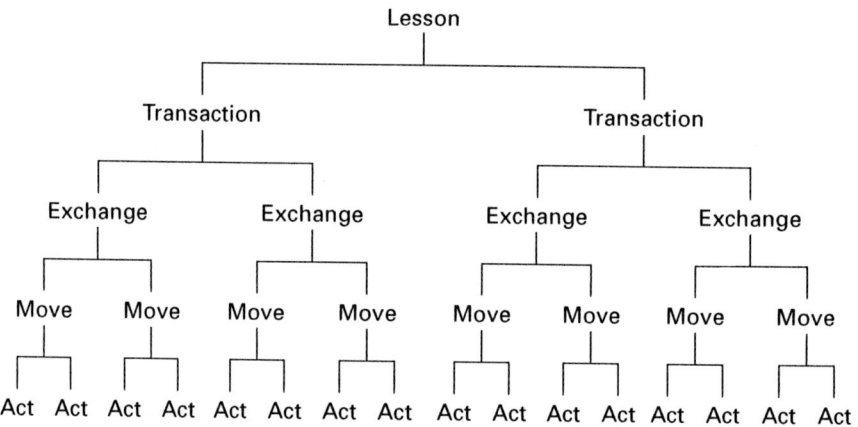

Limitations of IRF

The IRF model has certain limitations as a model of classroom transactions. It does not accommodate easily to the real-life pressures and unruliness of the classroom, such as a pupil not responding to the teacher but asking a friend to respond, or a pupil returning the question with another question. Another limitation of the model is that it reflects the traditional teacher-centred classroom, in which the teacher is permitted long turns and the students can have short turns in response but cannot interrupt. In the 2001 British classroom, pupils work in pairs and groups, and the exchanges with the teacher are generally more interactive.

The IRF approach as described here is rarely used today. It was explicitly restricted to classroom discourse and there have been adaptations of this framework (Stenstrom 1994). Although the structure of classroom transactions is not typical of everyday talk, it is typical of transactions of a formal and ritualistic nature with one person in a position of power over the other(s), controlling the discourse and planning it to a certain extent: interviews and trials are examples. The doctor–patient exchange in the medical surgery or accident and emergency ward context, is another example. The following excerpt is taken from the British TV series *Casualty*, which takes place in the accident and emergency department of a hospital. 'D' is the doctor, 'N' the nurse, and 'P' the patient:

D   So how long have you been having these symptoms?
P   This morning.
D   What did you eat yesterday?
P   What did I eat?
D   Uhuh.
P   Er. I don't really remember.
N   Er his temperature's 38.5. Pulse 1/10
D   Well have a think, because you may be suffering from food poisoning.
S   Food poisoning?

(*Casualty*, 16 December 2000)

Notice that the doctor has all the initiations and the patient all the responses. We could begin to analyse this excerpt like this: I (elicit with question), R (reply with answer), I (elicit with question), but then the pattern alters. The patient wants to avoid answering what he ate, because he stole it, and so he replies with a question 'checking': 'What did I eat?' The doctor implies a repetition of his question with his 'Well have a think, because you may be suffering from food poisoning.'

Another speech event that the IRF model has been applied to is the TV quiz show. The following excerpt is taken from the British TV programme *Who wants to be a millionaire?*, in which individual contestants are given a series of multiple choice questions, and on getting each question right are offered larger sums of money. The quiz master is Chris Tarrant and, on this occasion, the aspirant millionaire is Gary.

CT   Which of these countries is not a member of the Commonwealth: Ghana,
     Malaysia, India, the Philippines?
G   It's the Philippines.
CT   Sure?
G   Yeah.
CT   Final answer?
G   Final answer.
CT   It's the right answer. You've got eight thousand pounds.

(*Who wants to be a millionaire?*, 14 December 2000)

This transaction has such a formulaic structure that the moves used are all predictable: I (elicit with a question with four optional answers), R (reply with one of the options), I (check), R (reply reaffirming), I (check), R (reply reaffirming), F (accept/reject and reward/consolation).

Conversation analysis

A4.4

The exchange structure approach looked at discourse as a predetermined sequence. It started with the theory of a patterning of units, and showed how what people say fits the model, thus viewing conversation as a product. Conversation analysis (CA), on the other hand, takes a 'bottom-up' approach: starting with the conversation itself, it lets the data dictate its own structure. CA looks at conversation as a linear ongoing event, that unfolds little by little and implies the negotiation of cooperation between speakers along the way, thus viewing conversation a process. CA differs too, in its methodology, from discourse analysis. Whereas discourse analysis takes the concepts and terms of linguistics and then examines their role in real data, conversation analysis takes real data and then examines the language and demonstrates that conversation is systematically structured. Unlike exchange structure, both CA and discourse analysis are approaches that have evolved over the last decades and are very much alive today.

Let us start by defining conversation. Conversation is discourse mutually constructed and negotiated in time between speakers; it is usually informal and unplanned. Cook (1989: 51) says that talk may be classed as conversation when:

1   It is not primarily necessitated by a practical task
2   Any unequal power of participants is partially suspended
3   The number of the participants is small
4   Turns are quite short
5   Talk is primarily for the participants not for an outside audience

This is why classroom transactions, doctor–patient interviews and TV quiz shows are not conversations: they do not have all the properties listed here. Remember that we said, in analysing the geography lesson teacher–pupil exchange above, that it was not a conversation, because of the unequal power balance. We can add now that it was necessitated by a practical task and that it might have been partly 'for an outside audience', if the instructions were intended to be overheard by the children nearby. The doctor–patient interview was primarily necessitated by the practical task of diagnosing and prescribing, and there is unequal power in that the doctor is in control of the event. The quiz show is primarily for an outside audience.

On the other hand, the dialogue about option courses on Language Planning/ SLA, that we started this unit with, can be classified as a conversation, following Cook's list of properties. It is informal (note the 'Yeah', 'Wow') and unplanned (note the two–second pause, the sentence emerging in separate clauses as in 'Before we forget each other's faces', and the spontaneous laughter). It is neither for an outside audience (the topic is interpersonal) nor necessitated by a practical task (they are just socialising, not doing serious planning). In addition, neither BM nor DM is asserting power. They are the only two participants, and their average length of turn is just six words.

Many linguists would contend Cook's property of 'not primarily necessitated by a practical task', and say that most of what we say is outcome oriented. Even the most casual of conversations have an interactional function (see Unit D3). Casual conversations in parties can have the practical task of ascertaining whether future social cohesion is possible and desirable and, for some, whether establishing an intimate relationship is going to be feasible. Chats between old friends over coffee can have the goal of establishing norms and priorities in a particular situation, and determining the course of action that one participant should take. Other linguists, such as

Fairclough (1989: 12), would contend the property 'Any unequal power of participants is partially suspended', pointing out that in all exchanges, there is unequal power, in varying degrees, and that conversation *can* occur when there are significant power differentials between participants.

Let us now turn to the patterns that CA linguists find emerge as interaction unfolds. Typically, these are unwritten conventions about taking turns, and observable pairs of utterances.

Turn-taking

Cooperation in conversation is managed by all participants through turn-taking. In most cultures, generally speaking, only one person speaks at a time: speakers take turns, first one talking and then another. All cultures have their own preferences as to how long a speaker should hold the floor, how they indicate that they have finished and another speaker can take the floor, when a new speaker can start, whether the new speaker can overlap and interrupt, when speakers can pause and for how long. For example, Latin Americans have pauses of a fraction of a second and it is socially acceptable to overlap and interrupt, whereas North American Indians expect a two-second pause between turns, and for the Japanese it is unacceptable to interrupt.

A point in a conversation where a change of turn is possible is called a **transition relevance place** or TRP. Next speakers cannot be sure that the current speaker's turn is complete, but they will usually take the end of a sentence to indicate that the turn is possibly complete. When speakers do not want to wait until the TRP, this is called an interruption. In the following example, adapted from Gumperz (1982: 175), the moment when the interruption begins is indicated with a //.

B   yes. Tell, tell me what it // is you want
A   // umm. Um, may I first of all request the introduction please?

When hearers predict that the turn is about to be completed and they come in before it is, this is an overlap. In the following example, adapted from Schiffrin (1994: 240), the overlap is indicated with a =.

Interviewee   But not no more. Yeah =
Interviewer   = What happened to them?

Note that in the orderly classroom, doctor–patient exchange and quiz show, there are neither overlaps nor interruptions. This is partly because of the power structure and the conventions: students are not supposed to interrupt the teacher but to wait till the turn is handed to them, and quiz contestants do not usually challenge the quiz master but wait until they are asked to speak. The lack of overlaps and interruptions in the serials and shows can also be explained by the fact that they are scripted or semi-scripted: the language is more 'tidy' than real-life discourse, and the turns are pre-planned.

Each culture seems to have an unwritten agreement about the acceptable length of a pause between two turns. In any culture, if the pause is intended to carry meaning, analysts call it an 'attributable silence'. In the following sort of exchange:

A   Did you have a good time last night?
B   (3) Yeah.
A   So he asked you out then?
B   He did.

B pauses for three seconds before her 'Yeah', and A attributes to this silence an affirmative answer and very positive sentiments. In the cultures in which there is a low level of tolerance of silence between turns, if there is a lull in the conversation extending past about ten seconds, speakers tend to utter something like 'um' or 'So there you go', in order to break the silence. For those who do not know each other well, a long non-attributable silence can feel awkward.

Adjacency pairs

CA analysts say that there is a relation between acts, and that conversation contains frequently occurring patterns, in pairs of utterances known as 'adjacency pairs'. They say that the utterance of one speaker makes a certain response of the next speaker very likely. The acts are ordered with a first part and a second part, and categorised as question-answer, offer-accept, blame-deny and so on, with each first part creating an expectation of a particular second part. This is known as preference structure: each first part has a preferred and a dispreferred response. The pairs are endless; here are a few examples.

a question	has the preferred response of an answer
an offer	an acceptance
an invitation	an acceptance
an assessment	an agreement
a proposal	an agreement
a greeting	a greeting
a complaint	an apology
a blame	a denial

The dispreferred responses tend to be the refusals and disagreements. These are the more unusual responses, and they can be taken as meaningful or rude. An absence of response can be taken as the hearer not having heard, not paying attention, or simply refusing to cooperate.

We can express what is going on in the Language Planning/SLA dialogue above, in terms of CA. Their adjacency pairs are mainly 'assess' and 'agree': they want to show solidarity. Even when BM's assumption in the question 'You do you do Language Planning don't you?' is wrong, DM agrees first before putting him right: 'Yeah. I've stopped doing that though' (this is known as a pseudo-agreement). DM's 'We haven't got many things in common then' gets the preferred response of agreement in BM's 'We've parted ways' which almost echoes his sentiment. This is followed by a strong agreement: 'That's right. That's right. Yes.' Finally BM suggests an outing and DM gives the preferred response of an acceptance.

It can happen that the second part does not follow on from the first, and this is a dispreferred response. Let us imagine this scene in which a husband and wife are reading in the kitchen, while their dinner is cooking:

Wife	Do you want to test the potatoes?
Husband	Can I just finish this sentence?
Wife	Of course.

The question is not met with something that looks like an answer. Here the second question is presumably intended to mean that the husband will check the potatoes once he has finished his sentence. It implies a positive answer to the question.

Sequences

Conversation analysts claim that as speakers are mutually constructing and negotiating their conversation in time, certain sequences, which are stretches of utterances or turns, emerge. These can be pre-sequences, insertion sequences, and opening and closing sequences.

Pre-sequences prepare the ground for a further sequence and signal the type of utterance to follow. There are pre-invitations ('I've got two tickets for the rugby match . . .'), pre-requests ('Are you busy right now?') and pre-announcements ('You'll never guess!'). You will have heard conversations like the following, in which A uses a pre-invitation sequence:

A	You know that French film that's on in the Odeon?
B	Yes?
A	Do you want to go and see it tonight?
B	Yeah, why not?

In the case of an **insertion sequence**, the pairs occur embedded within other adjacency pairs which act as macro-sequences. The example above could have run like this:

A	You know that French film that's on in the Odeon?
B	Yes?
A	Do you want to go and see it tonight?
B	What time does it start?
A	Eight thirty-five
B	Yeah, why not?

Here, the 'What time does it start?' and 'Eight thirty-five' constitute the insertion sequence: the rest of the conversation could in theory stand without it, except that the timing seems to be important for B. Likewise:

Wife	Do you want to test the potatoes?
Husband	This is a really interesting article about racism in the police force. They're saying there's got to be a massive education campaign to change the way people think.
Wife	There certainly has.
Husband	Yeah.
Wife	Potatoes.
Husband	Fork.

The second part, about racism, is not a response to the first, unless the irrelevance of his answer can be interpreted as implying that he is refusing to check the potatoes.

The dispreferred response turns into an insertion sequence, because A repeats her request with 'Potatoes', and this time gets something that constitutes an acceptance ('Fork') even though it serves a double purpose of also making a request for a fork.

Finally, there are conventional **opening** structures and **closing** structures. Openings tend to contain a greeting, an enquiry after health and a past reference (as in 'How did it go last night?'). In the following example, Brenda, a 34-year-old housewife, greets Lee, a 15-year-old student, with a formulaic health enquiry:

Brenda	Hi, Lee.
Lee	Hi. Hi, Jean.
Jean	Hi, hi.
Brenda	How are you?
Lee	Not bad. I'll be in, in a minute.

(BNC: kbf Brenda, 1991)

The British and North Americans tend to have a pre-closing sequence rather than just ending with a farewell. This sequence can be long and drawn out on occasions. In the following exchange, we can see an insertion sequence within the 'saying goodbyes':

A	Anyway, I'm gonna have to go.
B	Yeah. See you.
A	See you tomorrow.
C	What time is it?
D	Oh. I've left my lights on.
E	Half three.
C	Three.
E	Tarrah.

(BNC: kb1 Albert, 1992)

Limitations of CA

One problem with CA is that there is a lack of systematicity in the sense that there is not an exhaustive list of all adjacency pairs, or a precise description of how adjacency pairs or TRPs might be recognised (Eggins and Slade 1997). In addition, researchers and students of language cannot and should not choose this form of analysis in the hope that it will lead to quantifiable results. CA sets out to be a qualitative not a quantitative approach. CA analysts do not count up instances of types of pairs, the most typical response or grammatical or lexical features, in order to find densities and distributions, or give empirical validity to claims about conversation organisation.

Another criticism levelled at CA is that it does not take into account pragmatic or sociolinguistic aspects of interaction, the background context of why and how people say what they say, the components of situation, and the features of the social world and social identity such as occupation and gender of participants. For CA analysts, text is context; they focus on the sequential progression of interaction, and the way that each utterance is shaped by the previous text and shapes the following text. CA sees context as something created in talk, rather than talk as something created by context. Although some background knowledge context is relevant to text, it is only in as much as it can be seen and understood in text. The drawback is, as Fairclough

(1989: 12) says, that conversation does not exist within a social vacuum. Conversation structures are connected to structures of social institutions and societies, and conventions of everyday action are determined by wider social structures. There is an approach to discourse analysis that takes into account both the structure of discourse and the social aspects of interaction: it is interactional sociolinguistics.

Interactional sociolinguistics

This approach takes into account the pragmatic and sociolinguistics aspects of interaction, as well as adjacency pairs, turn-taking and sequences, giving importance to the way that language is situated in particular circumstances in social life. It brings to the forefront the situational context, and the context of shared knowledge about speakers, their histories and their purpose in speaking. It looks at grammar, social structure and cultural patterns.

Interactional sociolinguistics focuses on the fact that social groups have their own ways of expressing meaning with their language. Gumperz (1982) says that language relates to context through 'contextualisation cues'. These are the linguistic features that indicate the aspects of the context relevant to what the speaker means, and that only take on their full meaning when the hearer is familiar with the rest of the context, as he or she is a member of the social group.

Let us return to the dialogue about Language Planning/SLA from the beginning of this unit. In this conversation, the speakers' adjacency pairs of agreement, echoing and acceptance, relaxed two-second pause and overlapped laughter suggest that they want to show solidarity with each other, and claim in-group membership of the student academic discourse community (Swales 1990).

Their language relates to the socio-cultural context of the course. They speak the in-group code of Edinburgh MSc Applied Linguistics students, described by Cutting (2000: 142) as containing vague and implicit grammatical and lexical features, heavily dependent on the context for their meaning. They use the general noun 'things', as in 'We haven't got many *things* in common then', referring in this context to 'option courses'. They use general 'do' verbs, as in 'You do you *do* Language Planning don't you?' and 'I've stopped *doing* that though. I did stop *doing* that last week', to mean specifically 'take the course'. They use in-group proper nouns, such as *Language Planning* and *SLA*, normally referring to fields and applications of language study, but referring here to courses.

Although the main goal of interactional sociolinguistics is not to describe the structure of discourse, and that is the main goal of conversation analysis, the two approaches are coming together now (Ochs, Schegloff and Thompson 1996), with analysts looking at the relationship between grammar and social interaction, within the larger schemes of human conduct and the organisation of social life.

THE COOPERATIVE PRINCIPLE   **A5**

Understanding concepts   A5.1

- ❑ observing maxims
- ❑ flouting and violating
- ❑ relevance theory

A5.2 **Introduction**

The excerpt that opens this unit comes from a sociological survey of the living conditions of senior citizens in Scotland, and the factors affecting their housing satisfaction. X is the interviewer and Y is a lady living in sheltered housing, (apartments for
retired people with a warden living on site, responsible keeping an eye on them and
alerting public services if help is needed):

X   Do you find the place is warm enough?

Y   Yes, oh yes. Very comfortable I think. It's all that you need really, you don't
need any more.

X   And you say that the warden is a nice person.

Y   Oh yes, you will get other opinions, but that's my opinion.

X   Well you can't please everybody can you?

Y   She's been very good to me.

X   What would the other people say?

Y   Ah well I don't know. I wouldn't like to repeat it because I don't really
believe half of what they are saying. They just get a fixed thing into their
mind. But it's always been, I mean, we had another one – this is our
second one. But if she's off ill and that it's, oh off ill again and I mean
she's got certificates to prove it. But they just seem, what irks them really
is we can't get a warden that will be overnight you see.

X   Right, sort of 24 hrs, 7 days a week.

(Wilson and Murie 1995)

Verbal exchanges, whether interviews, conversations or service encounters, tend to
run more smoothly and successfully when the participants follow certain social conventions. This interview is no exception. The interviewer asks questions and the lady
gives answers that give just the right amount of information, and which are relevant
to the question, truthful and clear. When asked if the place is warm enough, for example, her answer 'Yes, oh yes. Very comfortable I think', says all that is needed; she
is presumably being honest; she is keeping to the topic established by the interviewer;
and she is not saying anything that is ambiguous. She is following the conversational
maxims of the **cooperative principle** (Grice 1975). Let us look at the four maxims of
the principle, by seeing how they are observed.

A5.3 **Observing the maxims**

The first maxim of the cooperative principle is the maxim of **quantity**, which says
that speakers should be as informative as is required, that they should give neither
too little information nor too much. Some speakers like to point to the fact that they
know how much information the hearer requires or can be bothered with, and say
something like, 'Well, **to cut a long story short**, she didn't get home till two.' People

who give too little information risk their hearer not being able to identify what they are talking about because they are not explicit enough; those who give more information than the hearer needs risk boring them.

The second maxim is that of **quality**, which says that speakers are expected to be sincere, to be saying something that they believe corresponds to reality. They are assumed not to say anything that they believe to be false or anything for which they lack evidence. Some speakers like to draw their hearers' attention to the fact that they are only saying what they believe to be true, and that they lack adequate evidence. In

A   I'll ring you tomorrow afternoon then.
B   Erm, I shall be there **as far as I know**, and in the meantime have a word with Mum and Dad if they're free. Right, bye-bye then sweetheart.
A   Bye-bye, bye.

(BNC: kc8 Gillian, 1991)

B says 'as far as I know', meaning 'I can't be totally sure if this is true', so that if A rings up and finds that B is not there, B is protected from accusations of lying by the fact that she did make it clear that she was uncertain. Most hearers assume that speakers are not lying, and most speakers know that.

The third is the maxim of **relation**, which says that speakers are assumed to be saying something that is relevant to what has been said before. Thus, if we hear 'The baby cried. The mommy picked it up' (Garfinkel 1967), we assume that the 'mommy' was the mother of the crying baby and that she picked the baby up because it was crying. Similarly, in the following exchange:

A   There's somebody at the door.
B   I'm in the bath.

B expects A to understand that his present location is relevant to her comment that there is someone at the door, and that he cannot go and see who it is because he is in the bath. Some speakers like to indicate how their comment has relevance to the conversation, as in the following from a market research meeting:

A   I mean, **just going back to your point**, I mean to me an order form is a contract. If we are going to put something in then let's keep it as general as possible.
A   Yes.

(BNC: j97 British Market Research Monthly Meeting, 1994)

The last is the maxim of **manner**, which says that we should be brief and orderly, and avoid obscurity and ambiguity. In this exchange from a committee meeting, the speaker points to the fact that he is observing the maxim:

> Thank you Chairman. Jus – **just to clarify one point**. There is a meeting of the Police Committee on Monday and there is an item on their budget for the provision of their camera.

(BNC, j44 West Sussex Council Highways Committee Meeting, 1994)

Grice said that hearers assume that speakers observe the cooperative principle, and that it is the knowledge of the four maxims that allows hearers to draw inferences about the speakers' intentions and implied meaning. The meaning conveyed by speakers and recovered as a result of the hearers' inferences, is known as 'conversational implicature'.

A5.4

Flouting the maxims

Let us look at an example, now, of maxims *not* being observed:

> When Sir Maurice Bowra was Warden of Wadham College, Oxford, he was interviewing a young man for a place at the college. He eventually came to the conclusion that the young man would not do. Helpfully, however, he let him down gently by advising the young man, 'I think you would be happier in a larger – or a smaller – college'.
>
> (Rees 1999: 5)

Here, Sir Maurice was not adhering to the maxim of quality, since he was not really saying what he thought. Nor was he following the maxim of manner, since he was being ambiguous and contradictory. The question is, was Sir Maurice lying to the young man in order to deceive him, or was he telling a white lie, or was he just finding a nice way of letting the young man down gently? The answer hinges on whether he thought that the young man knew the painful truth and could infer what he was trying to communicate.

It is more likely that the young man did know that Sir Maurice was trying to tell him that he had failed the interview. Obviously, if Sir Maurice had said, 'You won't do', or even 'Unfortunately you're not quite good enough for this college', he might have hurt him. If the young man knew that his 'I think you would be happier in a larger – or a smaller – college' meant 'You won't do', then it is no longer a question of lying. It is a question of face saving (see Unit A6). The young man can answer, 'OK, thanks for the advice. I'll look somewhere else', and save Sir Maurice's face in his turn.

Of course, what is funny about the anecdote is that fact that Sir Maurice says 'in a larger – or a smaller – college'. His saying that the college is both too small and too large for the young man is ridiculous and implies 'go anywhere so long as it is not here'. Whether the young man perceives this or not is irrelevant to the joke, except that his lack of wit that prevents him from entering the college might prevent him from understanding the absurdity of the suggestion.

In many cultures, it can be socially unacceptable to always say exactly what is in one's mind unless one knows the hearer very well (see the explanation of the politeness principle and social variables in Unit A6). Thus, we might prefer not to say to a shop assistant, as we hand back a dress, 'This looks awful on; I don't want it after all', but rather 'I'll go away and think about it and maybe come back later.' We are not lying: we know that she knows that we have no intention of returning. Similarly, in Britain, if the response to an invitation to a romantic date is 'I'm washing my hair tonight', the inviter knows that it means, 'I'm free but I don't want to go out with you.' It is quite common and acceptable in Britain to say, 'Do you find it's getting a bit chilly in here?' and mean 'I want to put the fire on.'

When speakers appear not to follow the maxims but expect hearers to appreciate the meaning implied, as in the case of the dress shop assistant, the romantic date and the chilly room, we say that they are 'flouting' the maxims. Just as with an indirect speech act, the speaker implies a function different from the literal meaning of form; when flouting a maxim, the speaker assumes that the hearer knows that their words should not be taken at face value and that they can infer the implicit meaning.

Flouting quantity

The speaker who flouts the maxim of quantity seems to give too little or too much information. In

A   Well, how do I look?
B   Your *shoes* are nice . . .

B does not say that the sweatshirt and jeans do not look nice, but he knows that A will understand that implication, because A asks about his whole appearance and only gets told about part of it. If we look again at the old lady in the sheltered home, in the example that started this unit, we see that she flouts the maxim of quantity when she says, 'Oh yes, you will get other opinions, but that's my opinion.' The interviewer knows that she is not giving all the information that he needs in order to fully appreciate what is being said. This will be why he later asks 'What would the other people say?' The old lady knew that the interviewer would know that she had more information, but maybe she wanted to be pressured for it. It is similar to 'I had an amazing time last night', which invites 'Go on – tell me what happened then!'

Flouting quality

The speaker flouting the maxim of quality may do it in several ways. First, they may quite simply say something that obviously does not represent what they think. We saw an incidence of this in Sir Maurice's 'I think you would be happier in a larger – or a smaller – college', which flouts the maxim if he knew that the student would understand what he was getting at, and hear the message behind his words.

    Speakers may flout the maxim by exaggerating as in the **hyperbole** 'I could eat a horse', or

Lynn   Yes **I'm starving** too.
Martin   Hurry up girl.
Lynn   Oh dear, stop eating rubbish. You won't eat any dinner.

(BNC: kd6 Martin, 1992)

in which 'I'm starving' is a well-established exaggerating expression. No speaker would expect their hearer to say, 'What, you could eat a whole horse?' or 'I don't think you are dying of hunger – you don't even look thin.' Hearers would be expected to know that the speaker simply meant that they were very hungry. Hyperbole is often at the basis of humour. Take this example from *Social Studies*:

> Remember that as a teenager you are at the last stage in your life when you will be happy to hear that the phone is for you.
>
> (Leobowitz 1985: 368)

It is an exaggeration to say that adults are *never* happy to hear that the phone is for them, even though this may often be the case. Anybody reading this humorous line would know not to take it at its face value.

Similarly, a speaker can flout the maxim of quality by using a **metaphor**, as in 'My house is a refrigerator in January' or 'Don't be such a wet blanket – we just want to have fun.' Here again, hearers would understand that the house was very cold indeed, and the other person is trying to reduce other people's enjoyment. Similarly, we all know how to interpret the meaning behind the words 'Love's a disease. But curable' from *Crewe Train* (Macaulay 1926) and 'Religion . . . is the opium of the people' (Marx 1818–83). Conventional euphemisms can also be put into this category too. When people say 'I'm going to wash my hands' meaning 'I'm going to urinate', and when they say 'She's got a bun in the oven' meaning 'She's pregnant', or 'He kicked the bucket' meaning 'He died', the implied sense of the words is so well-established that the expressions can only mean one thing.

The last two main ways of flouting the maxim of quality are **irony** and **banter**, and they form a pair. As Leech (1983: 144) says, 'While irony is an apparently friendly way of being offensive (mock-politeness), the type of verbal behaviour known as "banter" is an offensive way of being friendly (mock impoliteness).'

Thus, in the case of irony, the speaker expresses a positive sentiment and implies a negative one. If a student comes down to breakfast one morning and says 'If only you knew how much I love being woken up at 4 am by a fire alarm', she is being ironic and expecting her friends to know that she means the opposite. **Sarcasm** is a form of irony that is not so friendly; in fact it is usually intended to hurt, as in 'This is a lovely undercooked egg you've given me here, as usual. Yum!' or 'Why don't you leave *all* your dirty clothes on the lounge floor, love, and then you only need wash them when someone breaks a leg trying to get to the sofa?'

Banter, on the contrary, expresses a negative sentiment and implies a positive one. It sounds like a mild aggression, as in, 'You're nasty, mean and stingy. How can you only give me one kiss?' but it is intended to be an expression of friendship or intimacy. Banter can sometimes be a tease, and sometimes a flirtatious comment. The following example contains a slightly different example of banter: BM has just told AF that his wife has got a job teaching English as a Foreign Language, and AF, herself a teacher of EFL pretends to be angry:

AF   I'm beginning to realise why em why jobs in language schools run out so sharply in the autumn and in the spring. It's all these damn MSc students and their wives, // (heh heh)

BM   // (heh heh heh heh)

AF   Now I know why I was never wanted after October.

BF   Yeah that's right. (heh)

(Students on EFL schools 1996)

This example shows that hyperbole and banter can coexist – she is both exaggerating and mock attacking. The danger with banter is that it can offend if the hearers do not recover the conversational implicature, or if they suspect that there is an element of truth in the words.

Flouting relation

If speakers flout the maxim of relation, they expect that the hearers will be able to imagine what the utterance did *not* say, and make the connection between their utterance and the preceding one(s). Thus, in

A   So what do you think of Mark?
B   His flatmate's a wonderful cook.

B does not say that she was not very impressed with Mark, but by not mentioning him in the reply and apparently saying something irrelevant, she implies it. Similarly, in the next, Noel Coward is said to have had this exchange, after his play *Sirocco* (1927) was booed:

Heckler   We expected a better play.
Coward   I expected better manners.

(Sherrin 1995: 29)

Using a Gricean analysis, we can say that the second comment seems irrelevant to the first: the heckler in the audience is talking about the play, and Coward's comment is about manners. However, Coward intends the heckler to infer that he expected better manners than booing and shouting about his play. The heckler will have understood that Coward found him as well as the others not just bad-mannered, but rude and offensive.

Grice thought that flouting the maxim of relation was possible, but many people have disagreed since (see the section below on relevance theory). Whether we observe or flout maxims, our utterances will always be taken as relevant to the preceding co-text.

Flouting manner

Those who flout the maxim of manner, appearing to be obscure, are often trying to exclude a third party, as in this sort of exchange between husband and wife:

A   Where are you off to?
B   I was thinking of going out to get some of that funny white stuff for somebody.
A   OK, but don't be long – dinner's nearly ready.

B speaks in an ambiguous way, saying 'that funny white stuff' and 'somebody', because he is avoiding saying 'ice-cream' and 'Michelle', so that his little daughter does not become excited and ask for the ice-cream before her meal. Sometimes writers play with words to heighten the ambiguity, in order to make a point, as in Katherine Whitehorn's comments in *Sunday Best* on 'Decoding the West':

> I wouldn't say when you've seen one Western you've seen the lot; but when you've seen the lot you get the feeling you've seen one.
>
> (Whitehorn 1976)

thereby implying that she agreed with the first point of view, even though she had just said that she did not agree with it.

A5.5   **Violating the maxims**

A speaker can be said to 'violate' a maxim when they know that the hearer will *not* know the truth and will only understand the surface meaning of the words. They intentionally generate a misleading implicature (Thomas 1995: 73); maxim violation is unostentatiously, quietly deceiving. The speaker deliberately supplies insufficient information, says something that is insincere, irrelevant or ambiguous, and the hearer wrongly assumes that they are cooperating.

If a speaker violates the maxim of **quantity**, they do not give the hearer enough information to know what is being talked about, because they do not want the hearer to know the full picture. The speaker is not implying anything; they are 'being economical with the truth'. You may know the Peter Sellers film in which the Pink Panther asks a hotel receptionist about a little dog beside the desk:

A   Does your dog bite?
B   No.
A   *[Bends down to stroke it and gets bitten]* Ow! You said your dog doesn't bite!
B   That isn't my dog.

The receptionist knew that he was talking about the dog in front of her and not her dog at home, yet she intentionally did not give him enough information, for reasons best known to herself. Let us take another example:

Husband   How much did that new dress cost, darling?
Wife   Less than the last one.

Here, the wife covers up the price of the dress by not saying *how much* less than her last dress.

The wife, when asked 'How much did that new dress cost, darling?' could have violated the maxim of **quality** by not being sincere, and giving him the wrong information: 'Thirty-five pounds'. If Sir Maurice Bowra, in the example above, knew that the young man did not realise that he had failed the interview because of his performance, and if he knew that the young man would believe that it was the size of the college that was wrong for him, then he could be said to be telling a lie, because he was violating the maxim of quality.

Needless to say, not all violations of the maxim of quality are blameworthy. In many cultures it is perfectly acceptable to say to a child of five, 'Mummy's gone on a little holiday because she needs a rest', rather than 'Mummy's gone away to decide whether she wants a divorce or not.' A lie that protects is a lie with good intentions, what we call a white lie. If Sir Maurice knew that the young man did not realise that he had failed the interview, and that he would be devastated to be told that, then he is telling a white lie, and covering up the truth to be kind.

In answer to 'How much did that new dress cost, darling?' the wife could have answered violating the maxim of **relation**, in order to distract him and change the topic: 'I know, let's go out tonight. Now, where would you like to go?' She could have violated the maxim of **manner**, and said, 'A tiny fraction of my salary, though probably a bigger fraction of the salary of the woman that sold it to me', in the hope that that could be taken as an answer and the matter could be dropped. In the sheltered home example, the old lady answers the interviewer's question in a way that could be said to be violating the maxim of manner, in that she says everything except what the interviewer wants to know:

X   What would the other people say?
Y   Ah well I don't know. I wouldn't like to repeat it because I don't really believe half of what they are saying. They just get a fixed thing into their mind.

Her 'half of what they are saying' is an obscure reference to the other people's opinion, and 'a fixed thing' contains a general noun containing vague reference. She may be using these expressions to avoid giving a brief and orderly answer, for the moment.

Other forms of non-observance of maxims

A5.6

Grice listed two other ways to fail to fulfil a maxim: to infringe it and to opt out. A speaker infringing a maxim or opting out of a maxim is not implying something different from the words or being intentionally misleading.

A speaker infringing a maxim fails to observe a maxim because of their imperfect linguistic performance. This can happen if the speaker has an imperfect command of the language (a child or a foreign learner), if their performance is impaired (nervousness, drunkenness, excitement), if they have a cognitive impairment, or if they are simply incapable of speaking clearly (Thomas 1995: 74). For example, there was an advertisement on British television about a woman waiting for her boyfriend Wain to find a way of proposing to her. He was so tongue-tied that she gave up waiting for him to ask her to marry him, desperately exclaiming, 'Oh Wain!' Similarly, some writing seems to observe the maxims but their unfortunate choice of words creates unintentional ambiguity. To use a newspaper quote:

> Bush, himself a former director of the CIA, said Gates would not routinely attend Cabinet meetings but would take part in sessions where intelligence was necessary for making decisions.
>
> (Lederer 1987: 77)

A speaker opting out of a maxim indicates an unwillingness to cooperate, although they do not want to appear uncooperative. They cannot reply in the way expected, sometimes for legal or ethical reasons, and they say so (e.g. 'I'm afraid I can't give you that information'). Examples are a priest or counsellor refusing to repeat information given in confidence, and a police officer refusing to release the name of an accident victim until the relatives have been informed (Thomas 1995: 74–5).

Limitations of the cooperative principle

A5.7

A major objection that one may have to Grice's model is that different cultures, countries and communities have their own ways of observing and expressing maxims for particular situations. Let us examine this with some cross-cultural examples of maxim observance. In Britain it is not acceptable to say, 'We'll call you in about two weeks' and then not call, as this would be considered a violation of the maxim of quality, whereas in some countries this is quite a normal way of flouting the maxim and saying 'We're not interested.'

The maxim of quantity is another that separates cultures. In Britain, to talk of a family member always giving them the label of the relationship, as in 'My nephew Paul came round last night', is thought to be unnecessary and an opting out of the maxim. In other cultures this is a routine form of reference. In the United States, the question 'How are you?' expects the answer 'Fine'; any interlocutor that launches into a full description of their state of health would again be thought to be violating the maxim of quantity. On the other hand, in other cultures, 'How are you?' is a genuine request after the state of health and expects a full report. The whole matter of conversational implicature in requests and suggestions may just be a very British thing. In the United States, instead of saying 'Do you find it's getting a bit chilly in here?' and flouting the maxims of quantity and manner, people tend to come straight to the point and say, 'I'm cold. Is it OK if I put the fire on?' This is related to the matter of politeness and cultural conventions. Politeness is the topic of Units A6 to D6.

The second problem with the cooperative principle is that there is often an overlap between the four maxims. It can be difficult to say which one is operating and it would be more precise to say that there are two or more operating at once. Take for example the following:

A   What did you have to eat?
B   Oh, something masquerading as chicken chasseur.

Here, B is flouting the maxim of quality by saying that his food was pretending to be something, and thus implying that it was not 'chicken chasseur'. However, it could also be said that he is flouting the maxim of manner because he does not say exactly what the 'something' was, or looked like it was. Then again, he could also be flouting the maxim of quantity because he does not give enough information to identify what he ate. In fact, all these maxims are operating together here. What he is not flouting is the maxim of relation, since his answer is relevant to the question.

In the next example, the meaning lies in a flouting of the maxims of both quantity and manner. A woman (we will call her Pat) telephoned a female friend (Melanie), whose boyfriend (Phil) was staying for the weekend, and part of the conversation ran like this:

Pat   How's it going with Phil?
Melanie   One of us thinks it's OK.

Melanie intended Pat to infer that Phil was satisfied but that she herself was not. The expression 'One of us' carried little explicit information and it was ambiguous, but Pat assumed that it was relevant to her question, and understood that Melanie was flouting maxims so that Phil, who must have been within earshot, would not know that he was the topic of conversation.

Sperber and Wilson (1995) say that all maxims can be reduced to the maxim of relation, since relevance is a natural feature of all exchanges in which speakers have the aim of achieving successful communication. The maxim of quantity can be expressed as 'give the right amount of relevant information', the maxim of quality can be stated as 'give sincere relevant information', and the maxim of manner 'give unambiguous relevant information'. We assume that everything we read and hear contains utterances that make sense, and that they are relevant to each other and form a coherent whole. Sperber and Wilson say that the principle of relevance applies without exceptions, so that it is not a question of communicators following, violating or flouting the principle.

Relevance theory

A5.8

Sperber and Wilson propose relevance theory and say that conversational implicature is understood by hearers simply by selecting the relevant features of context, and recognising whatever speakers say as relevant to the conversation. When hearers and readers make sense of a text, they interpret the connections between utterances as meaningful, making inferences by drawing on their own background knowledge of the world. They say that the purpose of communication is not to 'duplicate thoughts' but to 'enlarge mutual cognitive environments' (1995: 193).

The degree of relevance is governed by **contextual effects**, and **processing effort**. Contextual effects include such things as adding new information, strengthening or contradicting an existing assumption, or weakening old information. The more contextual effects, the greater the relevance of a particular fact. A new fact unconnected to anything already known is not worth processing, whereas a new fact taken with something already known is worth processing.

As far as the processing effort is concerned, the theory says that the less effort it takes to recover a fact, the greater the relevance. The speaker assumes which facts are accessible for the hearer and speaks in such a way that the hearer can make the correct inferences without too much effort. The context for the interpretation of an utterance is chosen by the hearer, and the speaker assumes that the facts are relatively accessible for the hearer. The hearer interprets what is said by finding an accessible context that produces 'the maximum amount of new information with the minimum amount of processing effort' (Trask 1999: 58).

To understand an utterance is to prove its relevance, and proving relevance is determined by the **accessibility** of its relevance to the addressee. Take a look at the next example, adapted from Grundy's (2000) data:

A   Well there's a shuttle service sixty pounds one way. When do you want to go?
B   At the weekend.
A   What weekend?
B   Next weekend. How does that work? You just turn up for the shuttle service?
A   That might be cheaper. Then that's fifty.

(Grundy 2000)

Here, B assumes that A will know that 'At the weekend' means 'Next weekend'. A may know that that is what he means, but she needs to be sure, since she is about to sell an air ticket. A's answer 'That might be cheaper. Then that's fifty' is not a full answer; a more explicit answer would have been, 'If you buy the shuttle now, you have a seat booked, and it's £60. If you just turn up on the day to buy the ticket, it's £50.' A assumes that B can infer all of this and fill in the missing words.

This filling in the missing words, elaborating or 'enriching the propositional form' is what Sperber and Wilson call **explicature** and they say that this is a necessary stage before implicature. They say that the explicature of an utterance consists of the propositions that are explicitly communicated by the speaker, and that some of this has to be inferred by relevance-driven processes. It is usually the context, or cognitive environment, that stops what we say being ambiguous and that helps the hearer fill in any incomplete parts of the utterance or understand the connection between utterances, and thus infer the meaning implied. Sperber and Wilson say that nothing is ambiguous, taken in its proper cognitive environment.

A5.9 | Limitations of relevance theory

Relevance theory too has its limitations, however. As Mey (1994: 81) says, the fact that Sperber and Wilson feel that their principle accounts for all Grice's maxims, and that it is without exception and irrefutable means that the notion of relevance is so encompassing that it loses its explanatory force. In fact, it could be said that everything implies something that is not said, since every utterance depends on associations and background knowledge. Even 'What's the time?' which may mean 'Don't you think we should be getting ready to go now?', 'You're boring me' or anything at all according to the context. On the other hand, some linguists feel that it is precisely the strength of relevance theory that does account for the general indeterminacy of language.

Another limitation of relevance theory is that it says nothing about interaction and does not include cultural or social dimensions, such as age, gender, status and nationality. An objection that one may have to Sperber and Wilson's model, as with Grice's cooperative principle model, is that different cultures, countries and communities have their own ways of observing and expressing maxims.

A6 | POLITENESS

A6.1 | Understanding concepts

- ❏ negative politeness
- ❏ positive politeness
- ❏ maxims of politeness

A6.2 | Introduction

In pragmatics, when we talk of 'politeness', we do *not* refer to the social rules of behaviour such as letting people go first through a door, or wiping your mouth on the serviette rather than on the back of your hand. The following anecdote is an example of the politeness that we are talking about:

> During her successful General Election campaign in 1979, Margaret Thatcher undertook various photo opportunities to emphasise how in touch she was with ordinary people. On one occasion, she was photographed standing on the back of a platform

bus*. As this was taking some time, she said, 'I'm beginning to feel like a clippie** ...'
And then, observers recall, you see the realisation in her eyes that she might have said
something patronising, so she added, '... who are all doing a *wonderful* job.'

(BBC Radio *Quote ... Unquote*, 1979)

* a double-decker bus which has an open entrance at the back
** a bus conductor, who sells and clips tickets

We refer to the choices that are made in language use, the linguistic expressions that
give people space and show a friendly attitude to them. This anecdote shows how important it is to be seen to show a friendly attitude, if one wants to save face and be appre-
ciated in return.

Politeness and face

A6.3

Brown and Levinson (1987) analysed politeness, and said that in order to enter into
social relationships, we have to acknowledge and show an awareness of the **face**, the
public self-image, the sense of self, of the people that we address. They said that it is a
universal characteristic across cultures that speakers should respect each others' expectations regarding self-image, take account of their feelings, and avoid face threatening
acts (FTAs). When FTAs are unavoidable, speakers can redress the threat with **negative politeness** (which does *not* mean being impolite!) that respects the hearer's **negative face**, the need to be independent, have freedom of action, and not be imposed
on by others. Or they can redress the FTA with **positive politeness**, that attends the
positive face, the need to be accepted and liked by others, treated as a member of the
group, and to know one's wants are shared by others.

There are many ways of achieving one's goals and showing an awareness of face.
Let us imagine that you are in a resource centre trying to find a particular website,
but since you are having no luck, you would like one of your fellow students to help
you. If you want to 'avoid an FTA', you can avoid saying anything at all. You can just
show to those around you that you are having difficulty, by sighing loudly and shak-
ing your head, and maybe someone will notice and ask if you need help.

Off record

On the other hand, you can say something. You are then faced with a choice: to do
the FTA on record or off record. If you do it **off record**, you ask for help *indirectly*,
and say, in a voice loud enough for your neighbours to hear, something like, 'I
wonder where on earth that website is. I wish I could remember the address.' This
particular off-record communicative act is an indirect speech act (see Unit A3 Speech
acts) in which you are using a declarative representative functioning as a question 'to
yourself', that also needs the hearers to interpret it as a directive, a request for help,
as in 'Help me find where on earth that website is.' This off-record communicative
act also constitutes a flouting of the maxim of quantity (see Unit A5 the cooperative
principle), if you consider that your not saying openly that you need help means that
you are not appearing to make your contribution as informative as possible. It is off
record, because if challenged to say that you were asking for help finding the website,
you could in theory deny that you were.

Indirectness in the form of indirect speech acts and maxim flouting allows a speaker to make suggestions, requests, offers or invitations quite casually, without addressing them to anyone in particular, therefore. The illocutionary force will most likely be understood by hearers, but they can choose to ignore it.

Indirectness also enables speakers to address particular people but be polite by giving them options and retreating behind the literal meaning of the words. You may recall the example of a flouting of the maxim of quantity that we saw in Unit A5, in which B was threatening A's face and passing negative judgement on his clothes:

A   Well, how do I look?
B   Your *shoes* are nice . . .

A speaker can also be polite off record by flouting the cooperative maxim of relation and dropping a hint, as in 'Interesting book. Pity I don't have $30 on me', or flouting the maxim of quality and pretending to ask a question, as in 'Why does no one ever throw out the rubbish in this house?', or flouting the maxim of manner by being obscure and ambiguous, as in 'Looks like someone had a good time last night.' Hearers usually know what is implied, but they have the freedom to respond to it or ignore it, without losing face. In this sense, the speaker is showing a great awareness of face and not imposing much at all.

On record – baldly

Back in the resource centre with your computer, you could turn to your neighbour and say, 'Mark, tell me the address for that website they were talking about this morning', and then he has to tell you, unless he wants to be rude or actually does not know the address. If a speaker makes a suggestion, request, offer, or invitation in an open and direct way, we say that they are doing an FTA **bald on record**. These are direct speech acts; such utterances tend to contain the imperative with no mitigating devices, as in 'This door handle's falling off. Fix it' or 'Give that note to me', which leave the hearers little option but do as they are told or be seen as uncooperative. For this reason, this is the most face-threatening mode of action.

On the other hand, sometimes bald-on-record events can actually be oriented to saving the hearer's face. In 'Have another biscuit' or 'Marry me', the risk that the hearer may not wish to be imposed upon is small, and the FTA is quite pleasant. The directness also makes the hearer less reluctant to threaten the speaker's face by impinging through accepting: they are unlikely to say 'No, I can't possibly deprive you of another biscuit' or 'No, I really shouldn't occupy your life like that.' For this reason, the firmer the invitation, the more polite it is (Brown and Levinson 1987). Besides, directness often indicates a wish to be seen as socially close, as we shall see later in this unit.

Most of the time, however, speakers do FTAs on record taking account of face, with 'face-management'. They can do this on record, with redressive action, using negative politeness or positive politeness.

On record – with negative politeness

Negative politeness strategies pay attention to negative face, by demonstrating the distance between interlocutors, and avoiding intruding on each other's territory. Speakers use them to avoid imposing or presuming, and to give the hearer options.

Speakers can avoid imposing by emphasising the importance of the other's time and concerns, using apology and hesitation, or a question giving them the opportunity to say no. In your resource centre, you could have asked for help with the website by saying to Mark, 'I don't want to be nuisance, but could you possibly tell me the address for that website they were talking about this morning?' Here are some more examples. Note that the politeness is quite formulaic:

> No I'm sorry but you can't have the cars and bikes out because it's tea-time and you're going home for your tea
>
> (BNC: kb8 Anne2, 1992)

Sorry to bother you. I couldn't borrow $30, could I, if you don't need it right now?

Feel free to come to the party if you have got the time.

Note that in the last two examples, the speaker gives the hearer the option to refuse the request for money and turn down the invitation to the party without losing face, by 'handing them an excuse on a plate': they needed the money and they did not have time.

The extent of the option-giving influences the degree of politeness. In many cases, the greater chance that the speaker offers the hearer to say 'no', the more polite it is. Thus in the following examples, (1) is more polite than (2):

1   I couldn't borrow $30, could I, if you don't need it right now?
2   Could I borrow $30?

In (1) the speaker's negative question 'I couldn't borrow $30 could I', which seems to anticipate a refusal, follows the negative politeness strategy that Brown and Levinson call 'be pessimistic'.

Speakers can minimise the imposition by making it seem smaller than it is, or by adding devices such as hedges that mitigate the imposition, such as 'if possible', 'sort of', 'in a way', 'I wonder', as in:

I sort of think that Fran is a bit of a mean person.

Would you mind moving just slightly? I can't see the screen very clearly.

Er, I think you may be late if you don't go now.

They can also emphasise the distance between interlocutors by impersonalising, stating the imposition as a general rule, or nominalising:

> The aim is not to – not to gain weight, and, the control has been lost when – when it's necessary to binge.
>
> (BNC: fl6 Eating Disorders: Television Discussion, date unknown)

Pre-sequences can also be used with a negative-face-saving function. As you may remember, in Unit A4 Conversation, there was this instance of a pre-invitation:

A   You know that French film that's on in the Odeon?
B   Yes?
A   Do you want to go and see it tonight?
B   Yeah, why not?

Here, A gives B space, in that she gives him time to predict what speech act is coming and stall it if he wishes.

On record – with positive politeness

Positive politeness strategies aim to save positive face, by demonstrating closeness and solidarity, appealing to friendship, making other people feel good, and emphasising that both speakers have a common goal. Asking about the website, in the resource centre, with on-record positive politeness would mean emphasising the strengthening of friendship and closeness: 'Marky, you're computer whiz-kid – I'd really appreciate it if you'd tell me the address for that website they were talking about this morning.'

Brown and Levinson (1987) say that one of the main types of positive politeness strategy is claiming common ground. Speakers can do this by attending to the hearer's interests, wants and needs. The invitation to the party that we saw in the discussion above on negative politeness can be re-phrased to show positive politeness thus

I know you hate parties, Jen, but come anyway. We'll all be there, and it'll be cool seeing if Ally is with Andrea! Come on – get a life!

This example contains many solidarity strategies – knowledge of personal information, nicknames, shared dialect and slang, and gossip. The inviter claims common ground by including her in a common activity, exaggerating the interest predicting that the party will be 'cool' and by using in-group identity markers: her familiar nickname 'Jen' and young people's in-group slang 'cool' and 'get a life'. The gossip about Ally and Andrea asserts common ground: the inviter is saying, 'I know that you know about them, just like we do.' In addition, the speaker here is optimistic that the hearer will accept the invitation.

A common positive politeness strategy is that of seeking agreement and avoiding disagreement. One way of avoiding disagreement is to use a pseudo-agreement as in:

Jean   Don't wash them and put them on the rack.
Raymond   But all //
Jean   // Get the dryer, dry them, do the tops, and then it's all done.
Raymond   Yes – yes but if you do that, your – your – your tea-towel's soaking, and at
                   the end of the night, nothing's getting dried.

(BNC: kdn Raymond2, 1992)

The speaker can also show that hearer and speaker are 'cooperators', by offering and promising, and assuming reciprocity, as in *The Love of a King*:

I will always do what you ask, but I'll never stop loving you. And if you need me, I'll always be here.

(Barnes and Dainty 1989)

Relationship with the cooperative principle

The politeness strategies sometimes conflict with the cooperative principle. Speakers can violate cooperative maxims if they want to show positive politeness. Witness:

A   How do I look?
B   Good! *(Thinks: 'Awful.')*

in which B prefers to tell a white lie and violate the maxim of quality, than offend A with the truth. Speakers may also choose to opt out of cooperative maxims to show negative politeness. In the next example, the speaker opts out of the maxim of quantity (giving more information than is required), making a polite request to strangers:

I'm terribly sorry to bother you but I couldn't help noticing that you seemed to have a copy of the programme, and I wondered whether you wouldn't mind me just having a look for a moment – I'd give it straight back to you.

Politeness maxims

A6.4

According to Leech (1983), there is a politeness principle with conversational maxims. He lists six maxims: tact, generosity, approbation, modesty, agreement and sympathy. The first and second form a pair, as do the third and fourth.

Let us start with the maxims of tact and generosity. The **tact** maxim ('perhaps the most important kind of politeness in English-speaking society', Leech 1983: 107) focuses on the hearer, and says 'minimise cost to other' and 'maximise benefit to other'. The first part of this maxim fits in with Brown and Levinson's negative politeness strategy of minimising the imposition, and the second part reflects the positive politeness strategy of attending to the hearer's interests, wants and needs:

'Could you I interrupt you for half a second – what was that website address?'
'If I could just clarify this then.'
'Would you like a birdtable commemorating your contribution to this historic bridge?'
(BNC: g2r, date unknown)

The paradox is that if the hearer is to accept the offer of the birdtable, they are deprived of the possibility of 'minimising cost to other'. If they both try to be polite at once, in this sense, they will reach a stalemate. The maxim of **generosity**, is the flip-side of the tact maxim since it focuses on the speaker, and says 'minimise benefit to self' and 'maximise cost to self'. This is present in:

'Could I copy down the website address?'
'You relax and let me do the dishes.'
'I'm sorry but I'll just have to lift you in then, one, two, three up he goes, ooh!'
(BNC: KB8 Anne2)

Let us move on to the second pair: approbation (other) and modesty (self). The maxim of **approbation** says 'minimise dispraise of other' and 'maximise praise of other'. The first part of the maxim is somewhat similar to the politeness strategy of avoiding disagreement. The second part fits in with the positive politeness strategy of making other people feel good by showing solidarity. We have:

'Mark, you're very efficient and make notes of everything – you must have a copy of that website address we were given today.'
'I heard you singing at the karaoke last night. It was, um . . . different.'

You may remember Sir Maurice Bewra's comment to the young man applying to his college (see Unit A5 The cooperative principle); he avoided telling him that he was no good by reducing his dispraise to an absolute minimum, with 'I think you would be happier in a larger – or a smaller – college.'

The **modesty** maxim, on the other hand, says 'minimise praise of self' and 'maximise dispraise of self'.

'Oh, I'm so stupid – I didn't make a note of that website address! Did you?'

> 'I don't dislike going to the dentist, but, but I'm terrible with dentists, hairdressers, and all these things, though, I work quite hard, I never really sort of . . . .'
>
> (BNC: kcb Graeme, 1992)

Modesty is possibly a more complex maxim than the others, since the maxim of quality can sometimes be violated in observing it. Cutting (1998) found that in conferences, members of the audience preface their questions to the speaker with self-deprecating expressions such as:

'A very obvious question from a non-specialist . . .'
'There is an idiot question I want to ask you . . .'
'Um, I don't know much about this area but I think that . . .'

Although on the surface, the questioners seem to be saving their own face, they are also saving the face of the speaker by reducing the threat of their question. The following story from *George* illustrates well how exaggerated modesty can be a counterbalance to exaggerated praise.

> In the 1930's, a critic described the actor Robert Donat as a 'half-Greek god who had winged his way from Olympus'. Donat's response was to sigh, 'Actually, I'm a half-Pole who's winged his way from Withington, Manchester.'
>
> (Williams 1973)

The last two maxims do not form a pair and Leech gives them less importance than the others. The maxim of **agreement**, 'minimise disagreement between self and other' and 'maximise agreement between self and other', is in line with Brown and Levinson's positive politeness strategies of 'seek agreement' and 'avoid disagreement', to which *they* attach great importance. We saw an example of this above in:

Raymond   Yes – yes but if you do that, your – your – your tea-towel's soaking, and at the end of the night, nothing's getting dried.

The **sympathy** maxim – 'minimise antipathy between self and other' and 'maximise sympathy between self and other' includes such polite speech acts as congratulate, commiserate and express condolences, as in, 'I was sorry to hear about your father.' This small group of speech acts is already taken care of in Brown and Levinson's positive politeness strategy of attending to the hearer's interests, wants and needs. Note that the speaker does not say 'I was sorry to hear about your father's *death*.' Speakers often soften the distress and embarrassment with euphemisms. We saw a polite euphemism when we discussed metaphors flouting the maxim of quality (see Unit A5 The cooperative principle): 'I'm going to wash my hands' meaning 'I'm going to urinate.'

Very close to this is a maxim proposed by Cruse (2000: 366): **consideration**, which is 'minimise discomfort/displeasure of other', and 'maximise comfort/pleasure of other'. Cruse points out that this is Leech's Pollyanna Principle – 'always look on the bright side of life', by softening painful, distressing, embarrassing, shocking events. We are back to Brown and Levinson's positive politeness strategy of making other people feel good. An amusing tale told by Billy Connolly, the Scottish actor and stand-up comedian, will serve as an example:

> Seeking to cheer up a patient in hospital, the visitor told her: 'You're lucky to be in here. It's pelting outside.'
>
> (Rees 1999: 108)

Overlaps and gaps

A6.5

Brown and Levinson differ from Leech, in that they are social psychologists who start from data, and he takes a philosophical approach starting from principles. This unit has shown, however, that there is considerable overlap between the categories of Brown and Levinson's model and the categories of Leech's model. There is also overlap within both Brown and Levinson's model and Leech's: the categories themselves are not mutually exclusive.

One utterance can contain both positive and negative politeness. The speaker in the following example mixes the two quite successfully: 'Could you be a pal and give me a lift home? Don't bother if you're not going my way.' Similarly, one utterance can obey two or more maxims. In the following, the speaker observes both tact and generosity: 'Have as many cakes as you want.'

Another criticism that could be levelled at Leech's model is that a new maxim could be added for every new situation that occurs. Remember that we saw that Cruse wanted to add a consideration maxim. There should also possibly be a **patience** maxim, which says 'minimise the urgency for other' and 'maximise the lack of urgency for other'. To give an example: 'Could I take a quick look at your paper? No hurry – whenever you're finished with it'. There may be endless gaps not covered by the maxims; no model can describe all human interactions.

Politeness and context

A6.6

Form and function

Politeness is a pragmatic phenomenon. Politeness lies not in the form and the words themselves, but in their function and intended social meaning. In the following, the form is polite but the intention is not:

Do me a favour – piss off.   (*The Older Woman*: BBC Radio 4 1994)

So, if you'd be as kind as to shut up, I'd appreciate it.   (Elmore: *Hombre* 1989)

If speakers use more polite forms than the context requires, hearers might suspect that there is an intention other than that of redressing an FTA, as in the playwright Richard Brinsley's invitation to a young lady (attributed in *The Perfect Hostess* 1980), 'Won't you come into my garden? I would like my roses to see you', which is aimed to flatter.

Another example of an inappropriate use of polite forms is the man's request to his pet, 'Cat, I wonder if you could possibly let me have my seat back?', which is simply meant to entertain whoever happens to be listening.

Politeness is not the same as **deference**, which is a polite form expressing distance from and respect for people of a higher status, and does not usually include an element of choice. Deference is built into languages such as Korean and Japanese, and can be seen in the pronouns of many European languages (*tu/vous, tú/Usted, du/sie*). It is rare to find it grammatically signalled in English, although it is present in honorifics such as 'Sir' and 'Madam', and, as the next example shows, they can play an important role:

> Shortly after being made a Dame of the British Empire, Edith Evans was appearing on the stage and heard herself addressed by a call-boy with the words, 'Ten minutes, Miss Evans.' She exclaimed: 'Miss Evans! It'll be Edie next!'
>
> (Wogan, BBC Radio: *Quote . . . Unquote* 1991)

Moreover, it is possible to be deferential without being polite (Thomas 1995: 153), as in the next example, in which Brian Wilson, Labour MP for Cunningham North, was addressing Nicholas Soames, Conservative MP for Crawley, during the 'poll tax' debate

> **BW** Does the honourable member for Crawley wish to intervene?
> **NS** No.
> **BW** The last time I saw a mouth like that it had a hook in it.
>
> (House of Commons: 28 March 1988)

Situational context

Since politeness is a pragmatic phenomenon, it is influenced by elements of the context. There are two situational context factors that influence the way that we make a request. One is the size of imposition, the routiness and reasonableness of task, and the rule seems to be 'the greater the imposition, the more indirect the language is'. For example, to borrow a large sum of money, one might employ a series of hedges and other negative politeness phenomena, as in, 'I couldn't borrow $30, could I, if you don't need it right now?', and to borrow a small sum, one's request could be bald on record, as in 'Give me 5 cents.'

The other factor is the formality of the context, and here the tendency is 'the greater the formality, the more indirect the language is'. Whereas a student, sitting informally in the common room over a coffee, might stop a colleague from interrupting her with a direct directive bald on record, 'Hang on – I haven't finished!', she would say to the same colleague, in the formal context of a seminar, 'I wonder if I might just finish what I'm trying to say', an indirect directive redressing the FTA with negative politeness.

Social context

The choice of the politeness formulation depends on the social distance and the power relation between speakers. When there is social distance, politeness is encoded and there is more indirectness; where there is less social distance, there is less negative politeness and indirectness. The variables that determine social distance are degree of familiarity, and differences of status, roles, age, gender, education, class, occupation and ethnicity.

The degree of familiarity between speakers is one of the most obvious social variables that affect how politeness is expressed. Speakers who know each other well do not need to use formulas encoding politeness strategies, and when they do use them, it can imply quite the opposite of politeness. In Thurber's short story *A Couple of Hamburgers* (1963), the wife asks her husband to hurry up, using formal language to express negative politeness: 'Will you be kind enough to tell me what time it is?' and 'If you'll be kind enough to speed up a little?' The result of her inappropriate indirectness is sarcasm, a flouting of the maxim of quality. Similarly, Basil Fawlty, in the English TV comedy series *Fawlty Towers*, over-applies Leech's generosity maxim to his wife with his 'Have another vat of wine, dear.' He flouts the maxim of quality since he is not offering her a vat of wine, but using a directive to imply an expressive, to deplore the amount that she drinks.

Differences of status, roles, age, gender, education, class, occupation and ethnicity can give speakers power and authority. It is those of the lower status, the less dominant role and so on who use more indirectness and more negative politeness features, such as hedges and mitigation, than those with higher status and so on do. Expressions that are bald on record are used by people who assume that they have got power. Thus is it that a lecturer, because of their role and status, is expected to give generalised orders when addressing a class of students, directly and bald on record, as in the following, taken from the transcription of a seminar entitled 'Using Video Clips in ELT':

> Now. What we're going to do is um a quick game of twenty questions: you'll get some points up here. Now these people can only answer Yes or No, so you must ask Yes/No questions. So you can't ask a question like: 'What happened?'
>
> (BASE 2000)

Conversely, a participant in a COHSE/NALGO/NUPE meeting has to address the chair using the negative politeness devices of hedges and requests for permission to speak:

> 'Erm chairman could I ask a question in relation to that?'
>
> (BNC: f7j business meeting, 1992)

Cultural context

However, the relationship between indirectness and social variables is not so simple: the whole issue of politeness and language is exceedingly culture-bound. As interactional sociolinguist Tannen says, the use of indirectness 'can hardly be understood without the cross-cultural perspective' (1994: 32–4). In some cultures, for example, a lecturer making suggestions to a student would do so directly, bald on record, because of their status. This explains why some international students interpret the option-giving literally, when faced with British lecturers' indirect suggestions, negative politeness hedges and mitigation, as in, 'I think this part of your essay could possibly come a little bit nearer the beginning, if you like.'

Travellers may find that the British put more emphasis on negative politeness than other cultures do. In Cuba, for example, friends should not show any distance at all, and to say 'thank you' for a cup of coffee, 'maximising praise of other', can cause offence as it appears to put up barriers. Thomas (1995: 161) mentions that Chinese hosts will choose a guest's menu for them and put the 'choicest pieces' on their plate, to show positive politeness. Here it seems that the tact maxim 'maximise benefit to other' of positive politeness in the Chinese mind overrides the 'don't impose' and 'give others options' maxim of negative politeness.

The use of the maxims of tact and generosity varies greatly from country to country. Thomas (1995: 161) quotes a Japanese PhD student who, on drafts of her thesis, wrote notes such as, 'This is a draft of Chapter 4. Please read it and comment on it.' To Thomas, this message seemed over-explicit and actually imposing in its directives; in fact the student intended to acknowledge how much work she was asking her to do and was going on record with the degree of her indebtedness. She was not observing the tact maxim of 'minimise cost to other' but observing the sympathy maxim of 'maximise sympathy between self and other'.

The use of the maxims of approbation and modesty are also deeply rooted in culture. The British reject praise in the form of a personal compliment, 'minimising praise of self', whereas the Japanese accept a compliment graciously. Cubans respond to a personal compliment about an article of clothing or an accessory with 'Es tuyo' ('It's yours whenever you want it'), a formula which appears to observe the tact maxim 'maximise benefit to other'. Similarly, in some Western cultures, refusals demand a specific excuse, if speakers are to avoid threatening positive face and 'minimise dispraise of other', whereas in other cultures, this is not necessary. Approbation in the form of positive feedback from a teacher to a student in a British lecture, 'maximising praise of other', is quite an acceptable teaching technique in Britain, but a study carried out on Chinese students in the University of Dundee (Catterick 2001) showed that they felt that their face was threatened by being praised by the teacher in front of everyone. On the other hand, British lecturers are unused to being praised by their students, whereas for the Chinese, this is a standard politeness routine.

This unit introduces the last theme in this book. As you will have seen, politeness is related to the context, the language used, the speech acts, the structure of the conversation and the principle of cooperation. Politeness is a basic form of cooperation and it underlies all language in some way or another.

DEVELOPMENT

STUDIES IN PRAGMATICS AND DISCOURSE

ANALYSING THE DISCOURSE IN CONTEXT

Analysing text using concepts

❏ situational context
❏ cultural and interpersonal background context
❏ exophora, deixis and intertextuality

Text

How are things going?

Here is another conversation between students. AF, the Scottish woman, comes in and sees CM, the Canadian man, and DM, the Englishman, sitting with the curtains drawn. They are joined by BM and MM, Englishmen.

1	AF	God it's hot in here.
2	DM	Is it?
3	AM	Yeah. (1) Really. (0.5) Are you shutting out this lovely sunshine?
4	DM	It's getting in my eyes.
5	AF	Oh no!
6	CM	Yeah. Not used to that are you?
7	DM	No. (6) What's that? Psycholinguistics?
8	AF	Mhm. I have difficulty getting my brain going first thing in the
9		morning.
10	DM	She certainly fills it up, doesn't she? She's got lots of things to tell you
11		I'm sure.
12	AF	Yeah. ((yawns)) Oh I just want to sit down. (1) You going to get on
13		your bike?
14	DM	Have you got to go?
15	NF	Yeah. I suppose I have. I shouldn't this morning.
16	DM	Yeah right. ((MM and BM enter))
17	MM	Anyone got the key to the photocopier? (1)

18	DM	No.
19	AF	Is it still not there? (2) Oh MM! I (0.5) brought the what what's a
20		name back.
21	MM	Yeah. Tell you what ((unintelligible)).
22	DM	How are you?
23	BM	All right.
24	DM	I haven't seen you very much.
25	BM	No I haven't seen you very much.
26	DM	We must not fit at all.
27	BM	You do you do language planning don't you.
28	DM	Yeah. I've stopped doing that though.
29	BM	Are you er (0.5) are going to do what you thought you'd do about
30		your project.
31	DM	I'm going to give out a questionnaire. And I'll give you one as well.
32		Sometime this week I hope t- tomorrow I'll get them all done.
33	AF	What your core project?
34	DM	Yeah. (0.5)
35	CM	Did he like did he like the idea?
36	DM	Well you know what he's like. It's difficult to tell isn't it? Yeah. He said
37		it wasn't terrible anyway. He said go ahead so (0.5) I'm going to go
38		ahead.
39	CM	Yeah he said this isn't terrible?
40	DM	No no he didn't tell me that. // (heh heh)

(Students on questionnaire 1996)

Text analysis

How are things going?

This conversation has all the signs of an exchange between people who know each other well. They are joking and teasing, and their language is informal: they omit the beginning of their sentences ('Not used to that are you?' and 'Anyone got the key to the photocopier?'). The most obvious sign is the high density of utterances assuming interpersonal knowledge.

Let us start by analysing the **situational context**. We can see two examples of reference to it.

❑ The first is in lines 1–7. AF's 'God it's hot in here' has place deixis in the form of a demonstrative adverb 'here' pointing to the room that they are in. The men know that she means the room, and not the whole building or indeed the whole of Edinburgh. Her words 'Are you shutting out this lovely sunshine?' contain a place deixis demonstrative adjective 'this' pointing to the sunshine shining through the curtains. Both of these are examples of exophoric reference.

❑   The second example occurs in line 7: 'What's that? Psycholinguistics?' Note again that we have an exophoric demonstrative pronoun in place deixis: 'that'. Presumably, the 'that' points to a book or lecture notes that AF is carrying.

In these two cases, the situational context means that the words do not have to be explicit because the surroundings provide the meaning. Note that AF does not say 'Are you shutting out this lovely sunshine that is coming through the curtains at the window behind you?' and DM does not ask 'What lecture is that file of notes, which is under your arm, for?' It would sound very strange if they did.

Moving on to the context of **cultural background** now, there are three stretches of discourse that show evidence of speakers assuming a common knowledge of the course, knowledge that only members of the student group would have.

❑   The first is in lines 8–12. AF implies that she thinks that the Psycholinguistics lectures require great mental effort, when she complains 'I have difficulty getting my brain going first thing in the morning.' DM infers that AF is making a comment about the lecturer's style and responds showing a similar attitude towards the lecturer: 'She certainly fills it up, doesn't she? She's got lots of things to tell you I'm sure.' Witness the fact that it is not necessary for DM to name the lecturer, because once 'Psycholinguistics' has been mentioned, the context of the lecture has been established and along with it all the associated context of the lecturer, her style, the materials, and so on.

❑   The second example is in lines 17–20. MM comes in and asks 'Anyone got the key to the photocopier?' He assumes that all those in the room know which photocopier and key he is referring to; he implies that the key is not where it should be, and that he thinks that someone in the room might have kept it. AF implies that she knows about the missing key, with her 'Is it still not there?', the 'still' suggesting that it was already missing before, and the 'there' showing that she knows where it should be.

❑   The third example comes in lines 36–42. They are talking about a lecturer that DM went to see. DM says 'Well you know what he's like. It's difficult to tell isn't it?', assuming that all hearers do indeed know what he is like, and have the same attitude towards him. DM seems to feel that the lecturer does not make himself clearly understood, and he asks his colleagues to share his attitude, with his 'isn't it?'

Finally, we come to stretches of dialogue assuming knowledge of **interpersonal background context**. There are five instances.

❑   The first is in lines 12–16. It appears that NF stands up to go. AF asks 'You going to get on your bike?' She knows that NF is not going upstairs to the lecture theatre but out of the building, and that she has a bike. DM knows where NF is going and that there is some doubt as to whether it is necessary: 'Have you got to go?' NF suggests that there is a good reason why she should stay: 'I suppose I have. I shouldn't this morning.' DM agrees. Neither AF nor DM needs to say where she is going or why.

❑   The second instance comes in lines 19–21. AF says 'Oh MM! I (0.5) brought the what what's a name back.' MM does not say 'What on earth are you talking about?' He just says 'Yeah' and mumbles something private to her. This is an example of intertextuality: they had possibly had a previous conversation in which MM asked AF to bring something back. Since they know what they mean, it is quicker and easier to use the vague, implicit expression 'the what's a name'. It also keeps it private.

❑ The next example is in lines 24–8. Not only do BM and DM show that they have an interpersonal context of not meeting up because their lectures do not coincide ('We must not fit at all'), but they also know what course options each has chosen. BM knows that DM had chosen the 'language planning' option. Because they had not interacted verbally recently, his knowledge is out of date, however.

❑ The fourth instance occurs in lines 29–34. BM refers to the topic of DM's project 'what you thought you'd do'. He may use this inexplicit noun clause because it is more convenient and economical than saying 'A study of native-speaker of English use of grammar in conversations', for example. On the other hand, he may use it because he has actually forgotten what DM said he was going to do. Whatever the reason, his 'what you thought you'd do' refers to a previous conversation. It is intertextual.

❑ The final example is in lines 36–41. CM mentions, out of the blue, an unnamed male person: 'Did he like did he like the idea?' He recalls a previous conversation in which DM said that he was going to take his project idea to a lecturer. The 'he' gains meaning from the context associated with the project and the questionnaire: it is an example of exophoric person deixis with intertextual reference. CM rightly assumed that DM could infer who 'he' refers to. Note that we said, above, that lines 35–41 contain reference to the cultural context. It is quite common to find an overlap of contexts when we analyse data. In this case, the whole student group is expected to have knowledge of the lecturer's manner, whereas maybe only CM and DM would have the specific knowledge of what DM went to see him for.

These stretches of language dependent on the interpersonal context are the most impenetrable to an outsider. Overhearers lacking knowledge of this context cannot begin to guess what is being talked about exactly in some of these lines. The inexplicit reference excludes everyone except people who were present at their last conversation: it is privileged information.

B1.2   **Further reading ▶▶▶▶**

❑ For good examples of the influence of context on meaning, see J. Mey (1993), P. Grundy (2000) and G. Brown and G. Yule (1983).

❑ For a further exploration of the relationship between context and deixis, see J. Thomas (1995) and A. Cruse (2000).

❑ P. Grundy (2000) has a deep and complex discussion of deixis, inference and common ground.

ANALYSING THE CO-TEXT

Analysing text using concepts

❑ grammatical cohesion
   – endophoric reference
   – substitution and ellipsis
❑ lexical cohesion

Text

The cesspool

This is taken from the opening page of chapter one of Virginia Woolf's *Between the Acts* (1941). Virginia Woolf was born in 1882, and during the years leading up to World War I, she became a prominent member of the famous literary group subsequently known as the 'Bloomsbury Group'. She had a mental breakdown in 1904 when her father died, and took her life in 1941. *Between the Acts* was published after her death.

```
 1   It was a summer's night and they were talking, in the big room with the
 2   windows open to the garden, about the cesspool. The county council had
 3   promised to bring water to the village, but they hadn't.
 4   Mrs Haines, the wife of the gentleman farmer, a goose-faced woman with
 5   eyes protruding as if they saw something to gobble in the gutter, said
 6   affectedly: 'What a subject to talk about on a night like this!'
 7   Then there was silence; and a cow coughed; and that led her to say how odd
 8   it was, as a child, she had never feared cows, only horses. But, then, as a
 9   small child in a perambulator, a great cart-horse had brushed within an inch
10   of her face. Her family, she told the old man in the arm-chair, had lived
11   near Liskeard for many centuries. There were the graves in the churchyard
12   to prove it.
13   A bird chuckled outside. 'A nightingale?' asked Mrs Haines. No,
14   nightingales didn't come so far north. It was a daylight bird, chuckling over
15   the substance and succulence of the day, over worms, snails, grit, even in
16   sleep.
17   The old man in the arm-chair – Mr Oliver, of the Indian Civil Service, retired
18   – said that the site they had chosen for the cesspool was, if he had heard
19   aright, on the Roman road. From an aeroplane, he said, you could still see,
20   plainly marked, the scars made by the Britons; by the Romans; by the
21   Elizabethan manor house; and by the plough, when they ploughed the hill
22   to grow wheat in the Napoleonic wars.
```

Text analysis

The cesspool

Analysis of this simple little passage shows how very closely woven it is in terms of both grammatical and lexical cohesion.

Let us start with grammatical cohesion, and **endophoric** reference. There are at least six instances of anaphoric reference and only one instance of cataphoric. This, as we have said, is a fairly typical ratio. Let us start with **anaphoric** reference, and list some examples.

❑ The first example is in lines 2–3 'The county council had promised to bring water to the village, but they hadn't', in which the 'they' links back to 'The county council'. Note that although 'The county council' is singular, it can have a plural personal pronoun since it is the members within the council who are being referred to.

❑ The link in lines 4–5 is simpler: 'Mrs Haines, the wife of the gentleman farmer, a goose-faced woman with eyes protruding as if they saw something to gobble in the gutter'. Here, the 'they' is cohesive with the preceding *eyes*.

❑ In lines 7–8, 'Then there was silence; and a cow coughed; and that led her to say how odd it was, as a child, she had never feared cows, only horses', the 'her' and 'she' refer back to the 'Mrs Haines' of the previous paragraph, not to the 'cow', of course.

❑ In lines 9–12, 'Her family, she told the old man in the arm-chair, had lived near Liskeard for many centuries. There were the graves in the churchyard to prove it' shows that a personal pronoun, as in *it*, can link back to a whole phrase or clause; it does not always have to be just one word. Here, it is 'Her family . . . had lived near Liskeard for many centuries.'

❑ The last example, in lines 17–19, 'The old man in the arm-chair – Mr Oliver, of the Indian Civil Service, retired – said that the site they had chosen for the cesspool was, if he had heard aright, on the Roman road' demonstrates that a pronoun, as in 'he', can relate back to two noun phrases ('The old man in the arm-chair' and 'Mr Oliver'), if they both refer to the same referent.

The **cataphoric** reference is typical of the opening sentence of a novel, as we saw in the Updike quote in Unit A2. We begin in lines 1–2: 'It was a summer's night and they were talking, in the big room with the windows open to the garden, about the cesspool.' The 'they' are not identified until line 4 ('Mrs Haines') and line 17 ('Mr Oliver'). This technique is aimed at creating expectation and interest, and throwing readers straight into the story, as if they had joined two people in the middle of the scene and the conversation.

Interestingly, we see 'the windows' and 'the garden' without being told anything about 'the house'. This is another way of throwing us into a story which is underway. We are given the components of the **presuppositonal pool** of 'a house', and are expected to work out through **associative anaphora** that before the story began, they were already in 'the house' where we find them.

There are no examples of **substitution**, but at least four of **ellipsis**.

❑ The first is in lines 2–3: 'The county council had promised to bring water to the village, but they hadn't.' The 'But they hadn't' is ellipsis because it is only the beginning of the clause – 'But they hadn't brought water.' Notice here that 'brought water' does not feature in the preceding text, but 'bring water' does; readers are expected to make the change of tense, albeit unconsciously.

❑ The next example takes the form of indirect speech, a report on what Mrs Haines said in lines 7–8: 'and that led her to say how odd it was, as a child, she had never feared cows, only horses'. The 'only horses' is ellipsis, this time because it is only the end of the clause: 'She had feared only horses.' Note again, that the clause that readers are expected to understand is not exactly the same as the preceding one, the preceding one being negative and the one ellipted affirmative.

❑ The third example of ellipsis omits the verb and subject of the sentence: in line 13, 'A bird chuckled outside. "A nightingale?" asked Mrs Haines', the ellipsis is exophoric. Although readers hear the bird at the same time as Mrs Haines, there is no form in the preceding discourse that would guide them, were they to try to express the question without ellipsis: it might be 'Is that a nightingale?', 'Is the bird chuckling outside a nightingale?', 'Is that sound a nightingale?' or 'Do you agree that's a nightingale?' Of course, it does not matter exactly how it is interpreted.

❑ The last example is a list: 'From an aeroplane, he said, you could still see, plainly marked, the scars made by the Britons; by the Romans; by the Elizabethan manor house; and by the plough, when they ploughed the hill to grow wheat in the Napoleonic wars.' Here, what is understood in each case is the beginning of the phrase, as in 'scars made by the Romans; scars made by the Elizabethan house; and scars made by the plough'. Mr Oliver sounds repetitive as it is: he would have sounded worse had he not used ellipsis.

It could be that these examples of ellipsis that require words to be retrieved that are not actually in the text in the same form are designed to involve readers, obliging them to contribute to the story.

Moving on now to lexical cohesion, we can see that by far the most used device is **repetition**. This threads right through this short passage and can best be demonstrated all at once like this:

---

1 It was a summer's <u>night</u> and they were talking, in the big room with the
2 windows open to the garden, about the <u>cesspool</u>. The county council had
3 promised to bring water to the village, but they hadn't.
4 Mrs Haines, the wife of the gentleman farmer, a goose-faced woman with
5 eyes protruding as if they saw something to gobble in the gutter, said
6 affectedly: 'What a subject to talk about on a <u>night</u> like this!'
7 Then there was silence; and a <u>cow</u> coughed; and that led her to say how

8   odd it was, as a <u>child</u>, she had never feared <u>cows</u>, only horses. But, then,
9   as a small <u>child</u> in a perambulator, a great cart-horse had brushed within an
10 inch of her face. Her family, she told <u>the old man in the arm-chair</u>, had lived
11 near Liskeard for many centuries. There were the graves in the churchyard
12 to prove it.
13 A <u>bird</u> chucked outside. 'A <u>nightingale</u>?' asked Mrs Haines. No,
14 <u>nightingales</u> didn't come so far north. It was a daylight <u>bird</u>, chuckling over
15 the substance and succulence of the day, over worms, snails, grit, even in
16 sleep.
17 <u>The old man in the arm-chair</u> – Mr Oliver, of the Indian Civil Service, retired
18 – said that the site they had chosen for the <u>cesspool</u> was, if he had heard
19 aright, on the Roman road. From an aeroplane, he said, you could still see,
20 plainly marked, the scars made by the Britons; <u>by the</u> Romans; <u>by the</u>
21 Elizabethan manor house; and <u>by the</u> plough, when they ploughed the hill to
22 grow wheat in the Napoleonic wars.

This way, it becomes clear that, whereas some repetition stretches across several lines, as in 'night' (in lines 1 and 6), 'cesspool' (in lines 2 and 18), and 'the old man in the arm-chair' (in lines 10 and 17), other repetition occurs within the same sentence or the same line, as in 'cow' (lines 7–8), 'child' (line 8), 'bird' (lines 13–14), and 'nightingale' (line 13). It can also be seen that repetition can take the form of parallel structures, as in the repeated 'by the' structure in line 18. Virginia Woolf chooses to repeat nouns not verbs, and the nouns repeated are the ones that tell the story. The noun 'night' sets the scene and then 'cow' and 'nightingale' introduce the background noise; 'the old man in the arm-chair' brings in one of the protagonists; and lastly 'cesspool', 'cow', 'child', 'bird' and 'nightingale' are the topics of conversation. Highlighting the nouns like this makes it obvious that this passage consists of not so much a conversation as two parallel monologues, since Mr Oliver is talking about the 'cesspool' but Mrs Haines wants to stop; and likewise 'cow', 'child', 'bird' and 'nightingale' are Mrs Haines' topics, (she wants to change the topic to one related to the beauty of the night), but they are not Mr Oliver's. The analysis brings out the lack of communication between the two of them: Mr Oliver resumes his topic of the 'cesspool' once Mrs Haines has stopped telling her stories and makes her look as if she was actually talking to the 'night'.

There are no **synonyms** but there are two **superordinates**.

❏   The first is 'What a subject to talk about on a night like this!' Mrs Haines dismisses Mr Oliver's topic, by putting it in the superordinate category of inappropriate 'subject'(s).

❏   The other instance is this one: 'A bird chuckled outside. "A nightingale?" asked Mrs Haines. No, nightingales didn't come so far north. It was a daylight bird, chuckling over the substance and succulence.' The superordinate 'bird' is needed here so that its identity can be left open; it could be 'a nightingale', or anything in the lower level superordinate category of 'daylight bird' such as 'a blackbird', 'a skylark' and 'a thrush'.

The only example of **general words** is the 'The old man in the arm-chair'. This is how Mr Oliver is introduced: as a faceless male person. This gives about as much information as the 'they' did in line 1. It seems to be part of the writer's technique of revealing her characters gradually. Mrs Haines has been described physically and her character is emerging; meanwhile Mr Oliver is still 'The old man in the arm-chair', sitting with a shadow over him.

Further reading ▶▶▶▶

❏   For a simple discussion of reference, substitution, ellipsis and lexical cohesion, see E. Hatch (1992) and B. R. Smith and E. Leinonen (1992).

❏   For a classic, central discussion of cohesion, read M. A. K. Halliday and R. Hasan (1976, 1989).

❏   G. Brown and G. Yule (1983) give a clear explanation of endophora, lexical chains, and substitution, and A. Cruse (2000) an advanced exploration of lexical hierarchies.

❏   G. Cook (1989) provides suggestions of how to teach language students about cohesion.

USING SPEECH ACTS   **B3**

Analysing text using concepts   **B3.1**

❏   direct speech acts
❏   felicity conditions
❏   indirect speech acts
❏   interactional/transactional function

Text

Fox hunting under cover

The following excerpt is taken from the BBC1 thriller series *Dalziel and Pascoe* (6 May 2001). Andrew Dalziel is an older detective of the grumpy-yet-amiable variety. In this scene, Dalziel's boss asks about one of the female police officers, to whom Dalziel had given the job of working under cover as a horse-rider in the fox-hunting world to discover who murdered one of the fox hunters. Dalziel's boss knows that he is against fox hunting, partly out of sympathy with the fox, partly out of antipathy for the aristocracy.

1	Boss	Under cover? This isn't your private army. Is she OK?
2	Dalziel	She's good. (0.5) In fact she spent half her childhood on a horse.
3	Boss	How do I know you're lying to me, Andy?
4	Dalziel	Look, we've even given her a full story; set up a liaison point.
5		Visitors often go on a ride with another hunt. They come for a
6		few days, stay at a local pub, borrow a horse. And since hunting
7		is about drinking as much as it is riding, it shouldn't be long
8		before someone becomes indiscreet. (0.5)

9	Boss	All right. But don't upset the locals. Hounsden is a nice village.
10	Dalziel	Pity it's not a bunch of miners – then we could have done what
11		we liked. (1)
12	Boss	Watch it superintendent! I'm not asking you to kow-tow to the
13		gentry. I'm telling you to go by the book. (0.5) You see I know
14		how you work.

Text analysis

Fox hunting under cover

Let us begin with the macro-function of this excerpt. This is a work conversation and it has a primarily 'transactional' function: they are not having a sociable chat, they are negotiating a plan of action. The boss's main aim is to transmit the information that will affect Dalziel's behaviour. She tells him 'Hounsden is a nice village' because she wants him to not 'upset the locals' but 'go by the book'. Dalziel gives his boss a full account of how he has organised the officer's task and cover because she needs the information. Between the factual points, there is language with a primarily 'interactional' function. The boss's 'All right' is an expression of agreement; Dalziel's 'Pity it's not a bunch of miners' comment is not essential to the negotiation; it is an attempt to share opinions and make the conversation more sociable.

Let us move on to the **perlocutionary** effect of the speakers' words on the hearers. The boss's 'How do I know you're lying to me, Andy?' makes Dalziel reassure her and convince her that his plan of action in this case is all well-thought-out and safe. He has to impress her since she is his superior and has the ultimate say in all his actions. The boss presumably hopes that the perlocutionary effect of her warning 'I'm telling you to go by the book' will be that he *will* work in the conventional way, and not offend any of the gentry.

Let us now analyse the **speech acts**, **direct** and **indirect**, and the **illocutionary force**. The boss gives orders indirectly to Dalziel first, and then they become more and more indirect.

❑ In line 1, her 'This isn't your private army' is, on the surface a declaration, functioning as a direct representative, a statement describing the people who work for Dalziel. Indirectly, it is a directive with the illocutionary force of forbidding him, as in 'Do not use these people for your own ends.'

❑ When Dalziel answers her enquiry about the police officer under cover saying that she is an experienced rider, she seems to be using an interrogative to ask a representative question in line 3: 'How do I know you're lying to me, Andy?' Again, this has the illocutionary force of an indirect directive forbidding him to lie as in the imperative 'Don't lie to me, Andy' or 'Tell me the truth.'

❑ When he tells her the theory behind his decision, she becomes more direct, giving him in line 9 a 'direct directive', in the form of a negative imperative, telling him, 'Don't upset the locals.'

❏   When Dalziel makes the point about the miners, she then uses, in line 13, something resembling a 'direct declaration' to make her command clear, so that there can be no doubt: 'I'm telling you to go by the book.' It comes across as the explicit performative, 'I hereby command you to go by the book.'

Let us look now at what Dalziel is doing in this brief exchange. He starts by showing respect, with neutral declaratives and indirect expressives, and then follows this with a show of anger, in the form of direct expressives.

❏   His declarative 'In fact she spent half her childhood on a horse' (line 2) is a 'direct representative', but 'indirectly', it is an 'expressive' that backs up the previous statement 'She's good', praising her skills. It could also be seen as an indirect commissive, implying 'I promise to you that I know what I'm doing and will not endanger her life.'

❏   Likewise his long story about her cover: lines 4 to 6 contain direct representatives that carry the 'indirect directive' message of 'Don't worry. Everything is in order.'

❏   In lines 10 to 11, his attitude changes. His words 'Pity it's not a bunch of miners – then we could have done what we liked' bear a reference heavy in cultural background knowledge of the closing of the British coal mines. In the 1980s the Thatcher government destroyed the mining industry, and the miners went on a very long strike; many felt that the closing of the mines was not accompanied by compassion or even consideration for the miners. By making this suggestion, Dalziel is implying an 'indirect expressive' deploring the double standards of the country that could be expressed as, 'We must make every effort not to upset the aristocracy, but we were not asked to make such efforts with the working class.' What might also be implied is a defiant indirect commissive of 'I'll do what I like.' This is what provokes the boss's 'Watch it superintendent!' She knows that he refuses to 'Kow-tow to the gentry'; what really worries her is that he may do something that does not 'go by the book'. As it happens, later in the programme he does step out of line and join the protesters in obstructing a hunt and saving a fox from being mauled to death by the hounds, a very topical theme for the year 2001, since fox hunting was coming under attack in Scotland and then England and Wales.

Let us look briefly at the 'felicity conditions'. This is closely related to the power structure: the boss's higher social status than Dalziel gives her the right to play the role of telling him what to do. Interestingly, although he seems to recognise that it is possible for her to carry out the act of directing him, he suggests that he cannot follow her orders, and asserts his rights as an individual with opinions. She reminds him in lines 12–14 that she can and will give him orders. It may be the case that other social dimensions are entering into play here. Dalziel is older than his boss and therefore more experienced; it may be this that gives him confidence to defy the felicity conditions. Then of course he is a man and is most likely unused to taking orders from a woman; this may be why she has to make it clear that she is boss.

All in all, it is a short but interesting little excerpt, with a great deal going on under the surface.

B3.2

Further reading ►►►►

❑ For a deeper and more detailed discussion of speech act classifications (slightly different terms), felicity conditions, performative verbs and the performative hypothesis, read A. Cruse (2000) and G. Leech (1983) and S. Levinson (1983).

❑ For a thorough, yet still accessible, explanation of indirect speech acts, looking at idioms, literal meaning and conventional meaning, with plenty of examples, read P. Grundy (2000).

❑ D. Schiffrin (1994) provides an advanced, careful explanation of the development of Austin's and Searle's theories, a discussion of their application to discourse analysis, and demonstrations of sample analysis.

❑ J. Thomas (1995) and D. Blakemore (1992) give an advanced, critical discussion of the development of Austin's and Searle's theories, the performative hypothesis and types of performatives, overlaps and cross-cultural differences.

❑ For a clear introduction to the sociolinguistic approach to speech functions, and an exploration of the effect of all social differences and contextual constraints on directives, go to J. Holmes (1992).

❑ For those needing guidance in speech act analysis, and suggestions for research projects in speech acts, and the applications to language learning, E. Hatch (1992) is helpful.

❑ Finally, D. Tannen (1994) reports on a specialised study report of indirect speech acts in male–female discourse, comparing Greeks and Americans, and the misunderstandings caused by stylistic differences.

B4

THE PRAGMATICS OF CONVERSATION

B4.1

Analysing text using concepts

❑ conversation analysis
❑ interactional sociolinguistics

Text

Scrabble

This extract is taken from British component of *The International Corpus of English* (ICE-GB). A mother and daughter are at the mother's house, eating, chatting and playing Scrabble ('a game in which players score points by putting rows of separate letters on squares of a board to form words' – (Longman Dictionary of Contemporary English 1978)).

1	Mother	I don't know what you're doing on that.
2	Daughter	Oh no.
3	Mother	No.

4	Daughter	No fear I should say =
5	Mother	= Well, do it somewhere else. I mean, look there's plenty of other
6		places to put it. How about here? // I like it like that.
7	Daughter	// Uhm it's OK. Oh God you don't –
8		First of all you don't score so much, and secondly you only get rid of
9		two letters // and you make your chances of picking up anything better
10	Mother	// Uhm
11	Daughter	that much more reduced by not // you know, getting rid of as many as
12	Mother	// Uhm
13	Daughter	you can. Two four six – seven twenty-four is eleven. I mean you could
14		do so much better than that if // you'd only
15	Mother	// Yeah. I'm busy eating as a matter of fact
16	Daughter	Oh.
17	Mother	I didn't really like that sandwich.
18	Daughter	(laughs) I wouldn't have noticed (laughs). You've // packed away most
19	Mother	// No but I
20	Daughter	of it (laughs) all the same.
21	Mother	kept hoping it would get better and it got worse. (laughs) Salty. Don't
22		like salty things.
23	Daughter	No.
24	Mother	Have some banana bread.
25	Daughter	Look. I'm not that much of a banana bread eater // and I wish you'd
26	Mother	// Oh I forgot //
27	Daughter	stop bothering.
28	Mother	Never mention it again.
29	Daughter	Yes, I mean, you know, I know where these things are. If I'm that
30		interested I'll ask if I may have a piece and then you can tell me you
31		haven't made any for months or don't make it any more (laughs) I've
32		got a whole load of my own banana bread in the fridge. I don't know.
33	Mother	Do we have 'sana' SANA?
34	Daughter	No. We have 'sauna' SAUNA. Right we have (unclear). A funny game.
35		That's a funny game. 'Go' and 'ox'. And the 'ox' is uh sixteen
36		seventeen eighteen nineteen twenty.
37	Mother	Mm. Mm.
38	Daughter	You're now eighty behind. If you'd listened to me (laughs) you'd only
39		be seventy behind. Anyway what else did Linda have to say for herself
40	Mother	Oh a lot. Never left off. When she's // finished with the kids, she
41	Daughter	// Oh.
42	Mother	goes back to Felicity and all her achievements. Actually you probably
43		wouldn't have enjoyed it here. (laughs)
44	Daughter	What do you mean about Felicity and her achievements, is it?
45		Oh no // I have been inured to that // for years.
46	Mother	// How wonderful she is, you know // how she talks.

(ICE-GB: Spoken dialogue, private, direct conversation: S1A–010, 1991)

Text analysis

Scrabble

The first comment to make about this excerpt is to emphasise that speakers are mother and daughter: they know each other very well and they are alone together in an informal environment. The 'interpersonal relations' and the **situational context** have a significant influence on how the conversation flows. They share background knowledge about the daughter's lack of interest in banana bread ('Oh I forgot. Never mention it again') and about the mother's friend Linda and her children ('do you mean about Felicity and her achievements?'). They know each other well enough to criticise how they play Scrabble (lines 7–14), to tease about how they eat (lines 18–20), and to pretend to take offence (lines 26–28). The criticisms and teasing are interspersed with laughter and they are not dwelt on.

CA says that this piece of talk shows that they know each other well, but not that their knowing each other well makes them talk like this. Indeed, in a more formal context and talking about less personal topics, the signs of their knowing each other well might not be so obvious. Whereas pragmatics, discourse analysis and interactional sociolinguistics say that all background context influences what interactants say, CA says that only some contexts are relevant in the understanding of the talk.

If we come to this real-life conversation and try to make it fit the *a priori* **exchange structure**, we find that the conversation is far too 'chaotic', especially as there is not one person with the role or status to initiate (as in teacher, doctor, quiz master) and the other to respond, and nor does the situational context require it. The only follow-up that stands out is the mother's responses – 'Uhm' (lines 10 and 12), and 'Mm. Mm' (line 37) – and they are more backchannelling and agreeing rather than evaluating what her daughter is saying.

The 'chaotic' nature of the conversation can be seen if we look at it using **conversation analysis**, which is designed to look at how real data unfolds and utterances affect each other. We cannot talk of turn-taking in the sense of respecting **transition relevance places**. Only in the middle of the excerpt, lines 28–39, do the speakers wait till the other has finished talking before they answer or contribute to the conversation. This is because the daughter is ranting about not wanting banana bread and telling her mother how far behind she is.

About half of the turns contain **overlaps** and **interruptions** (indicated with a //

in the text), and this is quite a high proportion, even for a casual conversation between familiars:

❑ In lines 6–7, the daughter takes the turn from her mother, with 'Uhm it's OK. Oh God you don't – First of all you don't score so much . . .' and she holds the floor arguing with her 'lesson' on Scrabble tactics, until line 14.
❑ In line 14, the mother interrupts and takes the turn back, with her 'Yeah. I'm busy eating as a matter of fact', and thus does not allow her daughter to extend her 'lesson' any further. Although the daughter overlaps and seems to take the floor in line 18, the mother takes it back with another interruption in lines 19–21: 'No but I kept hoping it would get better . . .'

- ❏ In lines 40–45, the daughter interrupts what her mother is saying about Linda and her talking about her children and Felicity, because she cannot and does not want to wait to say that she knows all about it: 'I have been inured to that for years.'

An analysis of the **adjacency pairs** shows that there is not a neat pairing of utterances or turns. The exception could be in lines 18 and 20 in which the daughter 'accuses', with 'You've packed away most of it all the same' and then the mother 'defends' in lines 19 and 21, giving the **preferred response**: 'No but I kept hoping it would get better . . .' More frequent is the **dispreferred response**:

- ❏ In line 13, the daughter 'advises', with 'I mean you could do so much better than that if only you'd . . .', but the mother neither 'accepts' nor 'rejects' the advice; she justifies her poor playing in line 15: 'Yeah. I'm busy eating as a matter of fact.'
- ❏ Again, in line 24, the mother 'offers' her daughter some banana bread, but instead of an 'accept', she is faced with a 'reject' ('Look. I'm not that much of a banana bread eater'), and the reject goes on for several lines.

This is not to say that there is a fight going on, to hold the floor. No offence is taken at the interruptions or the dispreferred responses, as it is an amicable exchange. There may, however, be the slightest of power struggles, in the sense that the daughter seems to need to show independence: she knows about Scrabble and she does not have to wait to be asked if she wants to eat. Likewise, the mother ignores the show of independence: her 'I'm busy eating *as a matter of fact*' shows that she is unimpressed, as does her 'Do we have "sana" SANA'?

Analysis of the **sequences** of the conversation shows that there are no 'opening' or 'closing' sequences, as this excerpt is part of a longer conversation. There are no **pre-sequences**, which is possibly a reflection of close relationship and the triviality of the task that they are engaged in: neither needs to prepare the other for a suggestion or invitation. It could be said that there are **insertion** sequences, however:

- ❏ In lines 15–32 the sandwich and the banana bread topics come as an insertion sequence within the main topic of playing Scrabble.
- ❏ Line 39 onwards about Linda and her family come as another.

Yet, it could also be said that the Scrabble commentaries are the insertions. It depends whether, in their mind, the chat is the background to the Scrabble, or the Scrabble is the background to the chat. The analyst cannot tell.

Returning to the relevance of the interpersonal relations and the situational context, we can analyse the conversation from the **interactional sociolinguistics** point of view and notice that the **contextualisation cues** point with imprecise reference to the knowledge that they share. The daughter's 'I know where *these things* are' refers presumably to other foods that the mother tends to offer and to the cupboards or shelves in the refrigerator where they are kept. Similarly, the mother's 'Actually you probably wouldn't have enjoyed *it here*' (lines 42–42) uses exophoric reference with a personal pronoun 'it' and a demonstrative adverb 'here', which only have meaning for them because they know the referring items because of their intertextual knowledge. The mother's 'you know how *she* talks' (line 46) is another example of the way that they refer to their shared knowledge in a way that would exclude an outsider. This interactional talk claiming common ground with vague reference, whether there is a mini power struggle or not, is a marker of their friendship.

B4.2

Further reading ►►►►

❑ For a simple check on classroom scripts, see E. Hatch (1992).

❑ For a simple explanation of IRF, see M. McCarthy and R. Carter (1994) and for a more thorough discussion, see M. Coulthard (1985) and S. Eggins and D. Slade (1997).

❑ You will find that P. Levinson (1983), J. Mey (1993) and M. Stubbs (1983) provide an in-depth explanation of turn-taking, TRP, adjacency pairs and sequences.

❑ For a comprehensive exploration of the history of conversation analysis and examples of the methodology, go to D. Schiffrin (1994).

❑ For an early paper on conversation analysis, try H. Sacks, E. A. Schegloff and G. Jefferson (1974).

❑ For a collection of lectures on conversation analysis, read H. Sacks (1992a and 1992b).

❑ For recent developments in conversation analysis and interactional sociolinguistics, try E. Ochs, E. A. Schegloff and S. A. Thompson (1996).

B5

COOPERATION AND RELEVANCE

B5.1

Analysing text using concepts

❑ observing maxims
❑ flouting/violating
❑ relevance theory

The following text is real data taken from the British National Corpus. It is part of a casual conversation between Lisa, a 30-year-old housewife from the South Midlands, and Melvin, a 29-year-old panel beater. The BNC does not give the situational context; the conversation suggests that the speakers share a certain amount of cultural background knowledge and interpersonal knowledge.

Text

Visiting Louise

1	Lisa	Oh your mum and dad er popped round last night to see Louise.
2		Guess what time they went round?
3	Melvin	About nine – ten o'clock?
4	Lisa	Quarter past eight. She was in bed. She normally goes to bed about
5		half past seven. They said that's the earliest they could get there.
6		I said that's a load of rubbish I said, cos they have fish and chips
7		on a Friday night.
8	Melvin	Yeah.
9	Lisa	So she didn't have to cook.

10	Melvin	Ah they would have had to wash up the plates and the knives and
11		forks. But she's just one of those women who don't like leaving
12		stuff around, you know what I mean? Once they've had something,
13		they've got to do it before they go, can you believe? She's a right
14		pain in the arse sometimes, me mum. That's why they don't go
15		anywhere, you see. Yeah, that's why they don't come out and
16		visit his brother very often. So why did they want to see Louise?
17	Lisa	It was her birthday.
18	Melvin	Oh yeah. They should have gone as soon as they got out of work.
19	Lisa	Yeah. And they could have got fish and chips on the way home,
20		couldn't they?
21	Melvin	Yeah.

(BNC: kd3 Lisa, 1992)

Text analysis

Visiting Louise

Because Melvin and Louise seem to share such a lot of cultural background knowledge and interpersonal knowledge, we can assume that they know each other and each other's worlds fairly well, and because of their shared knowledge, they can **flout** the maxims freely, in the certainty that they will each be able to infer the other's implied meaning.

❏ When Lisa says that Melvin's mother and father arrived at Louise's house or flat at quarter past eight, she adds, 'She was in bed. She normally goes to bed about half past seven. They said that's the earliest they could get there' (lines 4–5), which implies that it was not actually 'the earliest they could get there', and she feels that this was inconsiderate of them as they knew that she had to go to bed early and they wittingly disturbed her sleep. All of this information is not mentioned and yet it can be inferred by Melvin: the maxim of **quantity** is flouted.

❏ The maxim of **relation** may be flouted in the utterances 'They said that's the earliest they could get there. I said that's a load of rubbish I said, cos they have fish and chips on a Friday night' (lines 6–7), since the fact that they have fish and chips does not seem immediately relevant to their getting there early, yet Melvin infers it. Flouting too the maxim of quantity, Lisa omits the reference to the fact that they would have bought fish and chips in a chip shop, which would have meant that they did not have to spend time preparing, cooking or washing up, which in turn implies that they could have arrived before half past seven. Melvin corrects her, even though she said nothing about washing up: 'Ah they would have had to wash up the plates and the knives and forks. But she's just one of those women who don't like leaving stuff around, you know what I mean?' (lines 10–12).

❏ Melvin flouts the maxim of quantity when he says minimally, 'They should have gone as soon as they got out of work' (line 18). Lisa appears to infer that he means that they could have got there before 7.30, made a special effort for the special occasion and broken with their routine; her answer 'they could have got fish and chips on the way home' (line 19) shows that she is following on his idea.

❏ There is one example of the flouting of the maxim of **quality**: 'She's a right pain in the arse sometimes, me mum. That's why they don't go anywhere' (lines 13–15). This starts with a metaphor that is so well established that it has become a fixed expression and is no longer anything to do with pains or arses. The second part is a hyperbole; it is an exaggeration which his very next utterance would seem to contradict if we did not know that he was flouting the maxim of quality: 'that's why they don't come out and visit his brother very often' (lines 15–16).

A **violation** of the cooperative maxims is much harder to detect. It could be that Louise does not in reality go to bed at 7.30 normally, but that she goes at 9.30, and that Lisa is therefore lying, violating the maxim of quality. Note that Melvin asks if they went at nine or ten o'clock. It could be that the mother is a diabetic and needs to eat at fixed times, and that Melvin knows this but is not saying it, in which case he is violating the maxim of quantity. One would have to know the speakers and their context very well to know if they were trying to deceive each other and intentionally generate a misleading implicature.

There are no obvious examples of a speaker **infringing** a maxim because of imperfect linguistic performance. Nor is there an instance of either speakers opting out of a maxim: neither of them refuse to give information, for ethical reasons, and apologise for it, for example.

On the other hand, it could also be said that cooperative maxims are not flouted, violated, infringed or opted out of. For example, Lisa's,

She was in bed. She normally goes to bed about half past seven. They said that's the earliest they could get there. I said that's a load of rubbish I said, cos they have fish and chips on a Friday night.

(lines 4–7)

shows that she is in fact observing the maxim of quantity and giving Melvin just the amount of information that he needs, just as she is at the end of the excerpt. Sperber and Wilson would say that Lisa's utterances are held together by relevance, and indeed Melvin does not question the connection. **Relevance theory** holds true for this little passage: Lisa and Melvin communicate successfully, interpreting the connections between utterances as meaningful, making inferences drawing on their own background knowledge of Louise, the parents, birthdays, fish and chips, and so on and selecting the relevant features of context. Each new fact mentioned is relevant to something already known, and the interactants appear to recover the facts effortlessly, understanding each other by drawing on accessible information belonging to the context. This stops what they say being ambiguous and helps them fill in any incomplete parts of the utterance and infer the meaning.

Further reading ▶▶▶▶

❏ For a discussion of conversational implicature, with ample examples and explanations, see J. Thomas (1995) and for an advanced, critical discussion of implicature, try A. Cruse (2000).

❏ P. Grundy (2000), G. Leech (1983) and S. C. Levinson (1983) provide an extensive discussion of kinds of implicature and the limitations of each.

❏ D. Schiffrin (1994) looks at maxims and reference.

❏ For a more advanced explanation of the cooperative principle and an introduction to relevance theory, read J. L. Mey (1994).

❏ For a classic explanation of the principle of relevance, read D. Blakemore (1992).

❏ For an in-depth discussion of the most advanced explanation of the theory of relevance, study D. Sperber and D. Wilson (1982, 1987, 1995).

B5.2

THE PRINCIPLE OF POLITENESS

B6

Analysing text using concepts

B6.1

❏ negative and positive politeness
❏ maxims of politeness

Text

Imperialism

This excerpt comes from the British Academic Spoken English (BASE) corpus (see References). This excerpt features a lecture on European imperialism delivered by Dr Iain Smith.

1   Many of you here today are not from Africa but you are, many of you,
2   from parts of the world that have been affected by one of the great global
3   forces at work in world history – what we loosely call imperialism. And
4   that is why I thought what I should try to talk to you about today is this
5   phenomenon of imperialism, not just in terms of the nineteenth and
6   twentieth centuries, and as you will see, not just in terms of the impact
7   of Europe on the non-European world.
8   Because what we are grappling with in the phenomenon of imperialism is
9   a phenomenon that in various forms is as old as the formation of state
10 systems by human beings. So I'm going to, er, at considerable risk er to
11 myself, try to set this phenomenon in a much wider, er, more global
12 perspective. I hope that might be of interest to many of you who have
13 either been subjected to what you consider imperialism, or indeed have
14 been part of states and societies that have themselves been imperialistic
15 or are still being so. /.../
16 I think we have to begin by facing up to the fact that today we live in an
17 age of anti-imperialism. All over the world there is a reaction against the

18 things which we associate with the phenomenon of imperialism: the
19 domination of the weak countries or societies by the strong; the economic
20 exploitation of the natural resources of often poorer countries er in the
21 world, by the rich industrialised parts of the world; the gross, and in many
22 parts of the world, the widening gap in terms of political, military and
23 economic power and standards of the living between the rich and the poor
24 countries; the belief, in one society, of the absolute superiority of its
25 culture, its values and its beliefs and the attempt to impose these upon the
26 people of other cultures and often of different races.
27 Today in Europe and America, in the countries of the ex-Soviet Union and
28 in Asia, as well as in all those areas of what used to be called, the Third
29 World which were until so recently under European influence or indeed
30 colonial rule, imperialism is regarded as a bad thing. To call someone an
31 imperialist is a term of abuse, like calling him a racist or a fascist.
32 The very word imperialism, I think you'll agree, is loaded with emotional
33 and ideological overtones. If I say, for instance, that recently I have been
34 studying and contributing to a new Oxford History of the British Empire,
35 which I have, that is a clear, concrete and perfectly respectable historical
36 subject to study. It was indeed the most powerful and extensive empire in
37 world history. But if I say I'm studying and writing about the history of
38 British Imperialism, that's already a somewhat different thing. The kind of
39 books that are written about it are different too.

Text analysis

Imperialism

At first sight, this text might seem a strange one to use for the analysis of politeness. It is not a dialogue; it is not interactional; nobody is trying to order or suggest or invite; there is nothing said off record and nothing bald on record. Yet there is something friendly about the tone that the lecturer, Dr Smith, sets.

On close analysis, there are elements of what we have been looking at, throughout the excerpt. Let us start by noticing that there are examples of **positive politeness strategies**.

He establishes that his audience may have **common ground** with the topic of his lecture:

❏ by referring directly to the students, showing how what he has to say is going to be relevant to them (lines 1–3): 'Many of you here today are not from Africa but you are, many of you, from parts of the world that have been affected by one of the great global forces at work in world history – what we loosely call imperialism.'

❏ by involving the students by using the pronoun 'you' three times (lines 1, 2 and 3), and emphasising the wide appeal of his lecture by saying 'many of you' twice. In paragraph two, he again addresses them with 'many of you' (line 12).

- maintaining his friendly tone of positive politeness throughout this excerpt by the use of the inclusive pronoun 'we': 'Because what we are grappling with . . .' (line 8) and 'I think we have to begin by facing up to the fact that . . .' (line 16).
- using 'here today' (line 1) to bring out the closeness and solidarity by drawing their attention to the fact that they have common ground together in time and space.

He then appears to attend to the hearers' interests, wants and needs:

- by suggesting that it was because of the international consciousness and awareness of the students themselves that he chose the topic – 'And that is why I thought what I should try to talk to you about today is . . .' (lines 3–4). Note the repetition of 'today'.
- by using expressions that capture their attention, as in: 'I hope that might be of interest to many of you . . .' (line 12).

He exploits the **politeness maxims:**

- of **agreement**, by trying to win the students over to his point of view, and even assuming that they already have his point of view: 'as you will see' (line 6) and 'I think you'll agree' (line 32).
- of **modesty**, by suggesting tentatively that he is doing his best to serve the students in a very unassuming way: 'I thought what I should try to talk to you about today is . . .' (line 4) and 'I hope that might be of interest to many of you . . .' (line 12), and he even plays down the fact that he is writing an important book, adding the information in something that amounts to an 'aside', an afterthought: 'If I say, for instance, that recently I have been studying and contributing to a new Oxford History of the British Empire, which I have, . . .' (lines 33–5).
- of **generosity**, saying: 'So I'm going to, er, at considerable risk er to myself, try to . . .' (lines 10–11), and maximising the expression of cost to himself, without explaining exactly why it is a risk. It could be that this is in itself a ploy to make what he is saying interesting and intriguing for his audience.

Finally, the lecture contains a liberal sprinkling of **negative politeness**, in the sense that there are hesitations phenomena and hedges, minimising the imposition of his information and views, as it were:

- And that is why I thought what I should try to talk to you about . . . (lines 3–4)
- So I'm going to, er, at considerable risk er to myself, try to set this phenomenon in a much wider, er, more global perspective. (lines 10–12)
- I think we have to begin by facing up to the fact that . . . (line 16)

Of course, as an experienced lecturer, Dr Smith is not using these linguistic phenomena by chance. They reflect the friendly, relaxed attitude and welcoming tone that he is intentionally adopting, so as to make his lecture both more enjoyable and easier to understand. However, it is interesting that such an unlikely piece of data contains so many of the positive and negative politeness features and adheres to so many of the polite maxims.

B6.2

Further reading ➤➤➤➤

❏ For a thorough, yet still accessible, explanation of the relation between the cooperative principle and the politeness principle, and deeper explanation of the maxims of tact, generosity, approbation and modesty, go to G. Leech (1983) and J. Thomas (1995).

❏ For maxims of praise, sympathy and consideration, go to A. Cruse (2000).

❏ For a full description of strategies and social distance, power and status, as well as other cultural aspects of politeness see P. Brown and S. Levinson (1987), M. Coulthard (1986), P. Grundy (2000) and J. L. Mey (1994).

❏ For an introduction to the sociolinguistic approach to politeness looking at address forms, read J. Holmes (1992).

EXPLORATION

DATA FOR INVESTIGATION

EXPLORING THE CONTEXT OF WRITING

Studying further and exploring

❑ situational context
❑ cultural and interpersonal context
❑ discourse communities

The texts in this unit are further samples of language dependent on knowledge of the context for their full meaning. Texts A, B, D and E are all written examples, although text E contains dialogue. Texts A and B are full of specialised vocabulary dependent on cultural background knowledge, the former from the sphere of football, the latter from a medical context. Text D, about an interview with T. S. Eliot, shows a breakdown in communication due to cultural background knowledge wrongly assumed to be shared. Text E, from *Pride and Prejudice*, contains intertextual references in an interpersonal context. Text C is from a TV cookery programme, and is necessarily based on the situational context.

Activity

❑ For each one of these five texts, make a short list of the readers' assumed background knowledge.

Text A

Quarterbacking is an imperfect art

This written excerpt is taken from an Associated Press football news flash on the Internet, dated 9 October 2000, 12.27 pm., and written by Dave Goldberg, an AP football writer.

Peyton Manning threw three interceptions, the most he's had in a game since his rookie year.

Brett Favre threw three interceptions and fumbled twice.

And Mark Brunell fumbled four snaps, losing two, and threw interceptions on consecutive possessions before being pulled.

Yes, even the best of NFL quarterbacks can have off days. And when they do, their teams lose, as the Colts, Packers and Jaguars did Sunday.

"There was no bright side," Brunell said after the Jaguars (2–4) fell three games and a tiebreaker behind Baltimore in the AFC Central.

Activity

Text A is exclusively for the US discourse community of football fans: it assumes knowledge of the cultural background context of the game.

❑   It makes no concessions to those do not understand the reference of the specialised vocabulary of in-group terms. Why do you think this is?

❑   Find another sports news text, preferably not about football, and compare the density (percentage out of all words) of specialist terms in your text with the density in the football text. What do you think is the main influence on the density of specialist terms – the size of the discourse community that follows the sport, the place where the text is published, or something else?

Text B

The investigations for female patients

This written text is taken from a patient Information sheet of a Scottish hospital. It sets out to describe a research project to compare three outpatient methods for investigating endometriosis, and to ask for the patients' cooperation with the project.

Details of the different investigations are given below. All women in your age group will receive the investigation 'endometrial biopsy'. In addition you may receive other investigation(s) – this will be as specified in the envelope. Either –

❑   No additional investigation   *or*
❑   Hysteroscopy   *or*
❑   Pelvic ultrasound   *or*
❑   Both hysteroscopy and ultrasound scan

If you are to have hysteroscopy, then your biopsy will be taken at the same time as the hysteroscopy. This will sometimes be the same day as your clinic visit.

The ultrasound investigation requires a separate appointment at the Ultrasound department.

Hysteroscopy is examination of the interior of the womb with a small telescope passed through the cervix (neck of the womb)

Pelvic ultrasound uses sound waves to obtain an image of the structure of the womb, and is performed externally (abdominally) and when appropriate, also internally (vaginally)

Endometrial biopsy is a standard clinic procedure which involves taking a sample of the womb lining. It is currently performed using a small plastic tube known as a 'pipelle'. A newer 'brush' sampler is now available which may give us more information. We are therefore keen to compare the results obtained using the two methods, and this study provides an ideal opportunity to do so. We are therefore asking for your consent to use *both* methods of endometrial sampling – the standard pipelle biopsy plus the newer brush sample. This will add very slightly to the time taken for the procedure but should not cause any additional discomfort.

Activity

Text B is written by British medical staff for the general public, whom they assume to be non-medical specialists.

❑ Do you think that this is an example of writers using their knowledge to intentionally exclude those without the knowledge? What aspects of the procedures have not been mentioned? Why not?

❑ Think back to occasions when you have visited a doctor. To what extent do you feel that the way he or she speaks to you shows the power of knowledge, as in, 'I'm only going to tell you this much, because you are just a patient'? Do you think that this would vary according to the class, race or age of the patient? Is this different in other countries, in your experience?

Text C

Cookery class: unbaked chocolate cake

This excerpt comes from a BBC2 programme entitled *Delia's How To Cook: Part Two*. Delia Smith belongs to Britain's heritage of cookery programmes and simple cookery books. The programme (29 October 2000) is subtitled 'A guide to all things chocolate'. She starts by saying that the chocolate should be melted, and that two ounces of butter be beaten into it.

Now the next ingredient that's going to join the melted chocolate and butter is this one here, which is double cream. And it's been sort of lightly whipped to the floppy stage. So I'm just going to add that. And – just clean the bowl – and then I'm just going to stir the chocolate into the cream, combine the two thoroughly. This needs a bit more mixing, it looks sort of marbley, at the moment, and you just need to get all that sort of marble out of it so that it's a nice evenly blended colour.

And then the next ingredient is in my bowl here. It looks a bit peculiar but what it is actually – it's eight ounces of these, and these are oat biscuits that are very lightly sweetened. And what you do with them is you take the eight ounces and just break them up into little pieces. And I would say these are roughly sort of quarter of an inch, third of an inch, it's not vital, but not too small because you're going to get some crunch in this. Now they're going to go in to the cream and the chocolate. And we're just going to give them a little mix to be thoroughly combined.

And then the next ingredient I've got is the dried cherries that we used earlier in the series when we made the duck sauce, the dried sour cherries. I've got two ounces of those and two ounces of fat juicy raisins. And these have been soaked, um, overnight in three tablespoons of rum. So they're going to go in next.

And then finally I've got four ounces of pistachio nuts. You can buy these in packets ready shelled with no salt, er, specially for baking. And what I've done is I've just roughly chopped them. And they again shouldn't be too small because we want lots of nice crunch.

So we've got cherries, raisins, pistachio nuts and biscuits and now I'm just going to give this another mixing. Now the name of this cake is Un-baked Chocolate Cake. It's sometimes called Refrigerator Cake because the lovely thing about it is that it doesn't need any baking. It's just going to go into the refrigerator.

Activity

Text C is a TV cookery demonstration assuming very little cultural knowledge of the art of cooking.

❑ Out of all the referring expressions, roughly what proportion have exophoric reference and what proportion contain deixis? How much have you lost by reading the script as opposed to actually seeing the TV programme?

❑ How explicit is the language? Are there any parts that you would rewrite in a less explicit way if you were to aim at an audience of more experienced cooks?

❑ Do a simple experiment; you will need to find nine individuals willing to take part. Choose a series of connected actions to teach each individual (separately, not as a group); for example, you could demonstrate changing the battery for the flash in your camera or calling a friend using the address book in your mobile phone. Ask three of the individuals to watch you, listening to your instructions (using exophoric reference and deixis), and then, once you have finished, copy you exactly. Ask another three to watch and copy you, without you saying anything. Ask the other three to listen to the instructions and then do it, without you giving a demonstration. Compare how well each of the nine carry out the actions. What does this say about situational context and reference in instructions?

Text D

T. S. Eliot's Nobel Prize

The following anecdote is taken from *The Cassell Dictionary of Anecdotes*, edited by Nigel Rees (1999). This tale was told by Philip French of the *Observer* (17 April 1994).

> When it was announced that T. S. Eliot had been awarded the Nobel Prize for Literature in 1948, he was making a lecture tour of the United States. A Mid-Western reporter asked him if he had been given the prize for his great work *The Waste Land*. 'No', replied Eliot, 'I believe I have been given it in recognition of my whole corpus.' Accordingly, the journalist wrote: 'In an interview with our airport correspondent this morning, Mr Eliot revealed that the Swedish Academy had given him the Nobel Prize not for *The Waste Land* but for his poem *My Whole Corpus.*'

Activity

Text D is written for those who know something about T. S. Eliot's work. It shows a breakdown in communication.

❑ The breakdown occurs because the speaker implies one thing and the hearer infers another. Explain it in terms of background knowledge.
❑ Would you agree that this humorous piece of writing invites readers to share the attitude of the writer and laugh at those who know less than them, or do you think the humour lies in something more complex than this? To what extent is this typical of jokes, anecdotes and comedy in general? Can you think of any examples?

Text E

Elizabeth and Darcy declare their love

This is from Jane Austen's book *Pride And Prejudice* (1813). Elizabeth had loved Darcy for a long time but had always kept her distance because she had found him proud and supercilious. She had rejected his advances in the past because she had heard rumours about him being cruel to her sister's fiancé. Just before this extract, she learns that he had not in fact been cruel, and that he had secretly helped her sister out of serious financial difficulties. This scene takes place at the end of the book. They walk through the grounds of his estate, and finally alone, open their hearts for the first time.

Now was the moment for her resolution to be executed; and, while her courage was high, she immediately said –

"Mr Darcy, I am a very selfish creature; and for the sake of giving relief to my own feelings, care not how much I may be wounding yours. I can no longer help thanking you for your unexampled kindness to my poor sister. Ever since I have known it, I have been most anxious to acknowledge to you how gratefully I feel it. Were it known to the rest of the family, I should not have merely my own gratitude to express."

"I am sorry, exceedingly sorry," replied Darcy, in a tone of surprise and emotion, "that you have ever been informed of what may, in a mistaken light, have given you uneasiness. I did not think Mrs Gardiner was so little to be trusted."

"You must not blame my aunt. Lydia's thoughtlessness first betrayed to me that you had been concerned in the matter; and, of course, I could not rest until I knew the particulars. Let me thank you again and again, in the name of all my family, for that generous compassion which induced you to take so much trouble, and bear so many mortifications, for the sake of discovering them."

"If you *will* thank me," he replied, "let it be for yourself alone. That the wish of giving happiness to you might add force to the other inducements which led me on, I shall not attempt to deny. But your *family* owe me nothing. Much as I respect them, I believe I thought only of *you*."

Elizabeth was too much embarrassed to say a word. After a short pause, her companion added, "You are too generous to trifle with me. If your feelings are still what they were last April, tell me so at once. *My* affections are unchanged; but one word from you will silence me on this subject for ever."

Elizabeth, feeling all the more than common awkwardness and anxiety of his situation, now forced herself to speak; and immediately, though not very fluently, gave him to understand that her sentiments had undergone so material a change since the period to which he alluded, as to make her receive with gratitude and pleasure his present assurances. The happiness which this reply produced was such as he had probably never felt before, and he expressed himself on the occasion as sensibly and as warmly as a man violently in love can be supposed to do. Had Elizabeth been able to encounter his eyes, she might have seen how well the expression of heartfelt delight diffused over his face became him; but, though she could not look, she could listen, and he told her of his feelings which, in proving of what importance she was to him, made his affection every moment more valuable.

 Activity

❑ In Text E, Elizabeth and Darcy finally refer to their intimate interpersonal context.
   ❑ Can you find examples of intertextuality? How are they expressed?
   ❑ We have said that people who are close make vague and implicit reference to entities and events in their interpersonal context. Is this true of Elizabeth and Darcy? Why/why not?

❑ Do they have a shared attitude to conventions in their common socio-cultural context?

❑ Watch a film or a soap opera on TV, and record it if you can. Choose a ten-minute section of it with a substantial amount of dialogue, and make notes on the references to the situational, cultural background and interpersonal background context.

❑ Out of the three contexts, which one is referred to most?

❑ How often is there an overlap or a mixture of two or all of situational, cultural and interpersonal context at one time, assumed to be known?

❑ How much knowledge of the three contexts do you, as a viewer, have? How does the scriptwriter play on this?

INVESTIGATING CO-TEXT

C2

Studying further and exploring

C2.1

❑ cohesion

The texts on the next two pages have all the features of cohesion that we have been looking at, but you will find that they do not all occur in every text.

Text A, Shark Takes Leg, and Text B, Brad Pitt, are descriptive and informative, and they have a story line. Text C, Saving the Elk, is also descriptive and informative, but it deals in definitions and generalities. The type of text affects the form of cohesion.

Text D, Grammar stammers, contains sentences that are ambiguous because of cohesive devices that have not been used clearly.

Text A

Shark takes leg

This is the beginning of an article from the *Sydney Morning Herald* (7 November 2000).

The patrons at the Blue Duck café overlooking Perth's Cottesloe Beach were drinking coffee and having breakfast as the early morning swimmers splashed about just off shore.

Kim Gamble, owner of the café – a favourite spot of the city's business and political elite – was doing his paperwork on the balcony.

Suddenly, as he and his customers watched in horror, a five-metre white pointer shark ploughed into a group of swimmers, tearing one man's leg off and leaving him to die, and then chasing one of his companions towards the beach.

"From the balcony I could see this huge shark – it was really huge," a shaken Mr Gamble said soon after the attack. "There was a whole sea of blood and it was pulling the person."

Activity

Text A contains synonyms and anaphoric reference.

❑ Where are they?
❑ Why are they necessary?

Text B

Brad Pitt

Brad Pitt is a popular young film star who has sprung to fame since 1991. This excerpt comes from yahoo.com Internet. It is part of Rebecca Flint's *All-Movie Guide* to his career.

With looks that have inspired countless *People* magazine covers, Internet shrines, and record estrogen surges, Brad Pitt is an actor whose very name inspires more drooling platitudes about male beauty than it does about acting. Following his breakthrough as the wickedly charming drifter who seduces Geena Davis and then robs her blind in *Thelma and Louise* (1991), Pitt became one of Hollywood's hottest properties and spent most of the 1990s being lauded as everything from Robert Redford's heir apparent to the 'sexiest man alive.'

1991 marked the end of Pitt's sojourn in the land of obscurity, as it was the year he made his appearance in *Thelma and Louise*. Pitt's next major role did not come until 1994, when he was cast as the lead of the gorgeously photographed but woefully uneven *Legends of the Fall*. As he did in *A River Runs Through It*, Pitt portrayed a free-spirited, strong-willed brother, but this time had greater opportunity to further develop his enigmatic character. Following the film's release, *People* magazine dubbed Pitt 'the sexiest man alive.' That same year, fans watched in anticipation as Pitt exchanged his outdoorsy persona for the brooding, Gothic posturing of Anne Rice's tortured vampire Louis in the film adaptation of *Interview with a Vampire*. Starring opposite Tom Cruise, Pitt enjoyed the further helping of fame that was served up by the film's success.

Pitt next starred in the forgettable romantic comedy *The Favor* (1994) before going on to play a rookie detective investigating a series of gruesome crimes opposite Morgan Freeman in *Seven* (1995). In 1997, Pitt received a Golden Globe award and an Oscar nomination for his portrayal of a visionary mental patient in Terry Gilliam's *12 Monkeys*; the same year, Pitt attempted an Austrian accent and put on a backpack to play mountaineer Heinrich Harrar in *Seven Years in Tibet*. The film met with mixed reviews and generated a fair amount of controversy, thanks in part to the revelation that the real-life Harrar had in fact been a Nazi. Furthermore, due to its pro-Tibetan stance, the film also resulted in Pitt's being banned from China for life. In 1998, Pitt tried his hand at romantic drama, portraying Death in *Meet Joe Black*, the most expensive non-special effects film ever made. The film, which weighed in at three hours in length, met with excessively mixed reviews, although more than one critic remarked that Pitt certainly made a very appealing representative of the afterlife.

Activity

Text B demonstrates that in popular written English with a journalistic flavour, some features of cohesion or reference to co-text predominate at the expense of others.

❑ There are very few features of grammatical cohesion: which type of grammatical cohesion occurs most frequently?

❑ The cohesion is mainly lexical; what is the main device?

❑ Why do you think the characteristics described here in (a) and (b) are present in this text? What does it tell you about the text?

Text C

Saving the elk

This is taken from a Canadian Tourist Board website: CanadianParks.com. The website describes all the national parks, and Elk Island National Park is one on their list.

> Elk Island National Park is an island, not in the geographical sense, but in terms of its landscape of small hills and depressions surrounded by flat plains, and by virtue of its purpose, to create a fenced refuge for the protection and preservation of 3000 head of hoofed mammals, one of the highest concentrations of big game animals in the world. It was the first federally controlled area in Canada to be enclosed to protect a native mammal, the elk, and also the first large mammal sanctuary established in Canada. Set in the Beaver Hills, 45 kilometres east of Edmonton, Alberta, its 194 square kilometres rises 60 metres above the surrounding prairie, an oasis of boreal mixed forest and aspen parkland *vegetation*. It is also an island of protection for the heritage resources within its boundaries, and an island of tranquillity for the 350 000–400 000 visitors who each year approach the park as a destination for nature and wildlife viewing.

Activity

Text C differs from Texts A and B in that it deals in generalities. How is this reflected in the form of cohesion?

Text D

Grammar stammers

The following mini-extracts are taken from Richard Lederer's amusing *More Anguished English* (1987), which he calls 'An exposé of embarrassing, excruciating, and egregious errors in English'. These extracts come from the chapter entitled 'Grammar stammers', which lists funny cases of ambiguous grammar taken from US newspapers and magazines.

> ❏ During the summer, my sister and I milked the cows, but now that school has started, my father milks the cows in the morning, and us at night.
> ❏ Mrs McAllister watched as the giant airplane taxied out of the gate. Then like some wild beast she pointed her nose down the runway and screamed terrifically into the sky.
> ❏ Mr Yoshiko said the donkey owners should clearly state why they want to keep the animals. "If they cannot give good reasons why they need the donkeys, then they will be shot."
> ❏ Please place your garbage in this barrel. It will be here weekends for use.
> ❏ Recent visitors were Jonathan Goldings and their in-laws the Brett Packards, from Lake Placid, NY. Brett had his tonsils removed in Centerville. It was a pleasant surprise to have them for supper.

✪ Activities

❏ Take each of the sentences in Text D and
   a Explain their ambiguity in terms of cohesion.
   b Rewrite them so that the meaning is clear.
❏ Find a short text, of the same sort as Texts A and B, in that it contains popular written English with a journalistic flavour.
   a List the grammatical and lexical cohesive devices that predominate.
   b Compare the devices that predominate in your texts with the devices that predominate in Texts A and B.
   c To what extent can you say that the genre (type of text) determines the sort of cohesion that is used?
❏ Find a textbook which you have had to read for a course that you are doing or have done, and which you have found particularly difficult to follow.
   a Analyse the cohesive devices of a page or two that you remember having to read and reread in order to understand.
   b Decide whether you can say your difficulty in understanding is partly due to the presence of some devices or the absence of others.
❏ Do you think that children of 7–9 years use grammatical cohesion efficiently?
   a Find a child of about that age and record them.
   b Ask them to relate to you an incident that they witnessed or to tell you a story (not a well-known one).
   c Ask them to keep it short, so that they speak for only three or four minutes.
   d Transcribe it. This means writing every word that they say. Before you start, find a colleague who will work on it with you. Then look through the transcriptions of real spoken data in Units A1 and B1 to see how it is done, and check the transcription conventions mentioned in 'How to use this book'.
   e Look at each of the grammatical cohesion devices and see if they are used correctly.

f   See if there are any occasions in the recording when grammatical cohesion could have been used but was not.

g   Compare your findings with those of other students in your class.

h   Conclude whether children of 7–9 years use grammatical cohesion efficiently or not.

EXPLORING SPEECH ACTS

C3

Studying further and exploring

C3.1

❑   Speech acts and cultural variables

The texts and questions in this unit ask you to consider the sociolinguistic aspect of speech acts. They centre round the fact that the expression of speech acts is affected by the social differences that can dictate the need for indirectness (status, roles, age, gender, education, class, occupation and ethnicity) and the contextual constraints (the size of imposition; formality of situation). This unit also asks you to explore the rules surrounding speech acts and the effect of each country's culture on the choice and expression of speech acts.

Texts A, B and C are examples of speech acts in action. Text A comes from a newspaper and contains verbs that describe speech acts. Text B is from a children's book and illustrates the use of indirect speech acts in relations of unequal power. Text C is in fact two texts, both of which show that speech acts are bound by rules.

Text D is not an example of speech acts but a list of cultural dimensions which vary from country to country and reflect a view of life and society.

Text A

Aborigines' rights

This is from the national newspaper *The Australian*, dated 1 June 2000. It comes from an article written by Megan Saunders entitled 'Blacks in push for seats quota'. The issue is that the Aborigines' Commission and indigenous leaders (Ridgeway, Clark, Perkins and O'Donoghue) are calling for Aborigines to be represented in the Australian Parliament; they want a set number of seats to be reserved for Aboriginal Members of Parliament. This excerpt describes the discussions.

Two days after he refused to contemplate a treaty, the Prime Minister yesterday flatly rejected any suggestion of special or separate parliamentary representation for indigenous people, saying both issues would divide the nation.

Senator Ridgeway told *The Australian* that four seats should be set aside "in order not to alter the balance". He said it should be a temporary measure until the situation improved to the point where Aborigines were elected on their merits. "There would not be a need for the type of intervention that would currently be required once an indigenous person could get the sort of support others would," he said. The concept was backed by Mr Perkins, who suggested five seats in each house to give Aborigines an "opportunity to have their voice in parliament regardless of political parties". Ms O'Donoghue supported the proposal but said that she would prefer Aborigines to increase their representation in mainstream parties.

But Mr Howard publicly dismissed the idea. "I know that if we got into any kind of treaty negotiations, you would be talking about things like representation in parliament, special indigenous seats," he said. "You'd be talking about land ownership issues, you'd be talking about regional governance issues, and they would be seen quite widely by the rest of the community as divisive."

Mr Clark refused to comment until indigenous leaders met to develop a united front. But in his speech during Corroboree 2000 ceremonies last Saturday, he pointed to New Zealand, where Maoris had reserved seats, to Inuit home-rule in Greenland, and Sami parliaments in Finland, Norway and Sweden, as examples Australia could draw on in advancing indigenous rights.

Text B

Winnie the Pooh

Winnie the Pooh is the world-famous teddy bear created by the writer A. A. Milne (1882–1956). The characters of Milne's children's books are based on his son Christopher Robin's nursery toys; their adventures are set in Ashdown Forest, in southeast England, where the Milnes lived. This excerpt is from a chapter in *Winnie the Pooh* entitled 'In which Eeyore loses a tail and Pooh finds one'. Eeyore is a donkey who has a gloomy outlook on life and humanity; he assumes that someone has taken his tail. Pooh offers to find it and goes to consult Owl. The 'highly educated' Owl gives the highly lovable bear of very little brain his advice.

"Well," said Owl, "the customary procedure in such cases is as follows."

"What does Crustimoney Proseedcake mean?" said Pooh. "For I am a Bear of Very Little Brain, and long words Bother me."

"It means the Thing to Do."

"As long as it means that, I don't mind," said Pooh humbly.

"The thing to do is as follows. First, Issue a Reward. Then –"

"Just a moment," said Pooh, holding up his paw. "*What* do we do to this – what you were saying? You sneezed just as you were going to tell me."

"I *didn't* sneeze."

"Yes, you did, Owl."

"Excuse me, Pooh, I didn't. You can't sneeze without knowing it."

"Well, you can't know it without something having been sneezed."

"What I *said* was, 'First *Issue* a Reward'."

"You're doing it again," said Pooh sadly.

"A Reward!" said Owl very loudly. "We write a notice to say that we will give a large something to anybody who finds Eeyore's tail."

"I see, I see," said Pooh, nodding his head. "Talking about large somethings," he went on dreamily, "I generally have a small something about now – about this time in the morning," and he looked wistfully at the cupboard in the corner of Owl's parlour; "just a mouthful of condensed milk or what-not, with perhaps a lick of honey –"

"Well, then," said Owl, "we write out this notice, and we put it up all over the Forest."

"A lick of honey", murmured Bear to himself, "or – or not, as the case may be." And he gave a deep sigh, and tried very hard to listen to what Owl was saying.

But Owl went on and on, using longer and longer words, until at last he came back to where he started, and he explained that the person to write out this notice was Christopher Robin.

Text C

Invitations

a To garden parties

This text is taken from a fascinating book entitled *Home Management*, by Garth and Wrench, which aims to prepare newly-weds to run a household and behave correctly in society. Note that it was published in 1934 (Daily Express Publications, London).

When writing your notes of invitation to a garden party, it is well to mention whether tennis or any other game will be a feature of the afternoon. Guests at a garden party wear their very smartest frocks and hats, and probably carry parasols, but if the tennis players among them know that the tennis court will be in play, they will put on their tennis frocks or flannels, and bring their racquets with them.

Answers to all formal invitations must be in the third person: "Mr. and Mrs. Dugdale accept with pleasure Mrs. Wynston's kind invitation for Wednesday, June 15, at nine o-clock." Do be careful to avoid that very frequent mistake of writing "*will be*" pleased to accept. You are referring, remember, to the pleasure you feel at the moment of accepting, not to some future pleasure. Never answer an informal note in the third person. When the letters *R.S.V.P.* are not on an invitation card, an answer is neither expected nor necessary, but when they are, it is essential that a reply be sent – and PROMPTLY.

b To dinner parties

This text is from website of the Office of International Students Affairs, the University of Illinois, USA, which aims to prepare students to interact with their American hosts.

You may receive a verbal or written invitation from an American to visit his or her home. You should always answer a written invitation, especially if it says R.S.V.P. Do not say that you will attend unless you plan to do so. It is acceptable to ask your host about appropriate clothing. It is polite to arrive on time for special dinners and parties. If you will be late, call your host to explain. When you visit an American, especially for dinner, you will be asked what you would like to drink. You do not need to drink an alcoholic beverage. If you have any dietary restrictions you should tell the host at the time you accept the invitation.

 Activities

❑ Looking at the texts individually

a Which macro-class, direct speech acts and indirect speech acts are involved the most, in Texts A, B and C?

b In the three texts, what reasons can you see for the indirect speech acts being used? Consider the social differences and contextual constraints.

c In Text A, 'Aborigines' rights', why do you think there are so many verbs actually describing the speech acts? Find other national broadsheet newspaper reports about campaigns/negotiations and decide whether 'verbs naming speech acts' is part of the national broadsheet newspaper reporting genre or not.

d Would you say that Text B, 'Winnie the Pooh', shows a power-struggle? Is the indirect speech act and the way it is responded to appropriate for a book for children?

❑ Speech acts are governed by social conventions dependent on the context of culture.

a The two Text C 'Invitations' excerpts are about the speech acts of inviting and accepting invitations, and contain examples of a series of ways of expressing directives, giving advice. They illustrate how the social conventions vary from country to country, and from time to time. Compare the text's conventions and how they are expressed indirectly.

b Think of another situation in which a speech act is governed by conventions; write a description of it. You may want to look at the words used to ask someone out, or the words used to compliment someone on their clothes and the response of the complimented one, or the words used to apologise. The speech act situations and realisations are endless: the choice is yours.

c Ask 20 people to tell you what the conventions are. You can either write a questionnaire of responses for them to label true or false or you can give them a relatively free questionnaire in which you describe a situation and leave the respondents free to write what the participants would say.

d Write a brief description of your results and add a discussion, explaining why you think you got the answers that you did.

❑ Remember that speech act theory has limitations.

a As you were identifying the speech acts in Texts A, B and C, did you have a problem with overlap, or utterances that did not fit into macro-classes? Which was the greatest problem? Explain the problem and give examples.

b Do you feel that speech act theory is a satisfactory way of coding the function of language? Can you think of an improvement or better alternative?

❑ Think of a locution that constitutes a declaration speech act in your culture.
   a Explain the felicity conditions using Austin's model and then Searle's.
   b Which model do you prefer? Why?

Text D

Understanding the multi-cultural dimension

The findings summarised below are taken from the Royal Philips Electronic website (http://www.news.philips.com/mondial/archive/1999/august/artike14.html). The summary of the research is provided to guide people doing business with companies from other countries.

Understanding the multicultural dimension
Dutch engineer and social scientist Geert Hofstede has conducted extensive research into the problems of doing business across many cultures. After a comprehensive study of 80,000 IBM employees in 66 countries, he established four dimensions of national culture. These help managers identify areas in which they may encounter cultural difficulties:

❑ *Uncertainty avoidance*: this dimension refers to how comfortable people feel towards uncertainty. Cultures that ranked low (Great Britain) feel more comfortable with the unknown. Cultures high on uncertainty avoidance (Greece) prefer formal rules.

❑ *Power distance*: this is defined as "the extent to which the less powerful members of institutions and organizations accept that power is distributed unequally". In other words people in high power distance cultures (Philippines) are much more comfortable with a larger status differential than low power distance cultures (Sweden).

❑ *Masculinity-femininity*: this refers to expected gender roles in a culture. Masculine cultures (Japan) tend to have distinct roles for males and females, while feminine cultures (The Netherlands) have a greater ambiguity in what is expected of the genders.

❑ *Individualism-collectivism*: this is defined by the extent to which an individual's behavior is influenced and defined by others. Individual cultures (USA) prefer self-sufficiency while collectivists (Indonesia) recognize the obligations to the group.

For more information see *Cultures and Organizations* by Geert Hofstede (HarperCollins).

Activities

❑ Text D lists social dimensions that vary from culture to culture and can affect a speaker's choice of direct and indirect speech acts. To what extent would you agree that you can make blanket statements about cultural differences in this way? What difficulties might arise, if business people were to take these dimensions as scientifically proven for all occasions?

❑ How often do we really use indirect speech acts?

   a Over the next week, do one of the following alternatives:

      ❑ make a note of every single direct and indirect *directive* speech act that is addressed to you, word for word if you can, and make a brief note of the context, e.g. 'going through a door' or 'at a ticket office'.

      ❑ write down all written instructions that you see around you on notices, e.g. 'No Smoking', and make a brief note of the context, e.g. 'at a petrol station' or 'at the entrance to a park'.

   b See which you have more of – direct or indirect.

   c Examine how the indirect directives are expressed, to see which words and grammatical forms are used most.

   d Consider the extent to which the context affects the directness of the act.

   e Draw conclusions.

   f Write up your study.

❑ Look at all the texts to decide whether they have a mainly transactional or mainly international function, or whether they have an equal mix.

❑ Make a recording of two friends or relatives having a long casual conversation. You might have to wait until you know that they have settled down in a quiet place for an afternoon's chat over a coffee, or such like, so that you can get about an hour's recording. Do not give them any instructions as to what they should talk about or how; let it be spontaneous and natural.

   a Divide the recording up into three-minute chunks, regardless of what is happening at the three-minute interval; do not bother transcribing all this data.

   b Listen to each three-minute chunk and decide whether its function is primarily transactional or primarily interactional, or a 50/50 mixture.

   c Calculate what proportion of the 20 chunks is primarily transactional, what proportion is primarily interactional, and what proportion a 50/50 mixture, and say which proportion is biggest and why you think so.

   d Look at each of the three groups of chunks and see what direct speech acts are there.

   e Write up your findings under the title 'The overall function of a casual conversation'.

C4   THE ANALYSIS OF CONVERSATION

C4.1   Studying further and exploring

❑ conversation analysis
❑ interactional sociolinguistics
❑ social context

The data that you are invited to work with in this section is all to do with spoken language, since exchange structure and conversation analysis look at how people speak and interact orally, but not how people write to each other. However, Texts A and D are written versions of how people speak: Text A comes from a book that contains dialogue, and Text B is from a film. You will find some of the features of exchange structure and conversation analysis are present, despite the fact that it is not naturally occurring data. The features are exploited to dramatic advantage. By contrast, Texts B and C are transcriptions of real conversations. Text B takes place in a hospital kitchen and Text C in a lift. The difference between these conversations and the 'dramatic' ones of Texts A and D is striking.

Text A

Mr Kaplan

This excerpt comes from the light-hearted book *The Education of Hyman Kaplan*, by Leo Rosten (2000); it shows uninspired teaching methods of the between-the-wars period, the complications of the English language and the power struggles between students. Kaplan is a pupil in the English class of New York's Preparatory Night School for Adults. His teacher, Mr Parkhill has asked the students to write a sentence for each of three words, and read out their sentences. Mr Kaplan has just read his first sentence, and now Mr Parkhill prompts him to go on with his second. Be prepared for some strange English here: if you read the passage aloud, you will be able to understand what poor Kaplan means.

"Read your next sentence, Mr. Kaplan."

Mr. Kaplan went on, smiling. "De second void, ladies an' gentleman, is 'fascinate' – an' believe me is a planty hod void! So is mine santence: 'In India is all kinds snake-fescinators.'"

"You are thinking of snake-*charmers*." (Mr. Kaplan seemed to have taken the dictionary's description of "fascinate" too literally.) "Try 'fascinate' in another sentence, please."

Mr. Kaplan gazed ceilingward with a masterful insouciance, one eye half-closed. Then he ventured: "You *fescinate* me."

Mr. Parkhill hurried Mr. Kaplan on to his last word.

"Toid void, faller-students, is 'univoisity.' De santence usink dis void: 'Elaven yiss is married mine vife an' minesalf, so is time commink for our tvalft *univoisity*.'"

It was the opportunity for which Miss Mitnick had been waiting. "Mr. Kaplan mixes up two words," she said. "He means 'anniversary.' 'University' is a high college – the *highest* college."

Mr. Kaplan listened to this unwelcome correction with a fine sufferance. Then he arched his eyebrows and said, "You got right, Mitnick. Hau Kay! So I givink anodder santence: "Some pipple didn't have aducation in a *univoisity*'" – he glanced meaningfully at Miss Mitnick – "but just de same, dey havink efter elaven yiss de tvalft *annoiversery*.'"

Activity

Rewrite the dialogue parts of Text A as a play script, as in:

Teacher   Read your next sentence, Mr Kaplan.
Kaplan   De second void, ladies an' gentleman, is 'fascinate' – . . .

and then analyse it in terms of IRF. To what extent does it follow the model, and to what extent do you think it reflects what goes on in a real evening class for adults? How would you say that the writer exploits IRF and classroom traditions, and the deviations from it, to dramatic advantage?

Text B

Tamara's photos from the fancy dress

This excerpt is taken from a casual conversation in Diana Slade's (Eggins and Slade 1997: 11–12) database. It is a tea-break chat among three Australian women employees in a hospital kitchen. Slade says that the chat contains 'gossip', which 'involves participants engaging in exchanging negative opinions and pejorative evaluations about the behaviour of a person who is absent' and the purpose of which is interpersonal 'to do with the positioning of participants in relation to each other and to critical issues in their social world'. Note that in Slade's transcription system, = = indicates an overlap, . . . indicates a brief pause, and ( ) is a non-transcribable segment.

Jo   Did she see the photos in her coz*?
Jenny   She walks in . . . She stopped me she stopped me and she said, umm
         "Oh, by the way, have you have you seen any photos of = = me?" I
         thought, you know, you're a bit sort of, you know . . .
Jo   = = No one told her there were photos.
Jenny   She said, "Have you seen any photos of me at the fancy dress?" And
         I said, I said, "Well, as a matter of fact, I've seen one or two, um, of
         you Tamara, but you know, nothing . . ." And, um, she said "Do you know
         of anyone else who's taken = = any photos of me at the fancy dress?"
Donna   = = I wouldn't be taking any photos. = = I mean, I would have asked.
Jenny   = = I mean, if anyone had taken any of me at the fancy dress I'd want
         to = = burn them.
Jo   Why does she always want to get her picture? ( )
Jenny   She said, "I just wanted to see how well the costume turned out."
Jo   She's pretty insecure, that girl.

---

* As Slade explains 'Coz' is common Australian slang for costume.

 Activity

What features of turn-taking can you see in Text B? Why do you think they are present? Try and read it out with someone, and say whether you know of any films written with a script like that, and why.

Text C

Greetings in a lift

This excerpt is from Janet Holmes' (2000: 39) database. Here, Matt and Bob are male colleagues of equal status in a New Zealand government department. They meet and greet in the lift and the exchange is brought to an end when they reach Bob's floor. This is social talk with a reference to the shared context of work. Note that in Homes' transcription system, there are no capitals, commas or full stops, and she only uses? to indicate a rising intonation. The symbol + indicates a pause of up to one second.

> **M** hi how's things
> **B** hi good good + haven't seen you for ages how are you
> **M** fine busy though as always + must meet my performance objectives eh [laugh]
> **B** [laugh] yeah me too
> *Lift arrives at Bob's floor*
>   ah well see you later
> **M** yea bye

Activity

Describe Text C in terms of sequences and discuss why it has the characteristics that it does. Would you class it as a conversation?

Text D

The Full Monty

This text is from the British comedy film *The Full Monty* (1997). Six unemployed Sheffield steelworkers are driven to prepare a strip show to solve their money problems. As the blurb on the video says, 'Director Peter Cattaneo combines black comedy, roaring hilarity and all the absurdity, heartache and pathos of six men trying to keep body, soul and dignity together.' In this scene, Gaz and his ten-year old son Nathan are in the post office. The boy wants to withdraw the £100 that the owner of the club demands to cover his losses. Note the transcription convention of numbers in brackets to indicate the length of pause in seconds.

> **G** Nath – Nath – you can't give this, kid! It's your savings!
> **N** I can. It just needs your signature. It says in t'book. *[To the assistant at the counter]* I'd like to take out my money out please.
> **G** *[To Nathan]* Well you bloody well can't have it. *[To the assistant]* You – you're all right love. It's sorted.
> **N** *[To Gaz]* It's my money. I want it. *[To the assistant]* A hundred pounds please.
> **G** *[To Nathan]* Well, when you're eighteen, you-you-you you can walk in and get it yourself, can't you?

> N   You said you'd get it back.
> G   I know. (0.5) but you don't want to listen to what I say. (0.5)
> N   You said so. (0.5) I believe you. (0.5)
> G   You do? (1)
> N   Yeah. (2.5)
> G   Blimey, Nath.

✪ Activities

❏   Is it possible to look at Text D from the point of view of adjacency pairs and sequences? Discuss why/why not. Analyse, in terms of turn-taking, how the change in dramatic effect half way through this little extract is achieved.

❏   Going back now to interactional sociolinguistics, you will recall that it takes into account the context, and the fact that social groups have their own varieties or in-group codes. Look again at all four extracts and think about how the
    i   location that the exchange takes place in
    ii   relationship between the people (look at roles, status and power)
    iii histories they share
    iv   purpose in speaking

❏   affect the
    i   exchange structure
    ii   turn-taking
    iii adjacency pairs
    iv   sequences
    v   grammar
    vi   lexis.

❏   Record a lesson or seminar and analyse a stretch of it (no more than ten minutes) in which the teacher is talking and interacting with the students. Recording must of course be overt, so you will have to get the authorisation from the teacher before the session. Analyse the ten-minute stretch in terms of IRF.
    i   What are the factors that determine whether the IRF structure is followed?
    ii   Would you like to suggest a different model for classroom interaction?

❏   Design a questionnaire to see what language people use in pre-sequences. A way to do it would be to describe a situation and ask them what they would say, as in:

> You are in the library sitting next to a colleague whom you do not know very well. The colleague lives near you and has a car. You are feeling tired from your day's reading and want them to run you home (they have never given you a lift before). What might you say, to prepare the ground, before you actually come out with your request?

❑   As you can see, this question is phrased in such a way to ensure that your subjects would use a pre-sequence; otherwise, you may find that they just write their request sequence. Make sure that you include as many types of pre-sequence as possible, for example, pre-requests, pre-invitations, pre-announcements, pre-commands, pre-advice. Your question should also contain the socio-cultural dimensions of situational context, and the context of shared knowledge about speakers, their histories and their purpose in speaking. A list of ten situations should be enough. You will only start to get answers that you can group into trends and typical responses if you give the questionnaire to a minimum of twenty people. Write up your findings about the language that people use in pre-sequences and the socio-cultural factors influencing their choice. Include an appendix in your questionnaire.

FOLLOWING THE COOPERATIVE PRINCIPLE

Studying further and exploring

❑   cooperative principle
❑   relevance theory
❑   cultural variables

You are going to read five quite different scripts. Text A is a theatre's description of a member of staff, taken from its programme; Texts B and C are from the television, the first being a celebrity chat show and the second the news; and Text D is promotional web material for a concert. In all of these, there is evidence of conversational implicature but in each case it is quite different and is used for a different purpose. Text E is from a classic play, featuring a dramatic moment between a husband and wife, and it shows evidence of maxim violation.

Text A

Peter Pan programme

This excerpt is taken from a programme for *Peter Pan*, performed in the Royal Lyceum Theatre, Edinburgh, (Christmas 1999). *Peter Pan* is a children's story, written by J. M. Barrie in 1904, about a family of three children who fly away to the Never Never Land with Peter Pan, live with the Lost Boys and fight the pirates. This excerpt is part of the programme's description of the cast and the technical support: it describes Mike Travis, on percussion.

Mike Travis spends his life hitting things of various shapes and sizes. When he is not hitting things, he lives in the country with two dogs, two cats, two goats, twenty-one ducks, five geese, two pigs and eight hens (but not all in the same house, the smell would be minging!*) He loves playing for the Lyceum Christmas shows (Peter

Pan is his twelfth) because he gets to make up funny sounds for people like scratching, creeping, fighting, getting kicked on the bum and getting their noses tweaked. Mike really likes small children but he couldn't eat a whole one.

* Scots English meaning *smelly*

Activity

Describe Text A in terms of maxim observing, flouting and violating. How is maxim flouting used to reach the children in the text? Compare it with Text D below.

Text B

Parkinson

This excerpt is taken from a TV celebrity chat show hosted by Michael Parkinson, 31 March 2001, in which he talked to Tamsin from the London TV soap *Eastenders*. Tamsin described an incident in a celebrity party, when she was a barmaid. She dropped a bowl of punch and it spilt everywhere. Michael Palin, a famous TV personality, helped her by putting salt on the spill to dry up the wine and stop it staining the carpet. In the following text, she mentions meeting Ronnie Corbett, a very short stand-up comedian.

Tamsin	And Michael Palin and I spent the next two hours on our hands and knees with salt. Literally mopping it up. But you know I've never met Rennie – Ronnie Corbett and I remember – one thing I remember – I was kneeling down and the whole two hours he was at my eye-level. And I never knew how tall he was /.../
Parkinson	A – and also too you doing this er this drama series // called *Redcap*.
Tamsin	// It's a film actually It's a BBC1 film =
Parkinson	= BBC1 film.
Tamsin	And – er – it's about the special investigation branch within the army.
Parkinson	Yes.
Tamsin	Which basically entails being under cover em solving crime within the army and Patrick Harvinson and he's written *E.R.* and *Soldier Soldier* and the BBC's been kind enough to let me go and do it and then go back to *Eastenders* in the – er – summer.
Parkinson	Have you got to learn to be a soldier?
Tamsin	Got to learn how to hold a gun, and I've got to be three weeks training in the army.
Parkinson	That'll be fun eh?
Tamsin	Can't wait.
Parkinson	[heh heh heh]
Tamsin	Not like that.

Activity

Text B is full of maxim floutings – where are they? Explain how the audience understands the humour of the floutings.

Text C

Foot and mouth and elections

The year 2001 saw the worst outbreak of foot and mouth disease in the UK for a hundred years. In May, farmers' unions and opposition parties put pressure on the Prime Minister, Tony Blair, to delay the elections, and concentrate on wiping out the disease. On 2 April, he announced that he would put them off until June. This is from the BBC1 news.

Mr Blair	Any period of uncertainty is also bad for the economy as a whole. Business needs stability in order to plan ahead. Uncertainty is also bad for our public services, which would also lose from weeks or months of uncertainty.
Commentator	Does this mean the General Election's in June, too? Well of course it does and he can't say so.
Interviewer	Everybody watching and listening will take it from what you said that there is going to be a General Election on June 7th. Is it not possible simply to confirm that?
Mr Blair	I think it's very important (0.5) that (0.5) we ensure that the proper process of government goes on. I mean the very reason I've announced this d – delay to the local elections is precisely so that we can carry on with the business of government, putting in place the mechanisms to eradicate the disease. Now, you know, I've no doubt there'll be lots of speculation. I'm not (0.5) er – standing here and saying to you there won't be, but it's important that the formal process is gone through in the proper way.

Activity

Does Text C contain maxim violation? If you think so, which maxim does the Prime Minister violate? If you think not, how does he get round answering the interviewer's question? To what extent is this typical of politician-speak when they are interviewed by the media?

Text D

Australian Bach

This is an excerpt from a newspaper article entitled 'Playing it straight: Australian Bach Ensemble' from *The Sydney Morning Herald*, 19 March 2000. The reviewer, Harriet

Cunningham, discusses performances of Bach, the German eighteenth-century composer, which abound because it is the 250th anniversary of his death.

> How do you like your Bach? Hard, soft, poached or fried? The 250th anniversary of his death has prompted a rash of reinterpretations. Glenn Gould hums along, Paul Grabowsky scrambles the Matthew Passion, and this year's Melbourne Festival promises three weeks of technicolour Bach.
>
> The Australian Bach Ensemble does it straight. The ensemble has only just begun to explore the range of repertoire by this highly productive composer, and it shows. Clunky moments, and a stumble here and there were outweighed by some glorious playing.

Activity

Describe Text D in terms of maxim observing, flouting and violating. How is maxim flouting used to reach the children in Text A and to review the Australian Bach Ensemble in Text D? Would you say this is typical of programmes and reviews? Find some others, to back up your opinion.

Text E

Death of a Salesman

This excerpt is from the opening scene from *Death of a Salesman* (1949) by the American playwright Arthur Miller. The characters, Willy and Linda Loman live in New York. Willy is sixty and has to drive to New England every week to work.

> Linda   [*hearing Willy outside the bedroom, calls with some trepidation*]: Willy!
> Willy   It's all right. I came back.
> Linda   Why? What happened? [*Slight pause.*] Did something happen, Willy?
> Willy   No, nothing happened.
> Linda   You didn't smash the car, did you?
> Willy   [*with casual irritation*] I said nothing happened. Didn't you hear me?
> Linda   Don't you feel well?
> Willy   I'm tired to death. [*The flute has faded away. He sits on the bed beside her, a little numb.*] I couldn't make it. I just couldn't make it, Linda.
> Linda   [*very carefully, delicately*]: Where were you all day? You look terrible.
> Willy   I got as far as a little above Yonkers. I stopped for a cup of coffee. Maybe it was the coffee.
> Linda   What?
> Willy   [*after a pause*] I suddenly couldn't drive any more. The car kept going off on to the shoulder, y'know?

Linda   [*helpfully*] Oh. Maybe it was the steering again. I don't think Angelo knows the Studebaker.

Willy   No, it's me, it's me. Suddenly I realise I'm goin' sixty miles an hour and I don't remember the last five minutes. I'm – I can't seem to – keep my mind to it.

Linda   Maybe it's your glasses. You never went for your new glasses.

Willy   No, I see everything. I came back ten miles an hour. It took me nearly four hours from Yonkers.

Linda   [*resigned*]: Well, you'll just have to take a rest, Willy, you can't continue this way.

Activity

❏   In Text E, a husband violates maxims, talking to his wife. How does she react? Do you feel that this is typical of people who know each other well and for a long time (spouses, close friends, and so on)?

❏   Would you agree that children have to be taught to appreciate maxim flouting whereas maxim violating comes to them naturally? Think of examples to support your opinion, in your own experience.

❏   Make your own recording of a TV comedy show with well-known actors, or stand-up comedy, and pick out the instances of maxim flouting for comic effect. Which maxim is flouted most, would you say? Why do you think this is?

❏   Test the theory that a lot of what we say contains maxim flouting. Write an essay based on the following:

　i   Transcribe part of a spontaneous, unguided casual conversation between a husband and wife, or long-term girlfriend and boyfriend.

　ii   Categorise each utterance as 'maxim observing' or 'maxim flouting' (or 'maxim violating' if you know for sure) and calculate the percentage of utterances containing maxim flouting (and maxim violating).

　iii Interview the husband/boyfriend and wife/girlfriend, separately, about what they meant each time they meant more than what they said, why they violated a maxim.

❏   Do any of the texts contain examples of a speaker or writer infringing a maxim, or opting out? Explain why, or why not.

❏   Make a 10-minute recording of a casual conversation between people who know each other well, and transcribe it. Are there examples of them infringing or opting out of a maxim? If there are none, why is this? If there are instances,

　–   analyse the language that is used to infringe or opt out, to see if there are any interesting features of note

　–   have a look at the power relationship between speakers, and describe the social factors involved.

C6

APPLYING POLITENESS

C6.1

Studying further and exploring

❏   politeness and social variables

This unit contains a selection of authentic written texts demonstrating different aspects and uses of politeness strategies and maxims. The majority are written texts with spoken characteristics: Text A is a mobile phone text message, and Texts C and D are e-mails. Text B is a poem with a particular communicative objective requiring delicacy. Finally, Text E is a film transcript with an idiosyncratic brand of politeness. All the texts have been chosen for you to analyse because each offers an interesting dimension or problem, be it of a cultural nature or a social nature.

Text A

Mobile phone text messages

This is an exchange of text messages on a mobile phone. The names have been changed, and telephone number replaced with 'XXXX XXXX'. Joan did not know who sent the first text.

Robert	Hi, any chance of getting a copy of 2000 today at some point? Rob.
Joan	You are my first wrong number text message.
Robert	Why? Who are you? Not pete i assume?
Joan	No. Do you mean Smith?
Robert	Yes.
Joan	I'm Mary's mum.
Robert	I'm robert, petes mums partner. Sorry to bother you:)))
Joan	How funny! OK – now tell me what a copy of 2000 is. [*message sent twice*]
Robert	Do you want the answer twice?? :)) 2000 is an operating system for the computer. Just like windows 98 but better and more secure.
Joan	I wish I hadn't asked. How did you get my number? Can I put this conversation into a book on linguistics I'm writing?
Robert	It's the number ive had for peter for a while. Not had call to use it till now. You must have his old phone or sim card. Yes, feel free to use it:))
Joan	Thanks. This is not his phone or card.
Robert	Do you have the number he uses now? Sorry to hear about their split.
Robert	Sorry again. I really dont know where i got your number from.
Joan	XXXX XXXX. Have a nice day!
Robert	Thanks. And you.

Activity
In Text A, the mobile phone text message exchange, which predominates – positive politeness or negative politeness? Why? In what way is it similar to a casual conversation? How does it differ and why?

Text B

To his coy mistress

To his coy mistress is one of Andrew Marvell's (1621–78) most famous poems. This 'invitational lyric' (the editor Donno's term, Penguin, 1972) is addressed to his mistress, who is reluctant to consummate their relationship. The poem contains a balance of teasing humour and impatient passion.

> *Had we but world enough and time,*
> *This coyness, lady, were no crime.*
> *We would sit down and think which way*
> *To walk, and pass our long love's day.*
> *Thou by the Indian Ganges' side*
> *Shouldst rubies find: I by the tide*
> *Of Humber would complain. I would*
> *Love you ten years before the Flood;*
> *And you should, if you please, refuse*
> *Till the conversion of the Jews.*
> *My vegetable love should grow*
> *Vaster than empires, and more slow.*
> *An hundred years should go to praise*
> *Thine eyes, and on thy forehead gaze;*
> *Two hundred to adore each breast,*
> *But thirty thousand to the rest;*
> *An age at least to every part,*
> *And the last age should show your heart.*
> *For, lady, you deserve this state;*
> *Nor would I love at lower rate.*
>   *But at my back I always hear*
> *Time's winged chariot hurrying near;*
> *And yonder all before us lie*
> *Deserts of vast eternity.*
> *Thy beauty shall no more be found,*
> *Nor, in thy marble vault, shall sound*
> *My echoing song; then worms shall try*
> *That long-preserved virginity;*
> *And your quaint honour turn to dust,*
> *And into ashes all my lust.*

The grave's a fine and private place,
But none, I think, do there embrace.
Now, therefore, while the youthful hue
Sits on thy skin like morning dew,
And while thy willing soul transpires
At every pore with instant fires,
Now let us sport us while we may,
And now, like am'rous birds of prey,
Rather at once our time devour
Than languish in his slow-chapped pow'r.
Let us roll all our strength and all
Our sweetness up into one ball,
And tear our pleasures with rough strife
Thorough the iron gates of life.
Thus, though we cannot make our sun
Stand still, yet we will make him run.

 Activity

In Text B, the love poem, which predominates, positive or negative politeness, and why? How do the politeness maxims come into play with cooperative maxims?

Text C

Prospective PhD student

This text is an e-mail from a female Chinese postgraduate student, on an MA in teaching English to speakers of other languages. It is addressed to one of her female British lecturers, who already has linguistics PhD students in the area of TESOL and pragmatics.

I always consider you as a wise and honest mentor of mine. So, I would like to ask for your opinion about whether or not I am qualified to take up a doctoral study after I finish my MA here. And if your answer is yes, could you give me some suggestions on which schools I should choose for my study.

There are quite a number of fields I am interested in at present.

1 I do love to study pragmatics. I always have great curiosity in finding out how languages work. My dream is that some day I can decode the mystery of how a language is learnt and thus can make it easier for the second language learners.

2   I'm also very interested in the application of new technology (i.e. the Internet or computer or video conferencing) to the field of language teaching and learning. Maybe one day I will successfully run a language school on the Internet!

3   I feel that cultural study is very important for the learning of a second language, especially after students have all the 'correct' grammar in head, but can't communicate. So, I would also like to study how cultures are affecting the learning of a second language.

I know you are very busy, so I would appreciate it if you could give me some advice and directions. Thank you!

Activity

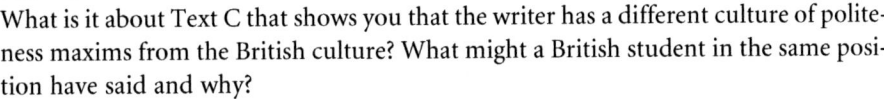

What is it about Text C that shows you that the writer has a different culture of politeness maxims from the British culture? What might a British student in the same position have said and why?

Text D

Rejections

These two texts are each the beginnings and ends of e-mails from journal editors responding to an author's proposal of an article. The [...] indicates where the central body of the e-mail has been omitted. Neither of the e-mails brings good news.

Dear [Name]

Thank you for your paper [title] submitted to [Journal].

I read your paper with interest. It is well and clearly written and argued, the data was interesting and you obviously know what you are writing about.

I must therefore admit that I hesitated a long time whether or not [Journal] would be the best forum for this paper, and I finally decided to recommend you to submit it elsewhere. This had little to do with quality, but rather with the fact that its topic is not squarely within the scope our new journal would like to establish in the field.

[...]

I am sorry I must recommend you to submit elsewhere, because it is an interesting and good paper, and I hope you'll be back with a paper that is a bit more within the scope of [Journal]

Best wishes [Name]

Dear *[Name]*

[Name] and I have now had an opportunity to share our reactions to your submission to *[Journal]*, *[Title]*. I am sorry to say that we think it doesn't reach the Journal's threshold for publication, so we have to decline it.

[...]

I am sorry to have to pass on this disappointing news, but *[Name]* and I hope the comments may be of some value to you if you decide to revise the paper and submit it to another journal.

With best wishes
[Name] *[Name]*

 Activity

Both e-mails in Text D have the goal of performing a very face-threatening act. Look at the politeness strategies and maxims obeyed and also label the speech acts. Finally, analyse in detail the language used to soften the blow, in terms of grammar and lexis. Are the two emails different in any way?

Text E

A touch of class

Basil Fawlty, of BBC TV's *Fawlty Towers*, is a part of British comedy heritage, and a master at politeness and deference pushed to obsequiousness. In this episode, 'A touch of class' (1975), the hotel owner sets out to attract a higher class of customer. In this scene, he is trying to impress an upper-class guest who calls himself Lord Melbury, and to make up for having made him fall off his chair at lunch. When Melbury asks if Fawlty will cash a cheque for £200 (equivalent to £400 today), he tries to cover up his shock.

Melbury	I was wondering, can you cash me a small cheque? I – I'm playing golf // this afternoon //
Fawlty	// Oh delighted! //
Melbury	// and I'd rather not go into the town =
Fawlty	= Absolutely! I mean, er, how much? If – if it's not a rude question . . .
Melbury	Could you manage – fif – er – oh – er a hundred?
Fawlty	A hun- ! (0.5) Oh! (laughs) Absolutely! Oh yes, I mean, a hundred and fifty? Two hun- a hundred and sixty? Or . . .
Melbury	Oh yes, well, let's see. Dinner tonight, a few tips, oh and it's the weekend, isn't it? Would two hundred be all right?

Fawlty	Oh, ha, ha, ha, ha. Oh please! Oh tremendous! Oh I'm so happy. I'll send someone out to town straight away and have it here when – when you get back.
Melbury	Yes, well, that'll be splendid.
Fawlty	Thank you. Thank you a lot.
Melbury	Thank you so much. *(Exits)*
Fawlty	Not at all. I mean, it's my privilege.

Activities

❏ In Text E, discuss Fawlty's polite formulas in terms of context and purpose, and social status and roles. Explain linguistically why we can say that he is being more obsequious than polite.

❏ Take all the texts together and think about politeness and the variables of status and roles. Can you see any tendencies emerging?

❏ If you use a mobile phone for text messages, or you use e-mail, or you have an answering machine, collect the messages that you receive in the next few days and analyse them from the point of view of politeness strategies and maxims. Compare the messages that you receive from people whom you consider to be good friends and those you would call acquaintances, to find if differences in degree of familiarity affect the way that politeness is expressed.

❏ In what way might written communications differ from spoken exchanges, in terms of politeness? What are the variables that might influence these differences?

EXTENSION

READINGS

CONTEXT: KNOWLEDGE AND STEREOTYPES

As you will see in this reading, Wardhaugh starts by saying that we 'assume that those with whom we deal share much specific information about the world' and then goes on to explain that 'there are differences between the parties in the specific that they know in contrast to the kinds of background knowledge that they share'. He makes the point that common knowledge is culture-loaded and varies from group to group.

Reading and researching

R. Wardhaugh (1985) *How Conversation Works*, pp. 16–20, Oxford: Blackwell.

We function in a world of normal appearances and usually do not probe beneath the surface of events, and in general, we believe that everybody else behaves in that respect much as we do, sharing with us a similar approach to daily existence. Those who probe are people like scientists and psychiatrists, but even their probing is restricted to a very narrow range of activities. Indeed, we go further and assume that those with whom we deal share much specific information about the world. One simple way of convincing yourself that this is so, that there is considerable shared background knowledge in any conversation, is to insist that each party make everything quite explicit in the very next conversation you have. That conversation will quickly degenerate: you may find yourself accused of being crazy, pedantic, or disruptive, or you may be assigned some other clearly antisocial label. Tempers are also likely to become frayed. Another way is to attempt to find out from newspapers, magazines, or radio and TV reports what is happening on some issue by using only the actual words you read or hear on a single specific occasion, completely disregarding any previous knowledge you might have of the topic. You will probably not be able to make much sense of what you either read or hear. One of the great difficulties you encounter in reading a local newspaper in a place you happen to be visiting is your lack of the background knowledge necessary to interpret what you are reading. This lack makes many items of local news either obscure or elusive: you lack knowledge of the people, the events, and the issues and have little or nothing on which to hang any details you are presented with. But the locals do not experience this difficulty.

Common knowledge, then – that is, 'what everyone knows' – is necessarily something that is culture-loaded and varies from group to group. Much of what everyone knows is also either scientifically unwarranted or very superficial. For example, there are numerous stereotypes in this kind of knowledge – ideas we have about the 'typical' behaviour and characteristics of people or objects. But that should not surprise us, because, after all, that is essentially what norms themselves are in one sense – abstractions based on certain kinds of experiences which apparently typify some kind of general behaviour. Many people go through life holding the view that common knowledge and stereotypes characterize a sort of truth about the world; others are somewhat more critical and conscious of the complexities that lie behind such a simple belief. What we must not assume, however, is that common knowledge is always false and stereotyping is always bad; social harmony is possible only if there are things we can agree on, and there are measures of agreement. What may be important is how fixed are the measures any society uses, not the existence of the measures themselves.

In periods of rapid social change old norms and stereotypes come under attack at a time when new ones are not available, so it is not surprising that confusion results. Linguistic behaviour at such times tends to reflect the disorder. Some strive to preserve the old ways, as conservative factions in Greece did in the 1960s to reimpose a 'high' variety of Greek. Others want to create a new set of conditions, for example, to rid a language of a *tu–vous* distinction in address forms, as did both the French and Russian revolutionaries (but eliminating the *vous* form in one case and the *tu* form in the other). Eventually new norms emerge, new appearances, new conventions, and new ways of using language to express these new norms with all the advantages, and disadvantages, of the old, offering as they do a way of constructing a certain kind of reality as well as providing blinkers which make other realities somewhat inaccessible to view.

One consequence of all this is that we must set limits on the amount of trust we place in others and in our view of the world. Similarly, in conversation we should not trust absolutely: that is too severe a demand to make both of ourselves and of others. Those who give their absolute trust to others are almost certain at one time or another to be disappointed. But we must also be aware that distrust cannot be the norm either, for a climate in which everyone distrusts everyone else would prohibit entirely all hope of mutually beneficial social contact. Therefore, we must err at all times on the side of trust. Unfortunately, those who would deceive us know that too, and, having confidence in their ability to exploit this basic social need, proceed to do so, often with impunity.

For any particular conversation it is also possible to show that there are differences between the parties in the specific things that they know in contrast to the kinds of background knowledge that they share. No two people have identical backgrounds, so in any conversation the participants will have different kinds of knowledge about almost any topic that is likely to be mentioned. If only two people, Fred and Sally, are involved, there will be certain matters known to both, some because 'everybody knows such things' and others because both Fred and Sally happen to know them. Then there will be matters known to only one of the speakers, so that Fred will know something that Sally does not know, or Sally something that Fred does not know. In addition, there will be partly known information: Fred or Sally, or both, may partly know something or know parts of something, but not necessarily the same parts. And Fred or Sally, or both again, may believe that the other knows something that the other actually does not know. As we can see, there are numerous possible permutations in who knows what, who believes who knows what, and so on. Again, there are predictable consequences: conversation can proceed only on the basis that the participants share a set of beliefs, that is, certain things must be known to all parties; others may be known; some will have to be explained; questions may be asked for clarification; difficulties will be negotiated or cleared up somehow; people will be understanding and tolerant; and the various processes that are involved will be conducted decently. If only one participant in a conversation refuses to subscribe to these beliefs and to conduct himself or herself accordingly, the others will become irritated, confused, or frustrated, and may well abandon any attempt to continue what they have begun.

Since most participants in a conversation usually do share a certain amount of background knowledge about 'proper' behaviour and the 'right' way to do things, much of what they say can be understood if we, too, are familiar with the knowledge they share. Their references to places, times, and events, and their accounts and descriptions are related to what they know and what they believe the others know. A participant in a conversation must believe that he or she has access to the same set of reference points that all the other participants have access to; all he or she needs do in conversing is use those points for orientation, and listeners will comprehend. And such a belief is largely justified. What is hardly ever necessary in a conversation is to begin at the very beginning of anything and to treat everyone and everything as unique and somehow without antecedents. In a trivial sense every occasion is unique, but procedures exist which minimize novelty and maximize normality – accepted ways of asking and giving directions, rules for regulating who speaks to whom and about what, and basic principles for conducting yourself, for example, with complete strangers.

A conversation between familiars offers a very special mix of knowledge. There are matters in it which the parties know but are reluctant to refer to directly, although they may allude to them if necessary. There are matters which are not in the conversation by reason of the fact that they are deliberately avoided – their absence is conspicuous. And then there are the actual topics of the conversation. However, these topics are not introduced logically, as it were, but rather in a variety of ways according to the needs of the individuals and of the occasion, with each participant willing to let a topic emerge as seems natural at the time in the expectation that its various bits and pieces will hold together.

In general conversation with others it is ordinary, everyday, 'commonsense' knowledge that we assume they share with us. In certain circumstances, as between professionals, we can also assume a sharing of specialized knowledge. We must always take great care when we refer to items outside these shared areas. We cannot rely on others knowing what we know. They may not even share the same assumptions about what it means to 'know' something. A physicist's knowledge of matter is different from a lay person's, and an actor's view of character is unlikely to be the same as that of a psychiatrist. Explanations may well become necessary, and they may not be easily provided. Briefing is one kind of explaining behaviour in such circumstances. But a recurrent difficulty is knowing just how much to say on a particular occasion and then judging how successful we have been in saying it. This is particularly crucial if we then proceed to treat this 'new' information we supply henceforth as part of our listeners' everyday knowledge. It may not be easily incorporated into existing knowledge, as anyone who has ever taught well knows, for it is one thing to teach something and quite another to learn it.

Activities

- ❏ Have a look at the Wardhaugh reading, and
    - a   explain, in terms of context, why tempers may become frayed if a speaker asks the people that she is talking to, to be explicit;
    - b   summarise the paragraph beginning 'In periods of rapid social change . . .' and ending '. . . somewhat inaccessible to view', giving an example;
    - c   explain the paragraph beginning 'For any particular conversation . . .' and ending '. . . attempt to continue what they have begun' in terms of attitude;
    - d   Explain the point that he makes about the language of discourse communities;
- ❏ Find a newspaper or magazine article, and
    - e   list all the assumptions of knowledge according to type of context: situational, cultural and interpersonal, and then draw a diagram of the cultural information assumed, that shows how some information is part of another bigger sphere of information – you may want to use concentric circles;
    - f   within each concentric circle, say what sort of person should be expected to have that sort of knowledge;
    - g   pick out examples of very inexplicit or vague language and suggest why you think the writer chose to use such vague reference;
    - h   find examples of exophoric reference, and say whether they come at the beginning, middle or end of the article, and how they fit into the article itself and are understood even though they are exophoric;
    - i   find examples of intertextual reference and say what you think it refers to.
- ❏ Test Wardhaugh's theory that we usually do not probe beneath the surface of events, that 'much of what everyone knows is . . . either scientifically unwarranted or very superficial', and that we usually deal with stereotypes.
    - j   Construct ten conditional sentences, just supplying the first half and leaving the second blank, as in
        - i   If you go into the bush in Australia, . . .
        - ii   If you stand by mistake on an Englishman's foot, . . .
        - iii   If you eat in a French restaurant, . . .

        Put, at the top of each sheet, spaces for them to write their sex, age and occupation. This is the social data of your subjects.

k   Then give out typed-up copies of the ten half-sentences for people to complete. Try to reach at least 50 people so that your results are significant.

l   Make a note of all the answers received for each question.

m   Count up the instances of an answer that comes again and again for particular questions.

n   Put together all the answers that come repeatedly for all the questions and look at the social data of the subjects and see if there is a definite tendency as to the characteristics of people who work in stereotypes.

o   Have a look at those unexpected, out-of-the-ordinary, outrageous and even 'funny' answers that some people have given back to you. What does this say about their attitude to being asked to stereotype?

p   Write up just the main findings of your test in a 250-word letter as you might for the opinion column of a newspaper, adding a short comment of your own.

❏ Test Wardhaugh's point that we have common background knowledge about 'proper' behaviour and the 'right' way to do things.

q   Record a group of people having a casual, natural, spontaneous conversation. They may be students having a coffee together in the kitchen of a student flat; they may be people making polite conversation together at the beginning of a meeting before it starts. The choice of who, where and when is yours.

r   Make sure that the people know that you are recording them and that they do not mind you doing it. If they do mind, take the machine away, and find another group of recordees, another time, another place.

s   Make sure that there is no extraneous background noise, such as voices, music or machines running, that is going to make it difficult for you to hear what they said, when you are playing it through afterwards.

t   Do *not* tell them that you are investigating common background knowledge about 'proper' behaviour and the 'right' way to do things; otherwise you might make them talk about topics that they might not have chosen, and in an unnatural way. Just say that you are studying their language in general.

u   Tell them to talk as naturally as possible, about anything they want. Do not give them a topic or prompt them in any way.

v   Keep out of the conversation, but close enough to the speakers to be able to turn the recorder off if they get particularly uncomfortable with it.

w   Record about 10 minutes' conversation when the speakers are in full flow. If you try to record before they have really got started, it will be stilted and awkward since they are still getting used to having the machine there.

x   When you turn the machine off, and they have finished talking, ask them very briefly what brings them together, how long they have known each other, where they meet, how often and why. Do not overdo this interrogation: all you are trying to find out is 'Is there reason for them sharing substantial cultural knowledge and even a little interpersonal knowledge?'

y   Now go back to Wardhaugh's point about us having common background knowledge about 'proper' behaviour and the 'right' way to do things, and answer the following questions:

i Are there any instances of some people knowing more about one particular topic than others do?

ii Does this upset the conversation or enhance it for the others, as far as you can see?

iii Is there an example of somebody wrongly assuming his/her hearers share knowledge of a context, and giving less information than is needed for people to understand?

iv Does a brief breakdown in communication occur as a result of this inexplicitness, or does it sound as if they let it pass by?

v Is there an example of someone wrongly assuming their hearers do not share knowledge of a context, and giving more information than they need in order to follow him/her?

vi Do the hearers protest about this over-explicitness: do they subtly interrupt with new information, or do they politely 'backchannel', saying 'Mhm', 'Aha', 'Right' and so on?

vii When you have tried to answer these questions, play your recording to someone from the group who was actually recorded, and see if you have got your answers 'right'.

viii Looking at all your answers above, what seems to be the 'proper' behaviour and the 'right' way to do things in conversations? What are the 'rules' about referring to common knowledge and new knowledge, as far as this conversation seems to show?

ix Write up your findings in a short essay. Your essay should contain brief answers to questions i to vii, and then the list of conversation rules that you made up in question viii.

CO-TEXT: REPETITION AND REFERENCE D2

The first excerpt is taken from a book which discusses types of lexical cohesion, and examines patterns of lexically cohesive links through texts. Whereas Units A2, B2 and C2 looked at cohesion from the point of view of analysing what speakers have said and writers have written, this unit looks at it the other way on, from the point of view of productive skills, and how we should write. We said in Unit A2 that pronouns, substitutes, ellipsis, synonyms, superordinates and general words avoid repetition, and give just the amount of information as is necessary, thereby suggesting that it is advisable to avoid repetition. This reading considers the importance of using repetition, and questions that idea that learners of English should use grammatical cohesion at the expense of lexical cohesion.

Be aware that what we have been calling 'grammatical cohesion' and 'grammatical cohesion devices', Hoey simply calls 'cohesion' and 'cohesive devices', and what we have been calling 'the lexical cohesive device of repetition' he calls 'repetition' and 'repetition devices'. Note that when he talks of 'complex repetition', he means related words that share a common root or base form, known as a lexical morpheme, e.g. 'drugs' and 'drugging', 'economist' and 'economy'.

Reading and researching

M. Hoey (1991) *Patterns of Lexis in Text*, pp. 242–5, Oxford: Oxford University Press.

Repetition and writing

Most of this chapter has been devoted to consideration of the implications of lexical patterning for reading. We cannot end this chapter, and with it the book, without brief consideration of the implications for writing. The teaching and practice of cohesion has become a regular part of many teaching programmes. It is not, however, certain that this is either necessary or sufficient to produce good writers. Brodine (1983) reported that when the essays of a group of Italian learners were compared with those of native speaker teachers, there was no significant difference between the two groups as regards frequency of use of various cohesive devices. Skuja (1984) reported a similar result; concerned to find out in what respects advanced learners in Singapore were failing to produce natural English, she compared her learners' essays with those elicited on the same topic from a group of experienced native speakers. Her results show that advanced learners in Singapore actually use slightly more cohesive ties than do native speaker users when writing on the same topic at the same length. This implies that the teaching of cohesive features for writing may, on occasion, be counter-productive and that mastery of the cohesive system does not automatically produce native style fluency in composition.

Interested by her findings, Skuja went on to consider the range of text covered by the cohesive features in the essays of both groups and found that what distinguished the work of the two groups was that the native speakers characteristically used repetition devices to connect over a considerable distance in a text, whereas the Singaporean students, skilled though they were in other ways, tended to repeat at shorter distances, typically within the paragraph boundaries. Mountain (1987) sought to replicate these findings for Italian students using English undergraduates as her point of comparison. Although her findings are not conclusive, they are supportive of the same general position.

In the light of what we have said in this book, we can suggest that one of the characteristics of mature native speaker writing is that the writer's sentences will relate to each other in non-linear ways, though not necessarily by the means we have been describing. Writers who fail to connect what they are saying in any particular sentence to what they have said earlier are likely to be open to the charge of drifting from topic to topic. We should, therefore, be encouraging those who are learning to write, whether in their own or another language, to think of their writing non-linearly. They need to make connections between what they are currently saying and what they have previously said and later intend to say.

The implications made earlier are that making connections across the text would be particularly important with regard to topic sentences. If topic-opening sentences are typically identifiable in terms of the number of sentences that later refer back to them, then it would seem advisable for writers to keep in mind their topic sentence(s) as they write, rather than allowing the difficulties of the composition process to swamp them. Although our findings do not support the distinction between macrostructure and microstructure, at least as it is usually defined, the implications of the existence of central sentences are that writers who see what they have to say in terms of a series of interconnected macropropositions are more likely to succeed in producing highly valued writing than those who make it up as they go along.

One thing seems certain: the traditional advice to avoid repetition needs to be couched with special care if it is not to interfere actively with the development of mature writing skills. The advice grew out of two quite reasonable worries. First, when an inexperienced writer does not know what else to say, they sometimes resort to restating what they have already said. Nothing in this book should have shaken the reader's conviction that this is an unsatisfactory practice; the existence of patterns of lexis in text is not to be interpreted as an incitement to padding.

Second, especially among less experienced writers, limitations of vocabulary and ignorance of the means whereby one can repeat in a language may lead a learner to juxtapose the same lexical item clumsily in adjacent sentences. Again, it has been noted in earlier chapters that the tendency for adjacent sentences to bond is not great; the reason is that, in English, care is usually taken to avoid the clumsy juxtaposition just referred to. So, here too, the advice as traditionally given still stands.

But it cannot rest there. Reasonable as the worries concerning repetition may be, the advice to avoid repetition may be harmful unless it is immediately supplemented by something more. To begin with, if a learner is to avoid clumsiness, he or she must be taught how to avoid it. One of the most important ways is by means of complex repetition. So, in the first sentence of the previous paragraph, I used the lexical item **clumsily**; in the following sentence it has become **clumsy** while in the third sentence of this paragraph it appears as **clumsiness**. Similarly, **juxtapose** becomes **juxtaposition**, and **repeat** becomes **repetition**. There is nothing contrived about these examples; my practice is that of most writers needing to repeat without making the repetition obtrusive. Stotsky (1983) comments that 'an increase in the use of morphologically complex words [i.e. complex repetition], rather than repetition of a simple word or the use of a cumbersome paraphrase, may be an important index of growth.'

If we need to protect our learners against this aspect of avoiding repetition, still more must we protect them against misuse of the counsel to avoid padding. Learners should not be encouraged to say the same thing over and over again, but they *should* be advised to make connections between what they are currently saying and what they said before. There should, in non-narrative text, be some relationship between sentences at a distance from each other. What this means for learners is that they need to take time out of grappling with the difficulties of composing the sentence they are currently working on to consider its relationship with what they have already written. This may impose on the writer an additional burden but it also relieves him or her of at least some of the task of lexical selection. Indeed, knowledge that it is legitimate to reuse in different combinations lexical items already brought into play, may actually serve to lighten some aspects of the writing task.

The advice a learner needs will vary from person to person and from group to group. For some the main need may be to avoid going around in circles; such learners will need reminding that new information always accompanies repetition in mature writing. For others the need may be to prevent the text drifting; such learners will need telling that repetition usually provides the grounding for new information. In either case, materials may need developing that give the student practice in bonding back to earlier sentences. The well-tried strategy of supplying the learners with an incomplete text and asking them to complete it may be adaptable to this purpose; indeed, there is no reason why more than one text organizing principle at a time might not be practised in this way.

All of this is rather obvious, but it is easy for second language learners to lose sight of the applicability of what they already know in their first language when faced with the twin tasks of selecting appropriate lexis and avoiding ungrammaticality. As so often is the case with language learning, encouraging the learners to transfer a skill from their first language is half the battle.

The short Wodak excerpt is quite different. It is taken from a book that looks at linguistic barriers to communication in a variety of institutional contexts. The excerpt focuses on the discourse of the media, specifically radio broadcasts of the news. Wodak mentions imprecise references in news stories, and says that because little background context is provided for those who do not already know about the news item so that they can identify the referent, the news is inaccessible to parts of the population.

D2.2 Reference and the news

Wodak, R. (1996) *Disorders of Discourse*, pp. 100–2, London: Longman.

Depending on the content of the item, we may identify three types of news story:

> fact-stories – individual facts are assembled according to their importance
> action (event)-stories – the same action is reported repeatedly but with ever more details
> quote-stories – quotations and summaries alternate, the importance decreasing gradually.

> (Warren 1953)

A typical story should contain suspense, highlights, a beginning and an end (Labov/Waletzky 1967). But stories of this structure just do not occur in news bulletins. There is evidence of this text-inherent deficiency at both the macro- and micro-levels. Important units of the kind Sacks has established for narratives, such as interaction units ('today'), justification units ('of course') and recognition type-descriptions ('aha', 'mm') are missing (Sacks 1986). These are units occurring naturally in spoken language, in conversations where backchannels are possible. That is a completely different setting than news in the media.

Imprecise references, pronominalizations, and a lack of feed-back are thus also characteristics of these texts. Typically they are produced unconstrained by a need for self-justification. Consequently, they cannot really be considered stories, as the latter are normally conceived. The relevance of the story is never really explained, background knowledge and hints as to orientation are absent, no frame is available within which to embed the news item. As a result there is almost no possibility of 'updating' it. This situation was confirmed by Larsen, who analysed the intelligibility of Danish news spots (Larsen 1983) (see Wodak/Lutz 1986: 202ff). This suggests that it is often impossible to integrate new information into already available knowledge as long as the present form of providing news items pertains. Little or no acquisition of new knowledge takes place. As Larsen writes:

> The main effect of news bulletins apparently is to confirm the listener's view of the current events, or occasionally, to put new topics on a mental list of current events.

(Larsen 1983: 36)

On the one hand, listening to the news is a process of opinion-making, where opinions are formed and then – often misunderstood and unreflected – integrated. Thus stereotypes, clichés and prejudices are confirmed instead of being subjected to critical evaluation.

On the other hand, a large part of the population is excluded altogether from the information provided. To meet its obligations regarding information and education, the Austrian Broadcasting Company (ORF) would have to alter the text and the style of presentation of the news and make it more comprehensible. And even then we would need tests to see whether simpler news reports are 'better understood'. As long as news broadcasts retain their inaccessibility, they will continue to present the large symbolic capital of the elites. The elites possess information, others are excluded (van Dijk 1993a). And even if news texts are made more comprehensible, the elites and better educated profit more from the greater accessibility (see below). As soon as one considers the complete news-cycle – from news agency report to newswriter, to radio reporter or the newspaper that accepts an item, and from there to the uncomprehending reader – one realizes all the more clearly what power there is in the passing of news information.

This leads us to our main questions: What do reformulations mean? What is their impact?

Activities

❑ Read through the Hoey excerpt and, to help you grasp his argument, give brief answers to these questions:

    a   What differences did Skuja find between the writing of native speakers of English and that of advanced learners of English in Singapore?

    b   What point does Hoey make about topic-opening sentences?

    c   What two reasons does Hoey give for the desire of linguists and teachers of writing skills to make inexperienced writers avoid repetition?

d   If we do advise students not to use repetition and padding, what should we tell them to use in their place?

    e   What do you think he means by 'learners will need reminding that new information always accompanies repetition in mature writing.'?

❑ Do you agree with everything that Hoey says? Explain your answer.

❑ Imagine that you are trying to show a small group of learners of English as a Foreign Language how they can avoid clumsy 'near repetition', and that you want to use an example. Write a short paragraph containing two or three sentences, full of clumsy 'near repetition'; then rewrite it using complex repetition, synonyms, superordinates and general words.

❑ Look now at the Wodak excerpt, and think about the following:

    a   What exactly does she mean by 'imprecise references, pronominalisations, and a lack of feedback', do you think? Give examples.

    b   Do you agree that it is impossible to update information, integrating new information?

    c   Do you agree that radio news broadcasts are only accessible to the elite? Who are the elite and why are they elite?

    d   Could the same be said of television news broadcasts?

❑ Take a newspaper article from a quality newspaper (broadsheet), and another from a more popular one (tabloid), and compare them in terms of the reference and the background context knowledge that they assume. Is one more imprecise and inexplicit than another? Do they demand different types of background context knowledge?

❑ Record a short television news programme, which is aimed at children. In Britain, you could use something like 'Newsround', which is part of BBC children's TV. Presumably the background context knowledge of the young viewers is assumed to be non-existent. What is it about the grammar and the vocabulary that makes it explicit, accessible and comprehensible?

❑ Take ten short essays of native speakers of English (they could be cooperative colleagues in your tutorial or seminar group).

    a   Which do they use most: repetition, complex repetition, synonyms, superordinates and general words? Which do you think makes for better reading?

    b   Analyse each essay from the point of view of lexical cohesion, quantifying how many instances there are of repetition, complex repetition, synonyms, superordinates and general words, in each.

    c   Give copies of the ten essays to ten people, and ask them to rate them (and order them) according to how well they think they are written.

    d   Put the essays in the most popular order, taking into account all the answers, and go back to your analysis of them from the point of view of lexical cohesion.

    e   Discover which features are most used in the most popular essays, and which features are most used in the least popular essays.

    f   Discuss with colleagues to see if they had the same findings and then draw conclusions about the possible reasons for this.

    g   Finally, give some thought to what implications your findings and your conclusions have for the teaching of writing to native speakers of English.

h   Write up your project. You could use the following headings, if you like, or
    adapt them:
    i   introduction: what lexical cohesion is and which device you thought would
         be the most popularly used;
    ii   method: how you analysed the essays, who you gave them to, how you
         analysed the responses, what difficulties you encountered;
    iii results: which device featured in the essays was felt to be the best written;
    iv   discussion: why you think this is so;
    v   conclusion: how your results compare with what you originally thought
         would be the most popular, what the implications are for the teaching
         of writing.

SPEECH ACTS AND POWER   D3

Fairclough says that the idea of speech acts, 'uttering as acting', is central to what he
calls CLS (Critical Language Study). CLS 'analyses social interactions in a way which
focuses upon their linguistic elements', and how language affects and is affected by
the system of social relationships (1989: 5).

   In the first extract, Fairclough criticises pragmatics for what he sees as its
individualism and its idealism. He says that individuals are not usually free to manipulate language to achieve their goals, but that they are constrained by social conventions. He also says that people do not have equal control in interactions, because there
are inequalities of power.

   In the second, he looks at the speech act of 'requesting' and the way in which
it relates to inequalities of power. He says that indirect requests leave the power relationship implicit, and he shows how the grammar of a request can express varying
degrees of indirectness.

   In the third extract, Fairclough says that speech acts are a central part of pragmatics, which is in turn concerned with the meanings that participants in a discourse
give to elements of a text. He refers to the multi-functionality of speech acts, and then
focuses on the way that they are related to the co-text, the intertextual context, and
the situational and cultural background context. He sees the social factors that
influence the use of indirect speech acts in terms of power relations, and concludes
that the discourse type dictates the conventions for speech acts, and that the conventions reflect the participants' ideology and social relationships.

Reading and researching   D3.1

N. Fairclough (1989) *Language and Power*, pp. 9–11, 54–5 and 155–7, Harlow: Longman.

Pragmatics
Anglo-American pragmatics is closely associated with analytical philosophy, particularly with the work of Austin and Searle on 'speech acts'. The key insight is that
language can be seen as a form of action: that spoken or written utterances constitute the performance of speech acts such as promising or asking or asserting or

warning; or, on a different plane, referring to people or things, presupposing the existence of people or things or the truth of propositions, and implicating meanings which are not overtly expressed. The idea of uttering as acting is an important one, and it is also central to CLS in the form of the claim, that discourse is social practice.

The main weakness of pragmatics from a critical point of view is its individualism: 'action' is thought of atomistically as emanating wholly from the individual, and is often conceptualized in terms of the 'strategies' adopted by the individual speaker to achieve her 'goals' or 'intentions'. This understates the extent to which people are caught up in, constrained by, and indeed derive their individual identities from social conventions, and gives the implausible impression that conventionalized ways of speaking or writing are 'reinvented' on each occasion of their use by the speaker generating a suitable strategy for her particular goals. And it correspondingly overstates the extent to which people manipulate language for strategic purposes. Of course, people do act strategically in certain circumstances and use conventions rather than simply following them; but in other circumstances they do simply follow them, and what one needs is a theory of social action – social practice – which accounts for both the determining effect of conventions and the strategic creativity of individual speakers, without reducing practice to one or the other.

The individuals postulated in pragmatics, moreover, are generally assumed to be involved in cooperative interactions whose ground rules they have equal control over, and to which they are able to contribute equally. Cooperative interaction between equals is elevated into a prototype for social interaction in general, rather than being seen as a form of interaction whose occurrence is limited and socially constrained. The result is an idealized and Utopian image of verbal interaction which is in stark contrast with the image offered by CLS of a sociolinguistic order moulded in social struggles and riven with inequalities of power. Pragmatics often appears to describe discourse as it might be in a better world, rather than discourse as it is.

Pragmatics is also limited in having been mainly developed with reference to single invented utterances rather than real extended discourse, and central notions like 'speech act' have turned out to be problematic when people try to use them to analyse real discourse. Finally, Anglo-American pragmatics bears the scars of the way in which it has developed in relation to 'linguistics proper'. While it has provided a space for investigating the interdependence of language and social context which was not available before its inception, it is a strictly constrained space, for pragmatics tends to be seen as an additional 'level' of language study which fills in gaps left by the more 'core' levels of grammar and semantics. Social context is acknowledged but kept in its place, which does it less than justice.

Cognitive psychology and artificial intelligence

One of the concerns of pragmatics has been with the discrepancies which standardly exist between what is said and what is meant, and with how people work out what is meant from what is said; but the detailed investigation of the processes of comprehension involved, as well as of processes of production, has been undertaken by cognitive psychologists, and workers in artificial intelligence concerned with the computer simulation of production and comprehension. From the perspective of CLS, the most important result of work on comprehension is the stress which has been placed upon its active nature: you do not simply 'decode' an utterance, you arrive at an interpretation through an active process of matching features of the utterance at various levels with representations you have stored in your long-term memory. These representations are prototypes for a very diverse collection of things – the shapes of words, the grammatical forms of sentences, the typical structure of a narrative, the properties of types of object and person, the expected sequence of events in a particular situation type, and so forth. Some of these are linguistic, and some of them are not. Anticipating later discussion, let us refer to these prototypes collectively as '*members' resources*', or MR for short. The main point is that comprehension is the outcome of interactions between the utterance being interpreted, and MR.

Not surprisingly, cognitive pyschology and artificial intelligence have given little attention to the social origins or significance of MR. I shall argue later that attention to the processes of production and comprehension is essential to an understanding of the interrelations of language, power and ideology, and that this is so because MR are socially determined and ideologically shaped, though their 'common sense' and automatic character typically disguises that fact. Routine and unselfconscious resort to MR in the ordinary business of discourse is, I shall suggest, a powerful mechanism for sustaining the relations of power which ultimately underlie them.

Conversation analysis and discourse analysis

Power is also sometimes hidden in face-to-face discourse. For instance, there is obviously a close connection between *requests* and power, in that the right to request someone to do something often derives from having power. But there are many grammatically different forms available for making requests. Some are *direct* and mark the power relationship explicitly, while others are *indirect* and leave it more or less implicit. Direct requests are typically expressed grammatically in imperative sentences: *type this letter for me by 5 o'clock*, for instance. Indirect requests can be more or less indirect, and they are typically expressed grammatically in questions of various degrees of elaborateness and corresponding indirectness: *can you type this letter for me by 5 o'clock, do you think you could type this letter for me by 5 o'clock, could I possibly ask you to type this letter for me by 5 o'clock*. There are also other ways of indirectly requesting – through *hints*, for instance: *I would like to have the letter in the 5 o'clock post*.

Why would a business executive (let us say) choose an indirect form to request her secretary to type a letter? It could be, particularly if a hint or one of the more elaborate questions is used, for manipulative reasons: if the boss has been pressurizing the secretary hard all day, such a form of request might head off resentment or even refusal. But less elaborate forms of indirect request (*can you/will you/could you type . . .*) are conventionally used in the sort of situation I have described, so the question becomes why business executives and other power-holders systematically avoid too much overt marking of their power.

Activities

- ❑ Take a look at the reading and discuss
  - a   what his criticisms of pragmatics are;
  - b   why he says that notions like 'speech act' are problematic;
  - c   what he means by the term 'members resources' (MR);
  - d   what he says comprehension is;
  - e   whether you agree with what he is saying.
- ❑ Go now to the reading and
  - f   summarise what he says about the power holder using both elaborate and less elaborate indirect forms to make a request;
  - g   think of another situation in which a power holder makes a request and list all the ways that they might express the request, and see if the power holder uses indirect forms; can we generalise, therefore?
- ❑ The following lines are taken from the third Fairclough reading. Do you agree with them? Explain your answer and give an example of your own.
  - a   'Speech acts cannot be assigned simply on the basis of formal features of an utterance.'
  - b   'Discourse types differ in their conventions for the directness of expression of speech acts.'
  - c   The paragraph beginning 'Let us take as a further example the first two turns', and ending 'one that just gives the information asked for'.
- ❑ This question aims to help you to write an essay on classroom talk. In order to make comparisons, it would be a good idea if you discussed the questions either with other people in your class or with friends outside class from different educational backgrounds.
  - a   Think back to the teaching approach used in your school.
  - b   Define the teaching approach as traditional or liberal, and the level of education.
  - c   Think about the extent to which indirectness would have been used, and in what situations and to do what.
  - d   See if your experience confirms Fairclough's theory that indirectness is used in traditional classrooms but not in liberal ones, and less in higher education than in schools.
  - e   Think about whether there any other factors apart from ideology in the class-room that might have influenced whether indirectness was used.
  - h   Write about your classroom language and the use of indirectness and say to what extent you agree with Fairclough (be sure not to include anecdotes).
- ❑ Look at the last paragraph of the penultimate paragraph, in which he talks of asymmetries of speech act conventions, and
  - a   think of situations in which conventions of speech acts and indirectness reflect asymmetrical social relationships (the second abstract gave a very useful example);

b   choose one of these situations, and find a video film that contains an ex-
     ample of the situation; make sure that it is a short episode of only about ten
     minutes; watch it several times;

c   make a note of who can use what speech act, who can be indirect and who
     cannot, and also transcribe the language used to realise the speech act;

d   decide whether you agree with Fairclough that the conventions of speech acts
     embody social relationships.

CONVERSATION AND RACE   **D4**

The first of the Gumperz excerpts begins with a formulation of 'contextualisation cues'
and miscommunications. It describes miscommunications that can occur when a speaker
from one social group addresses a member of another social group, and it discusses
an exchange that is unsatisfactory because of the differences in variety of English and
speech style between the two speakers. The formulaic phrases of any social group usually serve to establish personal contact between members.

The second Gumperz excerpt contains another example of miscommunication
in brief encounters. This time it is the intonation that causes the problem because it
is misinterpreted as communicating a negative attitude.

Reading and researching   D4.1

J. Gumperz (1982) *Discourse Strategies*, pp.133–4 and 173–4. Cambridge: Cambridge
University Press.

The conversational analyses described in this chapter extend the methodological
principle of comparing ungrammatical and grammatical sentences, by which linguists
derive generalizations about grammatical rules, to the analysis of contextualization
phenomena that underlie the situated judgements conversationalists make of each
other. Naturally occurring instances of miscommunication are compared with func-
tionally similar passages of successful communication in the same encounter or
findings from other situations to derive generalizations about subculturally and sit-
uationally specific aspects of inferential processes.

The following example illustrates the type of miscommunication phenomena
we look for and shows how we begin to isolate possible linguistic sources of misunderstanding. The incident is taken from an oral report by a graduate student in
educational psychology who served as an interviewer in a survey.

(1) The graduate student has been sent to interview a black housewife in a low
     income, inner city neighborhood. The contact has been made over the phone
     by someone in the office. The student arrives, rings the bell, and is met by the
     husband, who opens the door, smiles, and steps towards him:

     Husband: So y're gonna check out ma ol lady, hah?
     Interviewer: Ah, no. I only came to get some information. They called from
                   the office.

     (Husband, dropping his smile, disappears without a word and calls his wife.)

The student reports that the interview that followed was stiff and quite unsatisfactory. Being black himself, he knew that he had 'blown it' by failing to recognize the significance of the husband's speech style in this particular case. The style is that of a formulaic opening gambit used to 'check out' strangers, to see whether or not they can come up with the appropriate formulaic reply. Intent on following the instructions he had received in his methodological training and doing well in what he saw as a formal interview, the interviewer failed to notice the husband's stylistic cues. Reflecting on the incident, he himself states that, in order to show that he was on the husband's wave-length, he should have replied with a typically black response like 'Yea, I'ma git some info' (I'm going to get some information) to prove his familiarity with and his ability to understand local verbal etiquette and values. Instead, his Standard English reply was taken by the husband as an indication that the interviewer was not one of them and, perhaps, not to be trusted.

The opener 'So y're gonna check out ma ol lady' is similar to the 'Ahma git me a gig' discussed elsewhere. Both are formulaic phrases identifiable through co-occurrent selections of phonological, prosodic, morphological and lexical options. Linguists have come to recognize that, as Fillmore (1976) puts it, 'an enormous amount of natural language is formulaic, automatic and rehearsed, rather than propositional, creative or freely generated.' But it must be emphasized that although such formulas have some of the characteristics of common idioms like *kick the bucket* and *spill the beans*, their meaning cannot be adequately described by lexical glosses. They occur as part of routinized interactive exchanges, such as Goffman describes as 'replies and responses' (1981). Their use signals both expectations about what is to be accomplished and about the form that replies must take. They are similar in function to code switching strategies. Like the latter they are learned by interacting with others in institutionally defined networks of relationships. Where these relationships are ethnically specific they are often regarded as markers of ethnic background. But, as our example shows, their use in actual encounters is ultimately determined by activity specific pre-suppositions so that failure to react is not in itself a clear sign of ethnic identity. Basically, these formulaic phrases reflect indirect conversational strategies that make conditions favorable to establishing personal contact and negotiating shared interpretations. . . .

Interethnic communication

Chapters 6 and 7 outline a perspective to conversation that focuses on conversational inference and on participants' use of prosodic and phonetic perceptions as well as on interpretive preferences learned through previous communicative experience to negotiate frames of interpretation. Using this perspective we can account for both shared grammatical knowledge and for differences in communicative style that characterize our modern culturally diverse societies.

This approach to speaking has both theoretical and practical significance. On the theoretical level it suggests a way of carrying out Garfinkel's program for studying naturally organized activities through language without relying on a priori and generally untestable assumptions about what is or is not culturally appropriate.

Although it might seem at first glance that contextualization cues are surface phenomena, their systematic analysis can lay the foundation for research strategies to gain insights into otherwise inaccessible symbolic processes of interpretation.

On the practical level, the study of conversational inference may lead to an explanation for the endemic and increasingly serious communication problems that affect private and public affairs in our society. We can begin to see why individuals who speak English well and have no difficulty in producing grammatical English sentences may nevertheless differ significantly in what they perceive as meaningful discourse cues. Accordingly, their assumptions about what information is to be conveyed, how it is to be ordered and put into words and their ability to fill in the unverbalized information they need to make sense of what transpires may also vary. This may lead to misunderstandings that go unnoticed in the course of an interaction, but can be revealed and studied empirically through conversational analysis.

The main purpose of earlier chapters was to illustrate the nature of the cues and the inferential mechanisms involved. To that end, the discussion largely relied on examples of brief encounters. Miscommunications occurring in such brief encounters are annoying and their communicative effect may be serious. But the social import of the phenomena in question and their bases in participants' cultural background is most clearly revealed through case studies of longer events. The following two chapters present in depth analyses of two such events. To begin with, let me give one more brief example to illustrate the scope of the analysis and the subconscious nature of the interpretive processes involved.

In a staff cafeteria at a major British airport, newly hired Indian and Pakistani women were perceived as surly and uncooperative by their supervisor as well as by the cargo handlers whom they served. Observation revealed that while relatively few words were exchanged, the intonation and manner in which these words were pronounced were interpreted negatively. For example, when a cargo handler who had chosen meat was asked whether he wanted gravy, a British assistant would say 'Gravy?' using rising intonation. The Indian assistants, on the other hand, would say the word using falling intonation: 'Gravy.' We taped relevant sequences, including interchanges like these, and asked the employees to paraphrase what was meant in each case. At first the Indian workers saw no difference. However, the English teacher and the cafeteria supervisor could point out that 'Gravy,' said with a falling intonation, is likely to be interpreted as 'This is gravy,' i.e. not interpreted as an offer but rather as a statement, which in the context seems redundant and consequently rude. When the Indian women heard this, they began to understand the reactions they had been getting all along which had until then seemed incomprehensible. They then spontaneously recalled intonation patterns which had seemed strange to them when spoken by native English speakers. At the same time, supervisors learned that the Indian women's falling intonation was their normal way of asking questions in that situation, and that no rudeness or indifference was intended.

After several discussion/teaching sessions of this sort, both the teacher and the cafeteria supervisor reported a distinct improvement in the attitude of the Indian workers both to their work and to their customers. It seemed that the

Indian workers had long sensed they had been misunderstood but, having no way of talking about this in objective terms, they had felt they were being discriminated against. We had not taught the cafeteria workers to speak appropriate English; rather, by discussing the results of our analysis in mixed sessions and focusing on context bound interpretive preferences rather than on attitudes and stereotypes, we have suggested a strategy for self-diagnosis of communication difficulties. In short, they regained confidence in their own innate ability to learn.

The first of the longer case studies examines excerpts from an interview–counselling session recorded in an industrial suburb in London. The participants are both educated speakers of English; one is a Pakistani teacher of mathematics, who although born in South Asia went to secondary school and university in England. The other is a staff member of a center funded by the Department of Employment to deal with interethnic communication problems in British industry. The teacher has been unable to secure permanent employment and having been told that he lacks communication skills for high school teaching, he has been referred to the center. While both participants agree on the general definition of the event as an interview–counselling session, their expectations of what is to be accomplished, and especially about what needs to be said, differ radically. Such differences in expectation are of course not unusual even where conversationalists have similar cultural backgrounds. Conversations often begin with an introductory phase where common themes are negotiated and differences in expectation adjusted. What is unusual about this situation is that participants, in spite of repeated attempts at adjustment over a period of more than an hour, utterly fail to achieve such negotiation. Our analysis concentrates on the reasons for this failure and shows how it is based on differences in linguistic and socio-cultural knowledge.

 Activities

❑ Read through the first two pages of the first excerpt and summarise
   i   what is meant by 'contextualisation cues'
   ii what Gumperz means by 'miscommunication'.

❑ From your reading of Gumperz, what was it that separated the interviewer from the interviewee, socially? Discuss the exchange between them in terms of adjacency pairs and say whether you feel that conversation analysis can explain what happened, and why. Is it possible to explain it from the point of view of inter-actional sociolinguistics?

❑ Discuss the factors that caused the supervisor and cargo handlers to think that the Indian and Pakistani cafeteria assistants were being surly. Do you agree with Gumperz's interpretation of what went wrong or do you think that there was more to it than that?

❑ Over the next week, make a note of any miscommunication of this sort, that you happen to overhear. It could be that you have to sit or stand quite close to the people who are talking and in a good light because the miscommunications may be quite small or ambiguous, and only detectable in a hesitation or a slight flinch before the next speaker talks. What linguistic features are involved, and what socio-cultural factors? Are the features of overlaps, interruptions and pauses, the adjacency pair structure and sequences anything to do with the miscommunication?

❑ The miscommunications in the pages selected from Gumperz occur between people of different social class and different ethnic groups. Do you think that lessons can be learnt from these findings? Should courses be designed for social workers and immigrants with a different first language from the country that they are now in, to train them to appreciate the subtleties of language such as formulas and intonation and their socio-cultural effect? What sort of exercise could be given to sensitise those assistants in the airport cafeteria? Look at some advanced course books for teaching English as a Foreign Language and see how much of this is sort of thing is included.

❑ Have a look through several novels that you are familiar with and see if the writers have made their characters speak with overlaps, interruptions and pauses, the adjacency pair structure and sequences. What use do the writers make of all these features of natural speech? Is there always supposed to be a meaning or significance behind them? Which of the features is most represented in the books? Why do you think this is?

❑ Record a casual conversation between two or three people whom you know to be friends, and transcribe five minutes from the middle of the recording, including the overlaps, interruptions and pauses. Try and label each turn now, as part of an adjacency pair. What conclusions can you draw? To what extent would you say that the overlaps, interruptions and pauses, and the adjacency pair structure are a result of the speakers being friends?

❑ Record a cross-cultural programme on the TV or radio; this could be an interview between people from different countries or simply an informal exchange of ideas, or maybe even a travel programme. Observe the backchannels of each participant and observe the pauses.

i   Are there any differences?

ii   What seems to be the function of each?

iii Are there any misunderstandings or breakdown in communication that occur as a result of the differences?

iv   Why do you think this is?

COMMUNICATION AND RELEVANCE   D5

The Sperber and Wilson extract is more complex than the readings in this book have been so far. It contains part of the explanation of how relevance is achieved, supported by several examples illustrating the concepts that they discuss. Let us look briefly at the concepts.

Sperber and Wilson say that Grice's appeals to the maxim of relation are 'no more than dressed-up appeals to intuition'. In order to arrive at an understanding of relevance, they describe the 'cognitive environment', and say that cognition is relevance-oriented and that a communicator's intention is to alter the cognitive environment of the addressees. They then explore the concept of ostension and say that a speaker only draws the addressee's attention to something if they think it will be relevant enough to make it worth their attention.

They argue that in order for the addressee to process the information, they have to recognise and infer the speaker's intention behind the ostension. They conclude that, 'Ostensive-inferential communication consists in making manifest to an audience one's intention to make manifest a basic layer of information.' This intention is informative and communicative.

D5.1 Reading and researching

D. Sperber and D. Wilson (1995) *Relevance*, pp. 36–64, Oxford: Blackwell.

Problems of explanation: Grice's theory of conversation

The Gricean analysis of communication has been discussed almost exclusively by philosophers, whose main concern has been to define the terms 'meaning' or 'communication'. From our current, more psychological point of view, defining communication is not a primary concern. For one thing, communication does not necessarily involve a distinct and homogeneous set of empirical phenomena. Our aim is to identify underlying mechanisms, rooted in human psychology, which explain how humans communicate with one another. A psychologically well-founded definition and typology of communication, if possible at all, should follow from a theoretical account of these underlying mechanisms. We see Grice's analysis as a possible basis for such a theoretical account. From this perspective, the main defect of Grice's analysis is not that it defines communication too vaguely, but that it explains communication too poorly.

The code model has the merit of explaining how communication could in principle be achieved. It fails not on the explanatory but on the descriptive side: humans do not communicate by encoding and decoding thoughts. The inferential model, despite the technical problems discussed earlier, provides a description of human communication which rings true. By itself, however, it explains very little. The temptation to return to the code model will remain powerful as long as the inferential model is not developed into a plausible explanatory account of communication. However, the basis for such an account is suggested by another work of Grice's, his *William James Lectures*, in which he puts forward the view that communication is governed by a 'co-operative principle' and 'maxims of conversation'.

According to the inferential model, communication is achieved by the audience recognising the communicator's informative intention. However, it is not enough to point out, as we have done, that recognising intentions is a normal feature of human cognition. The recognition of informative intentions presents problems which the recognition of other human intentions does not.

How does one recognise another individual's intentions? One observes his behaviour; using one's knowledge of people in general and of the individual in particular, one infers which of the effects of this behaviour he could have both predicted and desired; one then assumes that these predictable and desirable effects were also intended. In other words, one infers the intention behind the behaviour from its independently observed or inferred effects. This pattern of inference is generally not available to an audience trying to recognise a communicator's informative intention. As we have seen, the informative effects of communication are normally achieved, if at all, via recognition of the informative intention. Hence, it seems, the audience cannot *first* observe or infer these effects, and *then* use them to infer the informative intention.

However, the problem is not that it is hard to come up with hypotheses about what the communicator might have intended to convey: it is that too many hypotheses are possible. Even a linguistic utterance is generally full of semantic ambiguities and referential ambivalences, and is open to a wide range of figurative interpretations. For non-coded behaviour there is, by definition, no predetermined range of information it might be used to communicate. The problem, then, is to choose the right hypothesis from an indefinite range of possible hypotheses. How can this be done? First, it is easy enough to infer that a certain piece of behaviour is communicative. Communicative behaviour has at least one characteristic effect which is achieved before the communicator's informative intention is recognised: it overtly claims the audience's attention.

Grice's fundamental idea in his *William James Lectures* is that once a certain piece of behaviour is identified as communicative, it is reasonable to assume that the communicator is trying to meet certain general standards. From knowledge of these general standards, observation of the communicator's behaviour, and the context, it should be possible to infer the communicator's specific informative intention. Grice, talking only of verbal communication, argues,

> Our talk exchanges . . . are characteristically, to some degree at least, co-operative efforts; and each participant recognizes in them, to some extent, a common purpose or set of purposes, or at least a mutually accepted direction. . . . at each stage, *some* possible conversational moves would be excluded as conversationally unsuitable. We might then formulate a rough general principle which participants will be expected (*ceteris paribus*) to observe, namely: Make your conversational contribution such as is required, at the stage at which it occurs, by the accepted purpose or direction of the talk exchange in which you are engaged.
>
> (Grice 1975: 45)

This Grice calls the *co-operative principle*. He then develops it into nine *maxims* classified into four categories:

Maxims of quantity
1   Make your contribution as informative as is required (for the current purposes of the exchange).
2   Do not make your contribution more informative than is required.

Maxims of quality
Supermaxim: Try to make your contribution one that is true.
1   Do not say what you believe to be false.
2   Do not say that for which you lack adequate evidence.

Maxim of relation
Be relevant.

Maxims of manner
Supermaxim: Be perspicuous.
1   Avoid obscurity of expression.
2   Avoid ambiguity.
3   Be brief (avoid unnecessary prolixity).
4   Be orderly.

This account of the general standards governing verbal communication makes it possible to explain how the utterance of a sentence, which provides only an incomplete and ambiguous representation of a thought, can nevertheless express a complete and unambiguous thought. Of the various thoughts which the sentence uttered could be taken to represent, the hearer can eliminate any that are incompatible with the assumption that the speaker is obeying the co-operative principle and maxims. If only one thought is left, then the hearer can infer that it is this thought that the speaker is trying to communicate. Thus, to communicate efficiently, all the speaker has to do is utter a sentence only one interpretation of which is compatible with the assumption that she is obeying the co-operative principle and maxims.

Recall, for instance, our example (16)–(18):

(16)   Jones has bought the *Times*.
(17)   Jones has bought a copy of the *Times*.
(18)   Jones has bought the press enterprise which publishes the *Times*.

There might be situations where only interpretation (17) of the utterance in (16) would be compatible with the assumption that the speaker does not say what she believes to be false (first maxim of quality). There might be situations where only interpretation (18) would be compatible with the assumption that the speaker is being relevant (maxim of relation). In those situations, the intended interpretation of (16) can easily be inferred. Hence the maxims and the inferences they give rise to make it possible to convey an unambiguous thought by uttering an ambiguous sentence.

Grice's approach to verbal communication also makes it possible to explain how utterances can convey not just explicit but also implicit thoughts. Consider dialogue (32):

(32)   *Peter*:   Do you want some coffee?
         Mary: Coffee would keep me awake.

Suppose that Peter is aware of (33). Then from the assumption explicitly expressed by Mary's answer, together with assumption (33), he could infer conclusion (34):

(33)   Mary does not want to stay awake.
(34)   Mary does not want any coffee.

In just the same way, if Peter is aware of (35), he could infer conclusion (36):

(35)   Mary's eyes remain open when she is awake.
(36)   Coffee would cause Mary's eyes to remain open.

Now in ordinary circumstances, Mary would have wanted to communicate (34) but not (36), although both are inferable in the same way from the thought she has explicitly expressed. This is easily explained on the assumption that Mary obeys Grice's maxims. The explicit content of her utterance does not directly answer Peter's question; it is therefore not relevant as it stands. If Mary has obeyed the maxim 'be relevant', it must be assumed that she intended to give Peter an answer. Since he can obtain just the expected answer by inferring (34) from what she said, she must have intended him to draw precisely this conclusion. There is no parallel reason to think that she intended Peter to infer (36). Hence, just as the Gricean maxims help the hearer choose, from among the senses of an ambiguous sentence, the one which was intended by the speaker, so they help him choose, from among the implications of the explicit content of an utterance, the ones which are implicitly conveyed.

Suppose now that the exchange in (32) takes place in the same circumstances as before, except that Peter has no particular reason beforehand to assume that Mary does not want to stay awake. Without this assumption, no answer to his question is derivable from Mary's utterance, and the relevance of this utterance is not immediately apparent. One of Grice's main contributions to pragmatics was to show how, in the event of such an apparent violation of the co-operative principle and maxims, hearers are expected to make any additional assumptions needed to dispose of the violation. Here Peter might first adopt (33) as a specific assumption jointly suggested by the utterance, his knowledge of Mary, and the general assumption that Mary is trying to be relevant. He might then infer, as in the previous example, that she does not want any coffee. To eliminate the apparent violation of the maxims, Peter would have to assume that Mary had intended him to reason just as he did: that is, that she was intending to convey implicitly both assumption (33) and conclusion (34).

Grice calls additional assumptions and conclusions such as (33) and (34), supplied to preserve the application of the co-operative principle and maxims, *implicatures*. Like his ideas on meaning, Grice's ideas on implicature can be seen as an attempt to build on a commonsense view of verbal communication by making it more explicit and exploring its implications. In his *William James Lectures*, Grice took one crucial step away from this commonsense view towards theoretical sophistication; but of course one step is not enough. Grice's account retains much of the vagueness of the commonsense view. Essential concepts mentioned in the maxims are left entirely undefined. This is true of *relevance*, for instance: hence appeals to the 'maxim of relation' are no more than dressed-up appeals to intuition. Thus, everybody would agree that, in ordinary circumstances, adding (33) and (34) to the interpretation of Mary's answer in (32) makes it relevant, whereas adding (35) and (36) does not. However, this fact has itself to be explained before it can be used in a genuine explanation of how Mary's answer is understood.

Grice's view of implicature raises even more basic questions. What is the rationale behind the co-operative principle and maxims? Are there just the nine maxims Grice mentioned, or might others be needed, as he suggested himself? It might be tempting to add a maxim every time a regularity has to be accounted for. However, this would be entirely *ad hoc*. What criteria, then, do individual maxims have to meet? Could the number of maxims be not expanded but reduced?

How are the maxims to be used in inference? Grice himself seems to think that the hearer uses the assumption that the speaker has observed the maxims as a premise in inference. Others have tried to reinterpret the maxims as 'conversational postulates' (Gordon and Lakoff 1975), or even as code-like rules which take semantic representations of sentences and descriptions of context as input, and yield pragmatic representations of utterances as output (Gazdar 1979). The flavour of such proposals can be seen from the following remarks:

> The tactic adopted here is to examine some of the data that would, or should be, covered by Grice's quantity maxim and then propose a relatively simple formal solution to the problem of describing the behaviour of that data. This solution may be seen as a special case of Grice's quantity maxim, or as an alternative to it, or as merely a conventional rule for assigning one class of conversational meanings to one class of utterance.
>
> (Gazdar 1979: 49)

The pragmatic phenomena amenable to this sort of treatment are rather limited: they essentially arise when the utterance of a certain sentence is so regularly correlated with a certain pragmatic interpretation that it makes sense to set up a rule linking the one to the other. For example, the utterance of (37) regularly suggests (38), the main exception being when it is already assumed that (38) is, or might be, false:

(37)   Some of the arguments are convincing.
(38)   Not all of the arguments are convincing.

The proposal is to deal with this by setting up a general rule associating (37) with the pragmatic interpretation (38), and effectively blocking its application in contexts where it is assumed that (38) is, or might be, false (Gazdar 1979: 55–9). However, in most cases of implicature, as for instance in example (32)–(34), the context does much more than filter out inappropriate interpretations: it provides premises without which the implicature cannot be inferred at all. The translation of Grice's maxims into code-like rules would thus reduce them to dealing with a narrow set of interesting but quite untypical examples of implicature.

What, then, are the forms of inference involved in the normal operation of the maxims? If, as seems plausible, non-demonstrative (i.e. non-deductive) inference is involved, how does it operate? Without pursuing these questions in any depth, most pragmatists have adopted one form or another of the Gricean approach to implicatures, and are otherwise content to explain the explicit core of verbal communication in terms of the code model. The results are as can be expected. Although based on an insight which seems quite correct, and although somewhat more explicit and systematic than the intuitive reconstructions supplied by un-sophisticated speakers, the analyses of implicature which have been proposed by pragmatists have shared with these intuitive reconstructions the defect of being almost entirely *ex post facto*.

Given that an utterance in context was found to carry particular implicatures, what both the hearer and the pragmatic theorist can do, the latter in a slightly more sophisticated way, is to show how in very intuitive terms there was an argu-ment based on the context, the utterance and general expectations about the behaviour of speakers, that would justify the particular interpretation chosen. What they fail to show is that on the same basis, an equally convincing justification could not have been given for some other interpretation that was not in fact chosen. There may be a whole variety of interpretations that would meet whatever standards of truthfulness, informativeness, relevance and clarity have been proposed or envis-aged so far. The theory needs improving at a fundamental level before it can be fruitfully applied to particular cases.

In his *William James Lectures*, Grice put forward an idea of fundamental import-ance: that the very act of communicating creates expectations which it then exploits. Grice himself first applied this idea and its elaboration in terms of the maxims to a rather limited problem of linguistic philosophy: do logical connectives ('and', 'or', 'if . . . then') have the same meaning in natural languages as they do in logic? He argued that the richer meaning these connectives seem to have in natural languages can be explained in terms not of word meaning but of implicature. He then suggested that this approach could have wider applications: that the task of linguistic semantics could be considerably simplified by treating a large array of problems in terms of implicatures. And indeed, the study of implicature along Gricean lines has become a major concern of pragmatics. We believe that the basic idea of Grice's *William James Lectures* has even wider implications: it offers a way of developing the analysis of inferential communication, suggested by Grice him-self in 'Meaning' (1957), into an explanatory model. To achieve this, however, we must leave aside the various elaborations of Grice's original hunches and the sophisticated, though empirically rather empty debates they have given rise to. What is needed is an attempt to rethink, in psychologically realistic terms, such basic questions as: What form of shared information is available to humans? How is shared information exploited in communication? What is relevance and how is it achieved? What role does the search for relevance play in communication? It is to these questions that we now turn.

Cognitive environments and mutual manifestness

We have argued that mutual knowledge is a philosopher's construct with no close counterpart in reality. This is not to deny that humans do, in some sense, share information. In the first place, the communication process itself gives rise to shared information; in the second place, some sharing of information is necessary if com-munication is to be achieved. Any account of human communication must thus incorporate some notion of shared information. In this section, we want to go beyond both the empirically inadequate notion of 'mutual knowledge' and the conceptually vague notion of 'shared information'. We will discuss in what sense humans share information, and to what extent they share information about the information they share.

All humans live in the same physical world. We are all engaged in a lifetime's enterprise of deriving information from this common environment and constructing the best possible mental representation of it. We do not all construct the same representation, because of differences in our narrower physical environments on the one hand, and in our cognitive abilities on the other. Perceptual abilities vary in effectiveness from one individual to another. Inferential abilities also vary, and not just in effectiveness. People speak different languages, they have mastered different concepts; as a result, they can construct different representations and make different inferences. They have different memories, too, different theories that they bring to bear on their experience in different ways. Hence, even if they all shared the same narrow physical environment, what we propose to call their *cognitive environments* would still differ.

To introduce the notion of a cognitive environment, let us consider a parallel case. One human cognitive ability is sight. With respect to sight, each individual is in a visual environment which can be characterised as the set of all phenomena visible to him. What is visible to him is a function both of his physical environment and of his visual abilities.

In studying communication, we are interested in conceptual cognitive abilities. We want to suggest that what visible phenomena are for visual cognition, manifest facts are for conceptual cognition. Let us define:

(39)   A fact is manifest to an individual at a given time if and only if he is
       capable at that time of representing it mentally and accepting its
       representation as true or probably true.

(40)   A *cognitive environment* of an individual is a set of facts that are manifest to
       him.

To be manifest, then, is to be perceptible or inferable. An individual's total cognitive environment is the set of all the facts that he can perceive or infer: all the facts that are manifest to him. An individual's total cognitive environment is a function of his physical environment and his cognitive abilities. It consists of not only all the facts that he is aware of, but also all the facts that he is capable of becoming aware of, in his physical environment. The individual's actual awareness of facts, i.e. the knowledge that he has acquired, of course contributes to his ability to become aware of further facts. Memorised information is a component of cognitive abilities.

We want to elaborate the notion of what is manifest in two ways: first, we want to extend it from facts to all assumptions; and second, we want to distinguish degrees of manifestness. Our point of view here is cognitive rather than epistemological. From a cognitive point of view, mistaken assumptions can be indistinguishable from genuine factual knowledge, just as optical illusions can be indistinguishable from true sight. Just as illusions are 'visible', so any assumption, whether true or false, may be manifest to an individual. An assumption, then, is manifest in a cognitive environment if the environment provides sufficient evidence for its adoption, and as we all know, mistaken assumptions are sometimes very well evidenced.

Anything that can be seen at all is visible, but some things are much more visible than others. Similarly, we have defined 'manifest' so that any assumption that an individual is capable of constructing and accepting as true or probably true is manifest to him. We also want to say that manifest assumptions which are more likely to be entertained are more manifest. Which assumptions are more manifest to an individual during a given period or at a given moment is again a function of his physical environment on the one hand and his cognitive abilities on the other.

Human cognitive organisation makes certain types of phenomena (i.e. perceptible objects or events) particularly salient. For instance, the noise of an explosion or a doorbell ringing is highly salient, a background buzz or a ticking clock much less so. When a phenomenon is noticed, some assumptions about it are standardly more accessible than others. In an environment where the doorbell has just rung, it will normally be strongly manifest that there is someone at the door, less strongly so that whoever is at the door is tall enough to reach the bell, and less strongly still that the bell has not been stolen. The most strongly manifest assumption of all is the assumption that the doorbell has just rung, the evidence for which is both salient and conclusive. We will have more to say, in chapter 3, about the factors which make some assumptions more manifest than others in a given situation. For the moment it is the fact rather than the explanation that matters.

Our notion of what is manifest to an individual is clearly weaker than the notion of what is actually known or assumed. A fact can be manifest without being known; all the individual's actual assumptions are manifest to him, but many more assumptions which he has not actually made are manifest to him too. This is so however weakly the terms 'knowledge' and 'assumption' are construed. In a strong sense, to know some fact involves having a mental representation of it. In a weaker sense, to say that an individual knows some fact is not necessarily to imply that he has ever entertained a mental representation of it. For instance, before reading this sentence you all knew, in that weak sense, that Noam Chomsky never had breakfast with Julius Caesar, although until now the thought of it had never crossed your mind. It is generally accepted that people have not only the knowledge that they actually entertain, but also the knowledge that they are capable of deducing from the knowledge that they entertain. However, something can be manifest without being known, even in this virtual way, if only because something can be manifest and false, whereas nothing can be known and false.

Can something be manifest without being actually assumed? The answer must again be yes. Assumptions are unlike knowledge in that they need not be true. As with knowledge, people can be said to assume, in a weak sense, what they are capable of deducing from what they assume. However, people do not assume, in any sense, what they are merely capable of inferring non-demonstratively – that is, by some creative process of hypothesis formation and confirmation – from what they assume. Although it presumably followed non-demonstratively from what you knew and assumed before you read this sentence that Ronald Reagan and Noam Chomsky never played billiards together, this was not, until now, an assumption of yours: it was only an assumption that was manifest to you. Moreover, something can be manifest merely by being perceptible, and without being inferable at all from previously held knowledge and assumptions. A car is audibly passing in the street. You have not yet paid any attention to it, so you have no knowledge of it, no assumptions about it, even in the weakest sense of 'knowledge' and 'assumption'. But the fact that a car is passing in the street is manifest to you.

We will now show that because 'manifest' is weaker than 'known' or 'assumed', a notion of mutual manifestness can be developed which does not suffer from the same psychological implausibility as 'mutual knowledge' or 'mutual assumptions'.

To the extent that two organisms have the same visual abilities and the same physical environment, the same phenomena are visible to them and they can be said to share a visual environment. Since visual abilities and physical environments are never exactly identical, organisms never share their total visual environments. Moreover, two organisms which share a visual environment need not actually see the same phenomena; they are merely capable of doing so.

Similarly, the same facts and assumptions may be manifest in the cognitive environments of two different people. In that case, these cognitive environments intersect, and their intersection is a cognitive environment that these two people share. The total shared cognitive environment of two people is the intersection of their two total cognitive environments: i.e. the set of all facts that are manifest to them both. Clearly, if people share cognitive environments, it is because they share physical environments and have similar cognitive abilities. Since physical environments are never strictly identical, and since cognitive abilities are affected by previously memorised information and thus differ in many respects from one person to another, people never share their total cognitive environments. Moreover, to say that two people share a cognitive environment does not imply that they make the same assumptions: merely that they are capable of doing so.

One thing that can be manifest in a given cognitive environment is a characterisation of the people who have access to it. For instance, every Freemason has access to a number of secret assumptions which include the assumption that all Freemasons have access to these same secret assumptions. In other words, all Freemasons share a cognitive environment which contains the assumption that all Freemasons share this environment. To take another example, Peter and Mary are talking to each other in the same room: they share a cognitive environment which consists of all the facts made manifest to them by their presence in this room. One of these facts is the fact that they share this environment.

Any shared cognitive environment in which it is manifest which people share it is what we will call a *mutual cognitive environment*. In a mutual cognitive environment, for every manifest assumption, the fact that it is manifest to the people who share this environment is itself manifest. In other words, in a mutual cognitive environment, every manifest assumption is what we will call *mutually manifest*.

Consider, for example, a cognitive environment E shared by Peter and Mary, in which (41) and (42) are manifest:

(41)   Peter and Mary share cognitive environment *E*.

(42)   The phone is ringing.

In this environment, (43)–(45) and indefinitely many assumptions built on the same pattern are also manifest:

(43)   It is manifest to Peter and to Mary that the phone is ringing.

(44)   It is manifest to Peter and to Mary that it is manifest to Peter and to Mary that the phone is ringing.

(45)   It is manifest to Peter and to Mary that it is manifest to Peter and to Mary that it is manifest to Peter and to Mary that the phone is ringing.

The more complex assumptions of type (43)–(45) get, the less likely they are actually to be made. However, in such a series, assumption *n* does not have to be actually made by the individuals it mentions for assumption *n* + 1 to be true. There is therefore no cut-off point beyond which these assumptions are likely to be false rather than true; they remain manifest throughout, even though their degree of manifestness tends asymptotically toward zero. (41)–(45) and all the assumptions in *E* are not only manifest to Peter and Mary; they are mutually manifest.

The notion of a mutually manifest assumption is clearly weaker than that of a mutual assumption (and *a fortiori* than that of mutual knowledge). Consider assumptions (46)–(48) and all the further assumptions that can be built on the same pattern:

(46)   Peter and Mary assume that the phone is ringing.

(47)   Peter and Mary assume that Peter and Mary assume that the phone is ringing.

(48)   Peter and Mary assume that Peter and Mary assume that Peter and Mary assume that the phone is ringing.

As before, the more complex assumptions of type (46)–(48) get, the less likely they are actually to be made. In this case, however, assumption *n* does have to be made by Peter and Mary for assumption *n* + 1 to be true. Moreover, there is sure to be some point – quite soon actually – at which Mary does *not* assume that Peter assumes that she assumes that he assumes, etc. At this point and beyond, all the assumptions in this series are false, and mutuality of assumptions is not achieved. Another way of seeing that mutuality of assumptions is stronger than mutual manifestness is to notice that (43) may be true when (46) is not, (44) may be true when (47) is not, (45) may be true when (48) is not, and so on, while the converse is not possible.

Mutual manifestness is not merely weaker than mutual knowledge or mutual assumption; it is weaker in just the right way. On the one hand, it is not open to the same psychological objections, since the claim that an assumption is mutually manifest is a claim about cognitive environments rather than mental states or processes. On the other hand, as we will show in section 12, the notion of mutual manifestness is strong enough to give a precise and interesting content to the notion of overtness discussed in section 6. However, by rejecting the notion of mutual knowledge and adopting the weaker notion of mutual manifestness, we deprive ourselves of a certain type of explanation in the study of communication.

Communication requires some degree of co-ordination between communicator and audience on the choice of a code and a context. The notion of mutual knowledge is used to explain how this co-ordination can be achieved: given enough mutual knowledge, communicator and audience can make symmetrical choices of code and context. A realistic notion of mutual manifestness, on the other hand, is not strong enough to explain such symmetrical co-ordination. However, before concluding that mutual manifestness is too weak after all, ask yourself what are the grounds for assuming that responsibility for co-ordination is equally shared between communicator and audience, and that both must worry, symmetrically, about what the other is thinking. Asymmetrical co-ordination is often easier to achieve, and communication is an asymmetrical process anyhow.

Consider what would happen in ballroom dancing if the responsibility for choosing steps was left equally to both partners (and how little help the mutual-knowledge framework would be for solving the resulting co-ordination problems in real time). Co-ordination problems are avoided, or considerably reduced, in dancing, by leaving the responsibility to one partner who leads, while the other has merely to follow. We assume that the same goes for communication. It is left to the communicator to make correct assumptions about the codes and contextual information that the audience will have accessible and be likely to use in the comprehension process. The responsibility for avoiding misunderstandings also lies with the speaker, so that all the hearer has to do is go ahead and use whatever code and contextual information come most easily to hand.

Suppose Mary and Peter are looking at a landscape where she has noticed a distant church. She says to him,

(49)   I've been inside that church.

She does not stop to ask herself whether he has noticed the building, and whether he assumes she has noticed, and assumes she has noticed he has noticed, and so on, or whether he has assumed it is a church, and assumes she assumes it is, and so on. All she needs is reasonable confidence that he will be able to identify the building as a church when required to: in other words, that a certain assumption will be manifest in his cognitive environment at the right time. He need not have accessed this assumption before she spoke. In fact, until she spoke he might have thought the building was a castle: it might be only on the strength of her utterance that it becomes manifest to him that the building is a church.

Inspired by the landscape, Mary says,

(50)   It's the sort of scene that would have made Marianne Dashwood swoon.

This is an allusion to Jane Austen's *Sense and Sensibility*, a book she knows Peter has read. She does not stop to think whether he knows she has read it too and knows she knows he has read it, and so on. Nor is she unaware of the fact that they may well have reacted to the book in different ways and remember it differently. Her remark is based on assumptions that she does not mention and that he need never have made himself before she spoke. What she expects, rightly, is that her utterance will act as a prompt, making him recall parts of the book that he had previously forgotten, and construct the assumptions needed to understand the allusion.

In both these examples Mary makes assumptions about what assumptions are, or will be, manifest to Peter. Peter trusts that the assumptions he spontaneously makes about the church and about *Sense and Sensibility*, which help him understand Mary's utterances, are those she expected him to make. To communicate successfully, Mary had to have some knowledge of Peter's cognitive environment. As a result of their successful communication, their mutual cognitive environment is enlarged. Note that symmetrical co-ordination and mutual knowledge do not enter into the picture at all.

The most fundamental reason for adopting the mutual-knowledge framework, as for adopting the code model, is the desire to show how successful communication can be guaranteed, how there is some failsafe algorithm by which the hearer can reconstruct the speaker's exact meaning. Within this framework the fact that communication often fails is explained in one of two ways: either the code mechanism has been imperfectly implemented, or there has been some disruption due to 'noise'. A noiseless, well-implemented code mechanism should guarantee perfect communication.

In rejecting the mutual-knowledge framework, we abandon the possibility of using a failsafe algorithm as a model of human communication. But since it is obvious that the communication process takes place at a risk, why assume that it is governed by a failsafe procedure? Moreover, if there is one conclusion to be drawn from work on artificial intelligence, it is that most cognitive processes are so complex that they must be modelled in terms of heuristics rather than failsafe algorithms. We assume, then, that communication is governed by a less-than-perfect heuristic. On this approach, failures in communication are to be expected: what is mysterious and requires explanation is not failure but success.

As we have seen, the notion of mutual manifestness is not strong enough to salvage the code theory of communication. But then, this was never one of our aims. Instead of taking the code theory for granted and concluding that mutual knowledge must therefore exist, we prefer to look at what kind of assumptions people are actually in a position to make about each other's assumptions, and then see what this implies for an account of communication.

Sometimes, we have direct evidence about other people's assumptions: for instance, when they tell us what they assume. More generally, because we manifestly share cognitive environments with other people, we have direct evidence about what is manifest to them. When a cognitive environment we share with other people is mutual, we have evidence about what is mutually manifest to all of us. Note that this evidence can never be conclusive: the boundaries of cognitive environments cannot be precisely determined, if only because the threshold between very weakly manifest assumptions and inaccessible ones is unmarked.

From assumptions about what is manifest to other people, and in particular about what is strongly manifest to them, we are in a position to derive further, though necessarily weaker, assumptions about what assumptions they are actually making. From assumptions about what is mutually manifest to all of us, we are in a position to derive further, and weaker, assumptions about the assumptions they attribute to us. And essentially, this is it. Human beings somehow manage to communicate in situations where a great deal can be assumed about what is manifest to others, a lot can be assumed about what is mutually manifest to themselves and others, but nothing can be assumed to be truly mutually known or assumed.

The situations which establish a mutual cognitive environment are essentially those that have been treated as establishing mutual knowledge. We have argued that assumptions of mutual knowledge are never truly warranted. Examples (49) and (50) are anecdotal evidence that they are unnecessary. The detour via mutual knowledge is superfluous: mutual cognitive environments directly provide all the information needed for communication and comprehension.

The notions of cognitive environment and of manifestness, mutual or otherwise, are psychologically realistic, but by themselves shed little light on what goes on in human minds. A cognitive environment is merely a set of assumptions which the individual is capable of mentally representing and accepting as true. The question then is: which of these assumptions will the individual actually make? This question is of interest not only to the psychologist, but also to every ordinary communicator. We will argue that when you communicate, your intention is to alter the cognitive environment of your addressees; but of course you expect their actual thought processes to be affected as a result. In the next section we will argue that human cognition is relevance-oriented, and that as a result, someone who knows an individual's cognitive environment can infer which assumptions he is actually likely to entertain.

Relevance and ostension

An individual's cognitive environment is a set of assumptions available to him. Which particular assumptions is he most likely to construct and process? There may, of course, be no general answer to this question. We want to argue that there is. This section is essentially an exploration of the idea that there is a single property – relevance – which makes information worth processing for a human being. Chapter 3 will contain a relatively technical discussion of relevance. In this section, we simply want to characterise the notion in very general, informal terms, and to make some suggestions about the role of relevance in communication.

Human beings are efficient information-processing devices. This is their most obvious asset as a species. But what is efficiency in information processing?

Efficiency can only be defined with respect to a goal. Some goals, such as catching a prey, winning a game or solving a problem, are absolute: they consist in bringing about a particular state of affairs which at any given moment either exists or does not exist. Other goals, such as multiplying one's offspring, improving one's backstroke, or understanding oneself, are relative: they consist in raising the value of some variable, and can thus only be achieved to a degree. Efficiency with respect to absolute goals is simply a matter of reaching them with the smallest possible expenditure of whatever resource (time, money, energy . . .) it takes. Efficiency with respect to relative goals is a matter of striking a balance between degree of achievement and expenditure. In the special case where the expenditure is fixed – say all the time available is going to be spent anyhow – efficiency consists in achieving the goal to the highest possible degree.

Most discussions of information processing, whether in experimental psychology or in artificial intelligence, have been concerned with the realisation of absolute goals. 'Problem solving' has become the paradigm of information processing. The problems considered have a fixed solution; the goal of the information-processing device is to find this solution; efficiency consists in finding it at the minimal cost. However, not all cognitive tasks fit this description; many tasks consist not in reaching an absolute goal, but in improving on an existing state of affairs. Hence, cognitive efficiency may have to be characterised differently for different devices.

Simpler information-processing devices, whether natural, such as a frog, or artificial, such as an electronic alarm system, process only very specific information: for example, metabolic changes and fly movements for frogs, noises and other vibrations for alarm systems. Their information-processing activity consists in monitoring changes in the values of a few variables. They could be informally described as engaged in answering a few set questions: 'Is there a fly-like object within reach?', 'Is there a large body moving in the room?' More complex information-processing devices, by contrast, can define and monitor new variables or formulate and answer new questions.

For the simpler devices, efficiency consists in answering their set questions at the minimal processing cost. Efficiency cannot be so easily defined for more complex devices such as human beings. For such devices, efficient information processing may involve formulating and trying to answer new questions despite the extra processing costs incurred. Formulating and answering specific questions must then be seen as subservient to a more general and abstract goal. It is in relation to this general goal that the efficiency of complex information-processing devices must be characterised.

On the general goal of human cognition, we have nothing better to offer than rather trivial speculative remarks. However, these remarks have important and non-trivial consequences. It seems that human cognition is aimed at improving the individual's knowledge of the world. This means adding more information, information that is more accurate, more easily retrievable, and more developed in areas of greater concern to the individual. Information processing is a permanent life-long task. An individual's overall resources for information processing are, if not quite fixed, at least not very flexible. Thus, long-term cognitive efficiency consists in improving one's knowledge of the world as much as possible given the available resources.

What, then, is short-term cognitive efficiency – efficiency, say, in the way your mind spends the next few seconds or milliseconds? This is a more concrete question, and one that is harder to answer. At every moment, many different cognitive tasks could be performed, and this for two reasons: first, human sensory abilities monitor much more information than central conceptual abilities can process; and second, central abilities always have plenty of unfinished business. The key problem for efficient short-term information processing is thus to achieve an optimal allocation of central processing resources. Resources have to be allocated to the processing of information which is likely to bring about the greatest contribution to the mind's general cognitive goals at the smallest processing cost.

Some information is old: it is already present in the individual's representation of the world. Unless it is needed for the performance of a particular cognitive task, and is easier to access from the environment than from memory, such information is not worth processing at all. Other information is not only new but entirely unconnected with anything in the individual's representation of the world. It can only be added to this representation as isolated bits and pieces, and this usually means too much processing cost for too little benefit. Still other information is new but connected with old information. When these interconnected new and old items of information are used together as premises in an inference process, further new information can be derived: information which could not have been inferred without this combination of old and new premises. When the processing of new information gives rise to such a multiplication effect, we call it *relevant*. The greater the multiplication effect, the greater the relevance.

Consider an example. Mary and Peter are sitting on a park bench. He leans back, which alters her view. By leaning back, he modifies her cognitive environment; he reveals to her certain phenomena, which she may look at or not, and describe to herself in different ways. Why should she pay attention to one phenomenon rather than another, or describe it to herself in one way rather than another? In other words, why should she mentally process any of the assumptions which have become manifest or more manifest to her as a result of the change in her environment? Our answer is that she should process those assumptions that are most relevant to her at the time.

Imagine, for instance, that as a result of Peter's leaning back she can see, among other things, three people: an ice-cream vendor who she had noticed before when she sat down on the bench, an ordinary stroller who she has never seen before, and her acquaintance William, who is coming towards them and is a dreadful bore. Many assumptions about each of these characters are more or less manifest to her. She may already have considered the implications of the presence of the ice-cream vendor when she first noticed him; if so, it would be a waste of processing resources to pay further attention to him now. The presence of the unknown stroller is new information to her, but little or nothing follows from it; so there again, what she can perceive and infer about him is not likely to be of much relevance to her. By contrast, from the fact that William is coming her way, she can draw many conclusions from which many more conclusions will follow. This, then, is the one truly relevant change in her cognitive environment; this is the particular phenomenon she should pay attention to. She should do so, that is, if she is aiming at cognitive efficiency.

Our claim is that all human beings automatically aim at the most efficient information processing possible. This is so whether they are conscious of it or not;

in fact, the very diverse and shifting conscious interests of individuals result from the pursuit of this permanent aim in changing conditions. In other words, an individual's particular cognitive goal at a given moment is always an instance of a more general goal: maximising the relevance of the information processed. We will show that this is a crucial factor in human interaction.

Among the facts made manifest to Mary by Peter's behaviour is the very fact that he has behaved in a certain way. Suppose now that she pays attention to this behaviour, and comes to the conclusion that it must have been deliberate: perhaps he is leaning back more rigidly than if he were merely trying to find a more comfortable position. She might then ask herself why he is doing it. There may be many possible answers; suppose that the most plausible one she can find is that he is leaning back in order to attract her attention to some particular phenomenon. Then Peter's behaviour has made it manifest to Mary that he intends to make some particular assumptions manifest to her. We will call such behaviour – behaviour which makes manifest an intention to make something manifest – *ostensive* behaviour or simply *ostension*. Showing someone something is a case of ostension. So too, we will argue, is human intentional communication.

The existence of ostension is beyond doubt. What is puzzling is how it works. Any perceptible behaviour makes manifest indefinitely many assumptions. How is the audience of an act of ostension to discover which of them have been intentionally made manifest? For instance, how is Mary to discover which of the phenomena which have become manifest to her as a result of Peter's behaviour are the ones he intended her to pay attention to?

Information processing involves effort; it will only be undertaken in the expectation of some reward. There is thus no point in drawing someone's attention to a phenomenon unless it will seem relevant enough to him to be worth his attention. By requesting Mary's attention, Peter suggests that he has reason to think that by paying attention, she will gain some relevant information. He may, of course, be mistaken, or trying to distract her attention from relevant information elsewhere, as the maker of an assertion may be mistaken or lying; but just as an assertion comes with a tacit guarantee of truth, so ostension comes with a tacit guarantee of relevance.

This guarantee of relevance makes it possible for Mary to infer which of the newly manifest assumptions have been intentionally made manifest. Here is how the inference process might go. First, Mary notices Peter's behaviour and assumes that it is ostensive: i.e. that it is intended to attract her attention to some phenomenon. If she has enough confidence in his guarantee of relevance, she will infer that some of the information which his behaviour has made manifest to her is indeed relevant to her. She then pays attention to the area that has become visible to her as a result of his leaning back, and discovers the ice-cream vendor, the stroller, this dreadful William, and so on. Assumptions about William are the only newly manifest assumptions relevant enough to be worth her attention. From this, she can infer that Peter's intention was precisely to draw her attention to William's arrival. Any other assumption about his ostensive behaviour is inconsistent with her confidence in the guarantee of relevance it carries.

Mary has become aware not only that there is someone coming who she wants to avoid, but also that Peter intended her to become aware of it, and that he is aware of it too. On the basis of his observable behaviour, she has discovered some of his thoughts.

Ostensive behaviour provides evidence of one's thoughts. It succeeds in doing so because it implies a guarantee of relevance. It implies such a guarantee because humans automatically turn their attention to what seems most relevant to them. The main thesis of section is that an act of ostension carries a guarantee of relevance, and that this fact – which we will call the *principle of relevance* – makes manifest the intention behind the ostension. We believe that it is this principle of relevance that is needed to make the inferential model of communication explanatory.

Ostensive-inferential communication

Ostension provides two layers of information to be picked up: first, there is the information which has been, so to speak, pointed out; second, there is the information that the first layer of information has been intentionally pointed out. One can imagine the first layer being recovered without the second. For example, as a result of Peter's leaning back, Mary might notice William coming their way, even if she paid no attention to Peter's intentions. And as for Peter, he might not care much whether Mary recognises his intention, as long as she notices William.

In general, however, recognising the intention behind the ostension is necessary for efficient information processing: someone who fails to recognise this intention may fail to notice relevant information. Let us modify our example slightly and suppose that William is in the distance, barely visible in a crowd. If Mary pays no attention to the fact that Peter's behaviour is ostensive, she might well look in the right direction and yet not notice William. If she pays attention to the ostension, she will be inclined to take a closer look and find out what information Peter thought might be relevant to her.

In our modified example, what Peter's ostension mostly does is make much more manifest some information which would have been manifest anyhow, though very weakly so. Sometimes, however, part of the basic information will not be manifest at all unless the intention behind the ostension is taken into account. Suppose a girl is travelling in a foreign country. She comes out of the inn wearing light summer clothes, manifestly intending to take a stroll. An old man sitting on a bench nearby looks ostensively up at the sky. When the girl looks up, she sees a few tiny clouds, which she might have noticed for herself, but which she would normally have paid no further attention to: given her knowledge – or lack of knowledge – of the local weather, the presence of these tiny clouds is not relevant to her. Now, however, the old man is drawing her attention to the clouds in a manifestly intentional way, thus guaranteeing that there is some relevant information to be obtained.

The old man's ostensive behaviour opens up for the girl a whole new strategy of processing. If she accepts his guarantee of relevance, she has to find out what makes him think that the presence of the clouds would be relevant to her. Knowing the area and its weather better than she does, he might have reason to think that the clouds are going to get worse and turn to rain. Such an assumption is of a very standard sort and would probably be the first to come to mind. The old man can thus be reasonably confident that, prompted by his behaviour, she will have no difficulty in deciding that this is what he believes. If it were not manifest to the old man that it was going to rain, it would be hard to explain his behaviour at all. The girl thus has reason to think that in drawing her attention to the clouds, he intended to make manifest to her that he believed it was going to rain. As a result of this act of ostension, she now has some information that was not available to her before: that he thinks it is going to rain, and hence that there is a genuine risk of rain.

In this example, the state of affairs that the old man drew the girl's attention to had been partly manifest to her, and partly not. The presence of the clouds and the fact that clouds may always turn to rain had been manifest and merely became more so. However, until that moment she had regarded the fact that the weather was beautiful as strong evidence that it would not rain. The risk of rain in that particular situation was not manifest to her at all. In other words, the clouds were already evidence of oncoming rain, but evidence that was much too weak. The old man made that evidence much stronger by pointing it out; as his intentions became manifest, the assumption that it would rain became manifest too.

Sometimes, all the evidence displayed in an act of ostension bears directly on the agent's intentions. In these cases, only by discovering the agent's intentions can the audience also discover, indirectly, the basic information that the agent intended to make manifest. The relation between the evidence produced and the basic information conveyed is arbitrary. The same piece of evidence can be used, on different occasions, to make manifest different assumptions, even mutually inconsistent assumptions, as long as it makes manifest the intention behind the ostension.

Here is an example. Two prisoners, from different tribes with no common language, are put in a quarry to work back to back breaking rocks. Suddenly, prisoner A starts putting some distinct rhythm into the sound of his hammer – one–two–three, one–two, one–two–three, one–two – a rhythm that is both arbitrary and noticeable enough to attract the attention of prisoner B. This arbitrary pattern in the way the rocks are being broken has no direct relevance for B. However, there are grounds for thinking that it has been intentionally produced, and B might ask himself what A's intentions were in producing it. One plausible assumption is that this is a piece of ostensive behaviour: that is, that A intended B to notice the pattern. This would in turn make manifest A's desire to interact with B, which in the circumstances would be relevant enough.

Here is a more substantial example. Prisoners A and B are at work in their quarry, each with a guard at his shoulder, when suddenly the attention of the guards is distracted. Both prisoners realise that they have a good chance of escaping, but only if they can co-ordinate their attack and overpower their guards simultaneously. Here, it is clear what information would be relevant: each wants to know when the other will start the attack. Prisoner A suddenly whistles, the prisoners overpower their guards and escape. Again, there is no need for a preexisting code correlating a whistle with the information that now is the moment to attack. The information is obvious enough: it is the only information that A could conceivably have intended to make manifest in the circumstances.

Could not the repetition of such a situation lead to the development of a code? Imagine that the two prisoners, caught again, find themselves in the same predicament: again a whistle, again an escape, and again they are caught. The next time, prisoner B, who has not realised that both guards are distracted, hears prisoner A whistle: this time, fortunately, B does not have to infer what the whistle is intended to make manifest: he knows. The whistle has become a signal associated by an underlying code to the message 'Let us overpower our guards now!'

Inferential theorists might be tempted to see language as a whole as having developed in this way: to see conventional meanings as growing out of natural inferences. This is reminiscent of the story of how Rockefeller became a millionaire. One day, when he was young and very poor, Rockefeller found a one-cent coin in the street. He bought an apple, polished it, sold it for two cents, bought two apples, polished them, sold them for four cents . . . After one month he bought a cart, after two years he was about to buy a grocery store, when he inherited the fortune of his millionaire uncle. We will never know how far hominid efforts at conventionalising inference might have gone towards establishing a full-fledged human language. The fact is that the development of human languages was made possible by a specialised biological endowment.

Whatever the origin of the language or code employed, a piece of coded behaviour may be used ostensively – that is, to provide two layers of information: a basic layer of information, which may be about anything at all, and a second layer consisting of the information that the first layer of information has been intentionally made manifest. When a coded signal, or any other arbitrary piece of behaviour, is used ostensively, the evidence displayed bears directly on the individual's intention, and only indirectly on the basic layer of information that she intends to make manifest. We are now, of course, dealing with standard cases of Gricean communication.

Is there a dividing line between instances of ostension which one would be more inclined to describe as 'showing something', and clear cases of communication where the communicator unquestionably 'means something'? One of Grice's main concerns was to draw such a line: to distinguish what he called 'natural meaning' – smoke meaning fire, clouds meaning rain, and so on – from 'non-natural meaning': the word 'fire' meaning fire, Peter's utterance meaning that it will rain, and so on. Essential to this distinction was the third type of communicator's intention Grice mentioned in his analysis: a true communicator intends the recognition of his informative intention to function as at least part of the audience's reason for fulfilling that intention. In other words, the first, basic, layer of information must not be entirely recoverable without reference to the second.

What we have tried to show so far in this section is that there are not two distinct and well-defined classes, but a continuum of cases of ostension ranging from 'showing', where strong direct evidence for the basic layer of information is provided, to 'saying that', where all the evidence is indirect. Even in our very first case of Peter leaning back ostensively to let Mary see William approaching, it is arguable that some of the basic information is made manifest indirectly, through Peter's intention being made manifest. Someone who engages in any kind of ostensive behaviour intentionally draws some attention to himself and intentionally makes manifest a few assumptions about himself: for instance, that he is aware of the basic information involved, and that he is trying to be relevant. Peter's ostension might make it manifest not just that William is approaching, but also that Peter expects Mary to be concerned, and that he is concerned too.

Would we want to say, though, that Peter 'meant something' by his behaviour? Like most English speakers, we would be reluctant to do so; but this is irrelevant to our pursuit, which is not to analyse ordinary language usage, but to describe and explain forms of human communication. Our argument at this stage is this: either inferential communication consists in providing evidence for what the communicator means, in the sense of 'meaning' which Grice calls 'nonnatural meaning', and in that case inferential communication is not a well-defined class of phenomena at all; or else showing something should be considered a form of inferential communication, on a par with meaning something by a certain behaviour, and inferential communication and ostension should be equated.

There are two questions involved here. One is substantive: which domains of facts are to be described and explained together? Our answer is that ostension is such a domain, and that inferential communication narrowly understood (i.e. understood as excluding cases of ostension where talk of 'meaning' would be awkward) is not. The second question is terminological (and hence not worth much argument): can the term 'communication' be legitimately applied to all cases of ostension? Our answer is yes, and from now on we will treat ostensive communication, inferential communication, and ostensive–inferential communication as the same thing. Inferential communication and ostension are one and the same process, but seen from two different points of view: that of the communicator who is involved in ostension and that of the audience who is involved in inference.

Ostensive–inferential communication consists in making manifest to an audience one's intention to make manifest a basic layer of information. It can therefore be described in terms of an informative and a communicative intention. In the next two sections, we want to reanalyse the notions of informative and communicative intention in terms of manifestness and mutual manifestness, and to sketch in some of the empirical implications of this reformulation.

The informative intention

We began this section by pointing out that any account of communication must answer two questions: first, what is communicated; and second, how is communication achieved? Up to now, we have considered only the second question. In this section, we return to the first. The generally accepted answer is that what is communicated is a meaning. The question then becomes, what is a meaning? And there is no generally accepted answer any more.

However much they differ, all answers to the what-is-a-meaning question share the view that the paradigm example of meaning is what is explicitly expressed by a linguistic utterance. The verbal communication of an explicit meaning is then taken as the model of communication in general. This is true of semiotic approaches, which are not only generalisations of a linguistic model, but are also based on the assumption that to communicate is always, in Saussure's terms, to transmit a 'signified' by use of a 'signifier'. It is true of inferential approaches, which regard all communicative acts as 'utterances' in an extended sense, used to convey an 'utterer's meaning'.

We believe that the kind of explicit communication that can be achieved by the use of language is not a typical but a limiting case. Treating linguistic communication as the model of communication in general has led to theoretical distortions and misperceptions of the data. The effects of most forms of human communication, including some of the effects of verbal communication, are far too vague to be properly analysed along these lines. Moreover, there is not a dichotomy but a continuum of cases, from vaguer to more precise effects.

Let us first illustrate this point with two examples of non-verbal communication. Mary comes home; Peter opens the door. Mary stops at the door and sniffs ostensively; Peter follows suit and notices that there is a smell of gas. This fact is highly relevant, and in the absence of contextual counterevidence or any obvious alternative candidate, Peter will assume that Mary intended to make it manifest to him that there was a smell of gas. Here, at least part of what is communicated could be reasonably well paraphrased by saying that there is a smell of gas; and it could be argued that this is what Mary *means*. She could indeed have achieved essentially the same result by speaking rather than sniffing ostensively.

Contrast this with the following case. Mary and Peter are newly arrived at the seaside. She opens the window overlooking the sea and sniffs appreciatively and ostensively. When Peter follows suit, there is no one particular good thing that comes to his attention: the air smells fresh, fresher than it did in town, it reminds him of their previous holidays, he can smell the sea, seaweed, ozone, fish; all sorts of pleasant things come to mind, and while, because her sniff was appreciative, he is reasonably safe in assuming that she must have intended him to notice at least some of them, he is unlikely to be able to pin her intentions down any further. Is there any reason to assume that her intentions were more specific? Is there a plausible answer, in the form of an explicit linguistic paraphrase, to the question, what does she mean? Could she have achieved the same communicative effect by speaking? Clearly not.

Examples like the one of Mary smelling gas, where it is reasonable to impute a meaning to the communicator, are the only ones normally considered in discussions of communication; examples like the one of Mary at the seaside – clearly communicating, but what? – are generally ignored. Yet these examples do not belong to distinct classes of phenomena, and it is easy enough to imagine intermediate cases: say, a guest sniffing appreciatively and ostensively when the stew is brought to the table, and so on.

The distortions and misperceptions introduced by the explicit communication model are also found in the study of verbal communication itself. Some essential aspects of implicit verbal communication are overlooked. Pragmatists assume that what is communicated by an utterance is a speaker's meaning, which in the case of an assertion is a set of assumptions. One of these assumptions is explicitly expressed; the others (if any) are implicitly conveyed, or implicated. The only difference between the explicit content of an utterance and its implicatures is supposed to be that the explicit content is decoded, while the implicatures are inferred. Now we all know, as speakers and hearers, that what is implicitly conveyed by an utterance is generally much vaguer than what is explicitly expressed, and that when the implicit import of an utterance is explicitly spelled out, it tends to be distorted by the elimination of this often intentional vagueness. The distortion is even greater in the case of metaphor and other figures of speech, whose poetic effects are generally destroyed by being explicitly spelled out.

In an effort to minimise the distortion, pragmatists have tended to focus on examples such as (32), where the implicit import is fairly precise, and to ignore equally ordinary cases of implicit vagueness such as (51):

(32)   Peter: Do you want some coffee?
        Mary: Coffee would keep me awake.

(51)   Peter: What do you intend to do today?
        Mary: I have a terrible headache.

In (32), Mary implicates that she doesn't want coffee (or, in some circumstances, that she does) and that her reason for not wanting it is that it would keep her awake. Here the implicatures can be spelled out without distortion. In (51), what does Mary implicate? That she will not do anything? That she will do as little as possible? That she will do as much as she can? That she does not yet know what she will do? There is no precise assumption, apart from the one explicitly expressed, which she can be said to intend Peter to share. Yet there is more to her utterance than its explicit content: she manifestly intends Peter to draw some conclusions from what she said, and not just any conclusions. Quite ordinary cases such as (51) are never discussed in the pragmatic literature.

Pragmatists tend to take for granted that a meaning is a proposition combined with a propositional attitude, though they may diverge considerably in the way they present and develop this view. In other words, they treat the communicator's informative intention as an intention to induce in an audience certain attitudes to certain propositions. With assertions, often taken to be the most basic case, the informative intention is treated as an intention to induce in an audience the belief that a certain proposition is true.

There is a very good reason for anyone concerned with the role of inference in communication to assume that what is communicated is propositional: it is relatively easy to say what propositions are, and how inference might operate over propositions. No one has any clear idea how inference might operate over non-propositional objects: say, over images, impressions or emotions. Propositional contents and attitudes thus seem to provide the only relatively solid ground on which to base a partly or wholly inferential approach to communication. Too bad if much of what is communicated does not fit the propositional mould.

At first sight, it might look as if semioticians had a more comprehensive view. They have an *a priori* account of how any kind of representation, propositional or not, might be conveyed: namely, by means of a code. However, studies by semioticians of what they call 'connotation', i.e. the vaguer aspect of what is communicated, are highly programmatic and do not offer the beginnings of a psychologically adequate account of the type of mental representation involved. The semiotic approach is more comprehensive only by being more superficial.

The only people who have been quite consistently concerned with the vaguer aspects of communication are the Romantics, from the Schlegel brothers and Coleridge to I. A. Richards, and their many acknowledged or unacknowledged followers, including many semioticians such as Roman Jakobson in some of his writings, Victor Turner, or Roland Barthes. However, they have all dealt with vagueness in vague terms, with metaphors in metaphorical terms, and used the term 'meaning' so broadly that it becomes quite meaningless.

We see it as a major challenge for any account of human communication to give a precise description and explanation of its vaguer effects. Distinguishing meaning from communication, accepting that something can be communicated without being strictly speaking *meant* by the communicator or the communicator's behaviour, is a first essential step – a step away from the traditional approach to communication and most modern approaches. Once this step is taken, we believe that the framework we propose, unlike the others we have discussed, can rise to this challenge.

Accounts of communication either are not psychological at all, and avoid all talk of thoughts, intentions, etc., or else they assume that a communicator's intention is to induce certain specific thoughts in an audience. We want to suggest that the communicator's informative intention is better described as an intention to modify directly not the thoughts but the cognitive environment of the audience. The actual cognitive effects of a modification of the cognitive environment are only partly predictable. Communicators – like human agents in general – form intentions over whose fulfilment they have some control: they can have some controllable effect on their audience's cognitive environment, much less on their audience's actual thoughts, and they form their intentions accordingly.

We therefore propose to reformulate the notion of an informative intention along the following lines. A communicator produces a stimulus intending thereby

(52)   *Informative intention*: to make manifest or more manifest to the audience a set of assumptions **I**.

We take an intention to be a psychological state, and we assume that the content of the intention must be mentally represented. In particular, the communicator must have in mind a representation of the set of assumptions **I** which she intends to make manifest or more manifest to the audience. However, to have a representation of a set of assumptions it is not necessary to have a representation of each assumption in the set. Any individuating description may do.

When the communicator's intention is to make manifest some specific assumptions, then, of course, her representation of **I** may be in the form of a list of assumptions which are members of **I**. Consider dialogue (53), for instance:

(53)   Passenger: When does the train arrive at Oxford?
        Ticket-collector: At 5:25.

Here the ticket-collector's informative intention is to make manifest to the passenger the single assumption that the train arrives at 5:25. Examples of this type, where the communicator wants to communicate one or more specific assumptions which she actually has in mind, are the only ones usually considered. Our characterisation (52) of informative intentions fits these cases quite straightforwardly, but unlike other approaches, is not limited to them.

Consider, at the other extreme, the vaguest forms of communication. Here the communicator may have a representation of **I** in which none of the assumptions in **I** is directly listed. For instance, Mary's informative intention when sniffing the seaside air might be that all the assumptions which became manifest to her when she opened the window and took a deep breath should, as a result of her ostensive behaviour, become manifest or more manifest to Peter. She need not intend to communicate any particular one of these assumptions.

If asked what she wanted to convey, one of the best answers Mary could give is that she wanted to share an impression with Peter. What is an impression? Is it a type of mental representation? Can it be reduced to propositions and propositional attitudes? What we are suggesting is that an impression might be better described as a noticeable change in one's cognitive environment, a change resulting from relatively small alterations in the manifestness of many assumptions, rather than from the fact that a single assumption or a few new assumptions have all of a sudden become very manifest. It is quite in line with common sense to think of an impression as the sort of thing that can be communicated, and yet this intuition is unexplainable within current theories of communication. In the model of ostensive–inferential communication we are trying to develop, impressions fall squarely within the domain of things that can be communicated, and their very vagueness can be precisely described.

In many – perhaps most – cases of human communication, what the communicator intends to make manifest is partly precise and partly vague. She may have in mind a characterisation of **I** based on a representation of some but not all of the assumptions in **I**. For instance, in (51), Mary's informative intention in saying that she has a headache might be described as follows: she intends to make manifest to Peter the assumption that she has a headache and all the further assumptions manifestly required to make this a relevant answer to Peter's question. Similarly, Mary's informative intention when sniffing the smell of gas might be to make manifest to Peter not only the assumption that there is a smell of gas, but also all the further assumptions that this initial assumption makes mutually manifest.

Instead of treating an assumption as either communicated or not communicated, we have a set of assumptions which, as a result of communication, become manifest or more manifest to varying degrees. We might think of communication itself, then, as a matter of degree. When the communicator makes strongly manifest her informative intention to make some particular assumption strongly manifest, then that assumption is strongly communicated. An example would be answering a clear 'Yes' when asked 'Did you pay the rent?' When the communicator's intention is to increase simultaneously the manifestness of a wide range of assumptions, so that her intention concerning each of these assumptions is weakly manifest, then each of them is weakly communicated. An example would be sniffing ecstatically and ostensively at the fresh seaside air. There is, of course, a continuum of cases in between. In the case of strong communication, the communicator can have fairly precise expectations about some of the thoughts that the audience will actually entertain. With weaker forms of communication, the communicator can merely expect to steer the thoughts of the audience in a certain direction. Often, in human interaction, weak communication is found sufficient or even preferable to the stronger forms.

Non-verbal communication tends to be relatively weak. One of the advantages of verbal communication is that it gives rise to the strongest possible form of communication; it enables the hearer to pin down the speaker's intentions about the explicit content of her utterance to a single, strongly manifest candidate, with no alternative worth considering at all. On the other hand, what is implicit in verbal communication is generally weakly communicated: the hearer can often fulfil part of the speaker's informative intention by forming any of several roughly similar but not identical assumptions. Because all communication has been seen as strong communication, descriptions of non-verbal communication have been marred by spurious attributions of 'meaning'; in the case of verbal communication, the difference between explicit content and implicit import has been seen as a difference not in what gets communicated but merely in the means by which it is communicated, and the vagueness of implicatures and non-literal forms of expression has been idealised away. Our account of informative intentions in terms of manifestness of assumptions corrects these distortions without introducing either *ad hoc* machinery or vagueness of description.

The communicative intention

When we introduced the notion of a communicative intention in an earlier section, we drew attention to a problem first discussed by Strawson (1964a). Strawson pointed out that a communicator's intentions must be 'overt' in a sense which is easy enough to illustrate and grasp intuitively, but hard to spell out precisely. One type of solution, proposed by Strawson himself, is to regard an intention as overt when it is backed by a series of further intentions, each to the effect that the preceding intention in the series should be recognised. Schiffer (1972) proposed another solution: he analysed 'overt' as meaning mutually known. We argued that both types of solution are psychologically implausible.

Our solution, which is closer to Schiffer's than Strawson's, though without suffering from the defects of either, is to replace the vague 'overt' by the more precise 'mutually manifest'. We therefore redefine a communicative intention as follows. To communicate intentionally by ostension is to produce a certain stimulus with the aim of fulfilling an informative intention, and intending moreover thereby

(54)   *Communicative intention*: to make it mutually manifest to audience and
        communicator that the communicator has this informative intention.

This takes care of the types of example which Strawson and Schiffer used to show that, in order to communicate, it is not quite enough to inform an audience of one's informative intention. For instance, in the example in an earlier section, Mary leaves the pieces of her broken hair-drier lying around, intending thereby to inform Peter that she would like him to mend it. She wants this informative intention to be manifest to Peter, but at the same time, she does not want it to be 'overt'. In our terms, she does not want her informative intention to be mutually manifest. Intuitively, what she does is not quite communicate. Our redefinition of a communicative intention accounts for this intuition.

What difference does it make whether an informative intention is merely manifest to the audience or mutually manifest to audience and communicator? Should this really be a criterion for distinguishing communication from other forms of information transmission? Is it more than a technicality designed to take care of implausible borderline cases dreamed up by philosophers? Our answer is that there is indeed an essential difference.

Consider first a more general question: why should someone who has an informative intention bother to make it known to her audience that she has this intention? In other words, what are the reasons for engaging in ostensive communication? Grice discussed only one of these reasons: sometimes, making one's informative intention known is the best way, or the only way, of fulfilling it. We have shown that people sometimes engage in ostensive communication even though the informative intention could be fulfilled without being made manifest: for example, by providing direct evidence for the information to be conveyed. However, even in these cases, ostension helps focus the attention of the audience on the relevant information, and thus contributes to the fulfilment of the informative intention. This is still the Gricean reason for engaging in communication, just slightly extended in scope.

However, we want to argue that there is another major reason for engaging in ostensive communication, apart from helping to fulfil an informative intention. Mere informing alters the cognitive environment of the audience. Communication alters the mutual cognitive environment of the audience and communicator. Mutual manifestness may be of little cognitive importance, but it is of crucial social importance. A change in the mutual cognitive environment of two people is a change in their possibilities of interaction (and, in particular, in their possibilities of further communication).

Recall, for instance, the case of Peter leaning back to let Mary see William coming their way. If, as a result of his behaviour, it becomes mutually manifest to them that William is coming, that they are in danger of being bored by his conversation, and so on, then they are in a position to act efficiently: i.e. promptly. All Mary may have to do is say, 'Let's go!'; she can feel confident that Peter will understand her reasons, and, if he shares them, will be ready to act without question or delay.

In the case of the broken hair-drier, if Mary had made mutually manifest her wish that Peter would mend it, one of two things would have happened. Either he would have mended it, thus granting her wish and possibly putting her in his debt; or he would have failed to mend it, which would have amounted to a refusal or rejection. Mary avoids putting herself in his debt or meeting with a refusal by avoiding any modification of their mutual cognitive environment. If Peter mends the hair-drier, he is being kind on his own initiative, and she does not owe him anything. If Peter decides not to mend the hair-drier, he might reason as follows: she doesn't know I know she intended to inform me of her wish, so if I ignore it, she will attribute this to her failure to inform me; she may find me stupid, but not unkind. As for Mary, she may have intentionally left this line of reasoning open to Peter. If he does not mend her hair-drier, she will find him unkind, but not hostile. His failure to grant her wish will not be in the nature of a rebuff. They will stand in exactly the same social relationship to each other as before. This shows how ostensive communication may have social implications that other forms of information transmission do not.

By making her informative intention mutually manifest, the communicator creates the following situation: it becomes mutually manifest that the fulfilment of her informative intention is, so to speak, in the hands of the audience. If the assumptions that she intends to make manifest to the audience become manifest, then she is successful; if the audience refuses to accept these assumptions as true or probably true, then she has failed in her informative intention. Suppose – we will soon see how this may happen – that the audience's behaviour makes it mutually manifest that the informative intention is fulfilled. Then the set of assumptions **I** that the communicator intended to make manifest to the audience becomes, at least apparently, mutually manifest. We say 'at least apparently' because, if the communicator is not sincere and some of the assumptions in **I** are not manifest to her, then by our definition of mutual manifestness, these assumptions cannot be mutually manifest to her and others.

A communicator is normally interested in knowing whether or not she has succeeded in fulfilling her informative intention, and this interest is mutually manifest to her and her audience. In face-to-face communication, the audience is generally expected to respond to this interest in fairly conventional ways. Often, for instance, the audience is expected to communicate its refusal to accept the information communicated, or else it becomes mutually manifest that the communicator's informative intention is fulfilled.

Where communication is non-reciprocal, there are various possible situations to be taken into account. The communicator may be in a position of such authority over her audience that the success of her informative intention is mutually manifest in advance. Journalists, professors, religious or political leaders assume, alas often on good grounds, that what they communicate automatically becomes mutually manifest. When the communicator lacks that kind of authority, but still wants to establish a mutual cognitive environment with her audience, all she has to do is adapt her informative intentions to her credibility. For instance, in writing this book we merely intend to make mutually manifest that we have developed certain hypotheses and have done so on certain grounds. That is, we take it as mutually manifest that you will accept our authority on what we actually think. The mutual cognitive environment thus created is enough for us to go on to communicate further thoughts which we would otherwise have been unable to communicate. (Of course we would also like to convince you, but we hope to do this by the force of our arguments, and not by making you recognise our informative intentions.)

We began this section by asking how human beings communicate with one another. Our answer is that they use two quite different modes of communication: coded communication and ostensive–inferential communication. However, the two modes of communication are used in fundamentally different ways. Whereas ostensive–inferential communication can be used on its own, and sometimes is, coded communication is only used as a means of strengthening ostensive–inferential communication. This is how language is used in verbal communication, as we will argue later.

Ostensive–inferential communication can be defined as follows:

(55) *Ostensive–inferential communication*: the communicator produces a stimulus which makes it mutually manifest to communicator and audience that the communicator intends, by means of this stimulus, to make manifest or more manifest to the audience a set of assumptions **I**.

As this definition stands, it does not exclude the possibility of unintentional communication: that is, a stimulus merely intended to inform might make mutually manifest the intention to inform, and this, by our definition, would count as communication. For instance, suppose Mary yawns, intending to inform Peter that she is tired, and hoping that her yawn will look natural. She does not do it too well: it is all too obvious that her yawn is artificial – and her informative intention becomes mutually manifest. We see no reason for refusing to call this a case of unintended ostensive communication. It would be easy enough, though, to modify definition (55) and make intentionality a defining feature of communication.

In any case, most human communication is intentional, and it is intentional for two good reasons. The first reason is the one suggested by Grice: by producing direct evidence of one's informative intention, one can convey a much wider range of information than can be conveyed by producing direct evidence for the basic information itself. The second reason humans have for communicating is to modify and extend the mutual cognitive environment they share with one another.

What we have offered so far is a good enough description of ostensive–inferential communication. However, we have not explained how it works. We have suggested that the explanation is to be sought in a principle of relevance. To make this principle truly explanatory, we must first make the notion of relevance much more explicit, and to do this we must consider how information is mentally represented and inferentially processed.

Activities

❑ Sperber and Wilson say 'There may be a whole variety of interpretations that would meet whatever standards of truthfulness, informativeness, relevance and clarity have been proposed or envisaged so far.' What do they mean?

❏ Explain in your own words, with examples, what they mean by each of the following:
   – cognitive environments and mutual manifestness
   – ostension
   – ostensive-inferential communication
   – the informative intention
   – the communicative intention
❏ Look at the examples that Sperber and Wilson discuss, and say what concepts they are being used to illustrate
   – (32) Do you want some coffee? . . .
   – (42) The phone is ringing . . .
   – (49) I've been inside that church . . .
   – Mary and Peter on the park bench, and he leans back . . .
   – The girl in light clothes, and the old man looks up at the sky . . .
   – Mary comes home, stops at the door and sniffs . . .
   – Mary and Peter at the seaside, Mary opens the window and sniffs . . .
   – (53) When does the train arrive at Oxford? . . .
   – Mary yawns . . .
❏ Make a 10-minute recording of a casual conversation between people who know each other well, and transcribe it. Describe it, as far as you can, in terms of Sperber and Wilson's
   – cognitive environments and mutual manifestness
   – ostension
   – ostensive-inferential communication
   – the informative intention
   – the communicative intention
❏ What is your opinion as regards the cooperative principle and relevance theory? Do you think that Sperber and Wilson's theory of communication cancels that of Grice? Which do you think best describes how exchanges hold together? Can you think of an alternative principle or set of maxims to show how people understand each other and how conversations run smoothly?

D6   READINGS IN POLITENESS

These two readings take our analysis of politeness further into the social and cultural dimension. Tannen suggests that women use polite indirectness for rapport and solidarity, and for getting their demands met and saving face at the same time. Her view is that indirectness can be a prerogative of the powerful or even a norm, but that indirectness is not associated with women or with power the world over.

D6.1   Reading and researching

Women and indirectness

D. Tannen (1994) *Gender and Discourse*, pp. 32–4, Oxford: Oxford University Press.

Indirectness

Lakoff (1975) identifies two benefits of indirectness: defensiveness and rapport. Defensiveness refers to a speaker's preference not to go on record with an idea in order to be able to disclaim, rescind, or modify it if it does not meet with a positive response. The rapport benefit of indirectness results from the pleasant experience of getting one's way not because one demanded it (power) but because the other person wanted the same thing (solidarity). Many researchers have focused on the defensive or power benefit of indirectness and ignored the payoff in rapport or solidarity.

The claim by Conley, O'Barr, and Lind (1979) that women's language is really powerless language has been particularly influential. In this view, women's tendency to be indirect is taken as evidence that women don't feel entitled to make demands. Surely there are cases in which this is true. Yet it can also be demonstrated that those who feel entitled to make demands may prefer not to, seeking the payoff in rapport. Furthermore, the ability to get one's demands met without expressing them directly can be a sign of power rather than of the lack of it. An example I have used elsewhere (Tannen 1986) is the Greek father who answers, 'If you want, you can go,' to his daughter's inquiry about going to a party. Because of the lack of enthusiasm of his response, the Greek daughter understands that her father would prefer she not go and 'chooses' not to go. (A 'real' approval would have been 'Yes, of course, you should go.') I argue that this father did not feel powerless to give his daughter orders. Rather, a communicative system was conventionalized by which he and she could both preserve the appearance, and possibly the belief, that she chose not to go rather than simply obeying his command.

Far from being powerless, this father felt so powerful that he did not need to give his daughter orders; he simply needed to let her know his preference, and she would accommodate to it. By this reasoning, indirectness is a prerogative of the powerful. By the same reasoning a master who says, 'It's cold in here,' may expect a servant to make a move to close a window, but a servant who says the same thing is not likely to see his employer rise to correct the situation and make him more comfortable. Indeed, a Frenchman who was raised in Brittany tells me that his family never gave bald commands to their servants but always communicated orders in indirect and highly polite form. This pattern renders less surprising the finding of Bellinger and Gleason (1982, reported in Gleason 1987) that fathers' speech to their young children had a higher incidence than mothers' of both direct imperatives (such as 'Turn the bolt with the wrench') *and* implied indirect imperatives (for example, 'The wheel is going to fall off').

The use of indirectness can hardly be understood without the cross-cultural perspective. Many Americans find it self-evident that directness is logical and aligned with power whereas indirectness is akin to dishonesty as well as subservience. But for speakers raised in most of the world's cultures, varieties of indirectness are the norm in communication. In Japanese interaction, for example, it is well known that saying 'no' is considered too face-threatening to risk, so negative responses are phrased as positive ones: one never says 'no,' but listeners understand from the form of the 'yes' whether it is truly a 'yes' or a polite 'no.'

The American tendency to associate indirectness with female style is not culturally universal. The above description of typical Japanese style operates for men as well as women. My own research (Tannen 1981, 1984, 1986) suggests that Americans of some cultural and geographic backgrounds, female as well as male, are more likely than others to use relatively direct rather than indirect styles. In an early study I compared Greeks and Americans with regard to their tendency to interpret a question as an indirect means of making a request. I found that whereas American women were more likely to take an indirect interpretation of a sample conversation, Greek men were as likely as Greek women, and more likely than American men *or women*, to take an indirect interpretation. Greek men, of course, are not less powerful vis-à-vis women than American men.

Perhaps most striking is the finding of Keenan (1974) that in a Malagasy-speaking village on the island of Madagascar, women are seen as direct and men as indirect. But this in no way implies that the women are more powerful than men in this society. Quite the contrary, Malagasy men are socially dominant, and their indirect style is more highly valued. Keenan found that women were widely believed to debase the language with their artless directness, whereas men's elaborate indirectness was widely admired.

Indirectness, then, is not in itself a strategy of subordination. Rather, it can be used either by the powerful or the powerless. The interpretation of a given utterance, and the likely response to it, depends on the setting, on individuals' status and their relationship to each other, and also on the linguistic conventions that are ritualized in the cultural context.

The Nelson, Al-Batal and Echols article below, compares Syrian Arabic speakers' and American English speakers' responses to compliments, and shows that, although both groups respond by accepting and mitigating rather than rejecting, the ways that they accept and mitigate are quite different. The authors hope that their article will contribute to an awareness of cross-cultural misunderstandings from pragmatic transfer.

<table>
<tr><td>**D6.2**</td></tr>
</table>

Compliment responses

G. L. Nelson, M. Al-Batal and E. Echols (1996), pp. 411–33, *Applied Linguistics* 18/3.

This study investigated similarities and differences between Syrian and American compliment responses. Interviews with Americans yielded 87 compliment/compliment response sequences and interviews with Syrians resulted in 52 sequences. Americans were interviewed in English and Syrians in Arabic. Data consisted of demographic information and transcriptions of the sequences. The entire set of data was examined recursively. This examination suggested three broad categories (acceptances, mitigations, and rejections) and subcategories. Two trained raters coded each of the English and Arabic compliment responses as belonging to one of the categories. Intercoder reliability for the American data was 92 per cent and 88 per cent for the Syrian data. Of the American compliment responses, 50 per cent were coded as acceptances, 45 per cent as mitigations, and 3 per cent as rejections. Of the Syrian compliment responses, 67 per cent were coded as acceptances, 33 per cent as mitigations, and 0 per cent as rejections. Results suggest that both Syrians and Americans are more likely to either accept or mitigate the force of the compliment than to reject it. Both groups employed similar response types (e.g. agreeing utterances, compliment returns, and deflecting or qualifying comments); however, they also differed in their responses. US recipients were much more likely than the Syrians to use appreciation tokens and a preferred Syrian response, acceptance + formula, does not appear in the US data at all.

1 INTRODUCTION

Recently, in a conversation with an American who had taught EFL in Damascus for two years, one of the researchers mentioned that she was investigating the strategies Syrians use in responding to compliments. The teacher looked surprised and asked, 'What's there to study? Syrians just say *Shukran* ("thank you"). When I'm complimented in Arabic, that's what I say — *Shukran*.' This teacher was applying a rule from his L1 speech community to an L2 speech community. The rule he was transferring is one that American parents teach their children and one that is taught in etiquette books: 'When you are complimented, the only response necessary is "Thank you"' (Johnson 1979: 43). Compliment responses in Syrian Arabic, as shall become clear later, are much more complex than saying *Shukran* when praised.

In this paper, we report on a study of Syrian Arabic speakers' and American English speakers' verbal responses to compliments. The purpose of the study is to better understand the strategies used by Syrians and Americans in responding to compliments, to discover similarities and differences between the two groups, and to relate the findings to second language acquisition and second language teaching.

2. THEORETICAL FRAMEWORK: CONTRASTIVE PRAGMATICS

In large part due to the theoretical paradigm of communicative competence (Habermas 1970; Hymes 1971, 1972, 1974; Canale and Swain 1980; Wolfson 1981, 1983), research on L2 learning and teaching has been extended to include learners' pragmatic knowledge. Thomas (1983: 92) defines pragmatic competence by contrasting it to grammatical competence. Grammatical competence consists of ' "abstract" or decontexualized knowledge of intonation, phonology, syntax, semantics, etc.', whereas pragmatic competence is 'the ability to use language effectively in order to achieve a specific purpose and to understand language in context' (ibid.: 94). She goes on to point out that if an L1 speaker perceives the purpose of an L2 utterance as other than the L2 speaker intended, pragmatic failure has occurred; the utterance failed to achieve the speaker's goal. The danger of pragmatic failure is that it is likely to result in misunderstandings, embarrassment, frustration, anger, and/or cross-cultural communication breakdowns (Beebe and Takahashi 1989).

Thomas identifies two kinds of pragmatic failure: pragmalinguistic failure and sociopragmatic failure. Pragmalinguistic failure occurs when 'the pragmatic force mapped by S onto a given utterance is systematically different from the force most frequently assigned to it by native speakers of the target language, or when speech act strategies are inappropriately transferred from the L1 to L2' (Thomas 1983: 99). Sociopragmatic failure refers to 'the social conditions placed on language in use' (ibid.) and includes variables such as gender, social distance, and intimacy of relationship.

In the context of language learning, one cause of pragmalinguistic failure is pragmalinguistic transfer, the use of L1 speech act strategies or formulas when interacting with members of an L2 speech community (Leech 1983). This transfer has been addressed in a number of speech act/event studies (e.g. Blum-Kulka 1982, 1983; Olshtain 1983; Olshtain and Cohen 1983; Edmonson, House, Kasper, and Stemmer 1984; Thomas 1984; Eisenstein and Bodman 1986; Garcia 1989; Wolfson 1989a; Beebe, Takahashi, and Uliss-Weltz 1990; Takahashi and Beebe 1993). In the anecdote at the beginning of this paper, the American, in responding to Arabic compliments by transferring an appropriate response from his L1 to an L2, believes that he is politely accepting the compliment. However, if the native Arabic speaker interprets the illocutionary force of the utterance differently (e.g. interprets the response as impolite and inappropriate) pragmatic failure has occurred.

It is, however, difficult, at times, to determine whether the pragmatic failure results from L1 transfer or from other factors. Hurley (1992), for example, notes that pragmatic failure may also result from developmental and proficiency factors or from L2 learners overgeneralizing the use of an L2 form to inappropriate settings. Stated differently, it is sometimes difficult to know *why* language learners experience certain kinds of pragmatic failure. In order to understand the reasons behind pragmatic failure, it is helpful, and perhaps even necessary, to conduct cross-cultural research to investigate students' L1 strategies (Wolfson 1989a).

Speech act and speech event studies have been criticized as being ethnocentric in that most have investigated variations of English (Blum-Kulka, House, and Kasper 1989). Rose (1994) further points out that, in particular, little work has been done in non-Western contexts. The present study is valuable, in part, because it was conducted in Arabic as well as English.

3. COMPLIMENT RESPONSES

Compliment responses were selected for cross-cultural study for two reasons. First, although a body of knowledge exists on the speech act of complimenting (Wolfson 1981, 1983; Manes 1983; Knapp, Hopper, and Bell 1984; Barnlund and Araki 1985; Holmes and Brown 1987; Nelson, El Bakary, and Al-Batal 1993), less research has been conducted on responses to compliments. For non-native English speaking (NNES) students, knowing how to compliment is important, but it is equally important to know how to respond to a compliment. In fact, it could be argued that for NNES students in the United States, appropriately responding to compliments is more important than complimenting because of the frequency with which Americans compliment (Wolfson 1983; Holmes and Brown 1987; Herbert 1988). In other words, ESL students may receive more compliments than they initiate. A second reason is that, although a few studies have been conducted on compliment responses in English-speaking countries (Pomerantz 1978; Herbert 1988; Herbert and Straight 1989), few, if any, cross-cultural studies have investigated compliment responses in an Arabic-speaking country.

For the purpose of this study, a compliment response is defined as a verbal acknowledgement that the recipient of the compliment heard and reacted to the compliment. Compliment/compliment response interactions have been referred to as adjacency pairs (Schegloff and Sacks 1973), action chain events (Pomerantz 1978), interchanges (Herbert 1988), and sequences (Wolfson 1989b). For ease of reference, Speaker$_1$ will refer to the person issuing the compliment and Speaker$_2$ to the recipient of the compliment.

4. PREVIOUS WORK ON COMPLIMENT RESPONSES

Pomerantz (1978) wrote the earliest and perhaps most detailed account of compliment responses among native speakers of English in the United States. She pointed out that, in the United States, compliment responses pose a dilemma for the recipient in that they involve two conversational principles that stand in potential conflict:

Principle I: Agree with and/or accept compliment.
Principle II: Avoid self-praise.

If recipients agree with the compliment, they are, in fact, praising themselves and therefore violating Principle II: Avoid self-praise. If they reject the compliment, they violate Principle I: Agree with and/or accept compliment. Neither of these alternatives, praising oneself or disagreeing with someone, contribute to the social solidarity of the relationship. Pomerantz submitted that compliment responses could be seen as solution types to this dilemma.

Pomerantz classified compliment responses as belonging to one of four categories: Acceptances, Agreements, Rejections, and Disagreements. Her analysis indicated that Acceptances were relatively infrequent when compared to Rejections and Disagreements (e.g. 'It's just a rag my sister gave me'). She suggested that self-praise avoidance accounts for the frequency of Rejections and Disagreements in compliment responses.

In their studies of complimenting behavior in the United States, Wolfson (1989a) and Manes (1983) included examples of compliment responses. They contended that one function of American compliments is to negotiate solidarity between the interlocutors. For recipients, however, negotiating solidarity is complicated by Pomerantz's (1978) dilemma. Wolfson (1989a) noted that one solution to the dilemma is to downgrade the compliment by referring to another characteristic of the object. In this way, the recipient mitigates the force of the compliment without disagreeing with the speaker and also without praising him/herself. Wolfson (1989a: 116) explained

> In response to a compliment on the beauty of a house, therefore, an American might say, 'Well, we would have liked to have a bigger one' or 'We wish the neighborhood were quieter,' but Americans would be very unlikely to suggest that the speaker was wrong and that the house was not beautiful at all.

The work of Pomerantz (1978), Manes (1983), Wolfson (1989a), and Wolfson and Manes (1980) was helpful in understanding how and why Americans compliment, but it did not provide a quantitative analysis of compliment response types and their frequency.

Herbert (1988) provided such an analysis in a study comparing the compliment/compliment response interchanges from American university students to South African university students. In analyzing his data, he grouped the responses as (a) Agreeing, (b) Nonagreeing, or (c) Requesting interpretation. Overall, nearly 66 per cent of the American compliment responses were broadly classified as Agreements, 31 per cent as Nonagreements, and 3 per cent as Request Interpretations. Of those Agreements (66 per cent), 7 per cent were categorized as Comment Acceptances and 29 per cent as Appreciation Tokens.[1] In contrast, 88 per cent of the South African compliment responses were categorized as Agreements and 43 per cent of those Agreements were categorized as Comment Acceptances. Holmes (1988) studied compliments and compliment responses in New Zealand, another native English speaking (NES) country. She categorized 61 per cent of the responses as acceptances, 29 per cent as deflections/evasions, and 10 per cent as rejections. Her distribution of New Zealand responses closely paralleled Herbert's (1988) study of American responses. The studies by Herbert (1988) and Holmes (1988) were helpful in providing information on the frequency of particular NES compliment response types. They did not, however, compare NES to NNES populations (such comparisons were not the purpose of their studies) and, therefore, did not contribute to an understanding of *why* a population of L2 learners might respond inappropriately to compliments based on transfer from their L1.

In a study comparing the compliment responses of American and Chinese speakers, Chen (1993) provided this type of explanation. His analysis presented information that helped explain the reasons Chinese speakers might experience pragmatic failure when responding to a compliment given by an American and the reasons Americans might experience pragmatic failure when responding to a Chinese compliment. His findings suggested that the strategies used by the American English speakers were largely motivated by Leech's (1983) Agreement Maxim: maximize agreements between self and others and minimize disagreement between self and others. In Chen's sample, 39 per cent of the US compliment responses were categorized as Acceptances, 19 per cent as Compliment Returns, 29 per cent as Deflections, and 13 per cent as Rejections. The Chinese speaker strategies, on the other hand, were governed by Leech's Modesty Maxim: minimize praise of self and maximize dispraise of self. Of the Chinese compliment responses, 96 per cent were categorized as Rejections: the most common types of rejections were disagreeing and denigrating (51 per cent).

5. THE PRESENT STUDY

The present study also contributes to an understanding of why a population of L2 learners may respond inappropriately to compliments. It builds on the work of Nelson *et al.* (1993) and their analysis of Egyptian Arabic and American English compliments. In the Egyptian/American study, 20 Egyptians and 20 American university students described in detail the most recent compliment they had given, received, and observed, providing a corpus of 60 Egyptian and 60 American compliments. Interview data were analyzed to determine compliment form and attributes praised. The analysis revealed that both Egyptian and American compliments tended to be adjectival (e.g. 'You look great'). A major difference between Egyptian and American compliments was that Egyptian compliments tended to be longer and contained more comparatives and metaphors than the US compliments (e.g. *shaklak 'ariis innaharda* ['You look like a bridegroom today']).

Both Egyptians and Americans complimented the attributes of physical appearance, personality traits, and skills/work. Because these are attributes complimented in both Arabic-speaking and English-speaking countries (see Holmes and Brown 1987; Holmes 1988 for studies on New Zealand compliments) these were the qualities complimented in this study.

5.1 Method of data collection

It is commonly argued that speech acts and events should be studied in their natural contexts using ethnomethodology (Wolfson 1983); however, ethnomethodology is difficult for cross-cultural studies due to problems of comparability (Blum-Kulka, House, and Kasper 1989) and a lack of ethnographers from non-English-speaking speech communities. Although this study did not use ethnomethodology, its method of data collection resulted in naturalistic, yet comparable, data.

In the United States, data were collected during audiotaped interviews. All of the interviewers were graduate students in Applied Linguistics at a large urban university in the southeastern part of the United States. Two were female, one was 26 years old and single and the other 46 and married. The third was male, 32, and single. All were Caucasian and middle class. Before the interviews, interviewers asked interviewees if they were willing to be interviewed on audiotape for a sociolinguistic study. If they agreed, the interviewer began the interview by asking demographic questions (e.g. What part of the United States are you from?). After a few questions, the interviewer complimented the interviewee on an aspect of his or her appearance, on a personality trait, or on a skill or well done job. For instance, one interviewer casually mentioned, 'By the way, you really gave a good presentation to the class last night'. In this way, the compliments were given as an aside, as an utterance not connected to the formal interview, and thus, resulted in naturalistic responses. Eighty-nine Americans were interviewed; two interviews were lost due to a malfunctioning tape recorder. Of the remaining 87 interviewees, 47 were female and 40 were male. At the completion of the interviews, interviewees were asked if their responses could be used in this study. All signed a consent form giving their permission. A total of 87 American compliment/compliment response interactions were analyzed.

The audiotapes were transcribed in English. The transcriptions included the gender, age, and relationship of the speakers. It is important to point out that the American male interviewer felt uncomfortable complimenting females on appearance, believing that the female recipients might interpret the illocutionary force of the compliment differently than he intended. Specifically, he was concerned that Speaker$_2$ might perceive the intent of the compliment as an expression of flirtation and a possible first move in the development of an intimate relationship.

The Syrian data were collected by four interviewers from Damascus (i.e. they were Damascenes and spoke Damascene Arabic). Two of the interviewers were female. One was attending college part-time and was 29 years of age, single, and a dental technician. The other was 25, single, a translator and secretary, and an English literature graduate from Damascus University. The other two interviewers were male. One studied English literature at the University, managed his family farm property, was 27 and was single. The fourth also studied English literature at the University and was 22. All four were middle class.

The Syrian compliment/compliment responses were not audiotaped. The Syrian interviewers reported that tape recorders were likely to make the interviewees feel uncomfortable; that, in general, Syrians are not familiar with the practice of conducting sociological or sociolinguistic studies about themselves; and that the tape recording would be culturally inappropriate. The Syrian interviewers praised 32 recipients, 20 males and 12 females, on physical appearance, on personality traits, or on a skill or job; listened to the responses; responded in turn; and after the interaction was completed, wrote down what was said. In some cases, the interviewers felt uncomfortable complimenting a person of a different gender or a person that was older. In these cases, they observed others giving and responding to compliments and wrote down what was said. These observations resulted in an additional 20 compliment/compliment response sequences. In 7 cases, males were complimented, and in 13 cases, females were complimented. These procedures resulted in naturalistic data and yielded 52 Syrian compliment/compliment responses from 52 recipients, 27 males and 25 females.

To insure the accuracy of the transcriptions, the Syrian interviewers were trained by one of the researchers. The trainer instructed them (1) to write down the exact words used in the complement/compliment response interaction, and (2) to do so as soon as possible after the interaction took place. In addition, the trainer gave each interviewer note cards and instructed them to write each interaction on a separate card. The trainer met with the interviewers at least once a week. At these meetings, the interviewers reported on their progress and the trainer again emphasized the importance of recording the interactions verbatim.

To native speakers of English, recalling compliment responses word-for-word may seem difficult, but the task is less difficult for native speakers of Arabic. Many of the Syrian utterances consist of set formulas. The Syrian interviewers would remember the responses because they exist as formulaic chunks of discourse. The potential for varying the formulas is minimal. For the non-formulaic responses, it is possible that an interviewer might have made a minor change in the wording. However, if such a change occurred, the wording of the compliment response would still be an appropriate Syrian response to the situation.

The Arabic compliments/compliment responses were translated into English, but the primary analysis was based on the Arabic transcripts, not the English translations.

5.2 Analysis
The US data consisted of demographic information and the transcripts of the audiotapes, and the Syrian data consisted of demographic information, the Arabic transcriptions, and the English translations. The entire set of data was examined recursively.

This examination suggested classification schemes similar to existing schemes (e.g. Pomerantz 1978; Herbert 1988; Herbert and Straight 1989). In the end, the classification scheme that most appropriately fitted the data was similar to, but still different from, earlier classifications. It consisted of three broad categories (i.e. acceptances, mitigations, and rejections) and subcategories. The specific subcategories are provided in the Results and Discussion section of this article in Tables D5.1 and D5.2. Following guide-lines set forth by Krippendorf (1980) and Holsti (1969), the categories were exhaustive (i.e. all data were represented in one of the categories) and mutually exclusive (i.e. a response could belong to only one category).

After the classification scheme was developed, one of the researchers and a graduate research assistant coded each of the English compliment responses as belonging to one of the categories. The Arabic compliment responses were coded by two of the researchers; one of whom is a native Arabic speaker. The coders worked independently and coded all of the compliment responses. Intercoder reliability was determined by comparing both coders' scores. Intercoder reliability was 92 per cent for the American data and 88 per cent for the Arabic. Next, the coders reviewed the coding guide-lines and the items on which there was disagreement. They recoded until they came to a consensus; thus, in the end, agreement on all compliment responses was achieved.

6. RESULTS AND DISCUSSION

This section presents the analysis of the American and Syrian compliment response types.

6.1 Compliment response types: US English data

Table D5.1 provides the frequency and representative examples of the English compliment response types.

6.1.1 Acceptances

The Acceptance category accounted for 50 per cent of the US compliment responses.

a. *Appreciation Token.* The most common response type in the Acceptance category of the American corpus was Appreciation Tokens. They were 'responses that recognize[d] the status of a previous utterance as a compliment' (Herbert 1988: 11), but were not 'semantically fitted to the specifics of that compliment' (Pomerantz 1978: 83). Examples included 'Thanks' and 'Thank you'.

(1) M_1: It's a really cool shirt
     M_2: Thanks (A1)[2]

For a response to be coded as an Appreciation Token, it included only the statement of appreciation. If additional information was given, the response was coded according to the additional information. Appreciation Tokens accounted for 29 per cent of the compliment responses in this corpus, a frequency identical to the 29 per cent reported by Herbert (1988) and Chen (1993), but one much higher than Pomerantz (1978) reported.

Table D5.1 Frequency distribution of American English compliment response types

	Number	Percentage
A. Accept		
1. Appreciation token (e.g. Thanks)	25	29
2. Agreeing Utterance (e.g. Well, I think so too.)	12	14
3. Compliment Return (e.g. Yours are nice, too.)	6	07
4. Acceptance + Formula	0	00
Subtotal	43	5
B. Mitigate		
1. Deflecting or Qualifying Comment (e.g. I bought it at REI.)	28	32
2. Reassurance or Repetition Request (e.g. Do you really like them?)	11	13
Subtotal	39	45
C. Reject		

1. Disagreeing Utterance
    (e.g. F_1: You look good and healthy.
        F_2: I feel fat.)
	3	03

Subtotal	3	03
D. No response	2	02
Total	87	100

n = 87

b. *Agreeing Utterance.* As illustrated below, Agreeing Utterances were responses in which Speaker$_2$ accepted 'the complimentary force of Speaker$_1$'s utterance by a response semantically fitted to the compliment' (Herbert 1988: 12). Agreeing Utterances occurred in twelve (14 per cent) of the American responses.

(2) F_1: That's really a great shirt.
    F_2: See, it matches my shorts. (A7)

(3) M_1: Sounds like you're pretty organized.
    M_2: Well, I think so. I try to be. Yeah. (A14)

This response type occurred more frequently in this sample than in the work of other researchers (Herbert 1988; Chen 1993). Pomerantz (1978: 84) found agreeing responses 'very prevalent' in her data; however, her examples suggested that these agreements occurred when two individuals were talking about a third party.

In none of her examples did a person agree with a compliment about him or herself.

c. *Compliment Return.* A Compliment Return consisted of two parts – (a) a stated or implied acceptance of the force of the compliment, and (b) praise for the original sender.

(4) M_1: Those are nice glasses.
     M_2: Yours are nice, too. (A9)

(5) F: You look great.
     M: So do you. (A52)

By returning the compliment, the recipient contributed to the equality of the relationship and maintained rapport. Compliment returns accounted for 7 per cent of the compliment responses in this sample, the same frequency found by Herbert (1988).

d.   *Acceptance + Formula.* This type of response did not occur at all in the English sample, but occurred frequently in the Arabic data.

6.1.2 Mitigating Responses

The general category of Mitigating Responses included two distinct compliment response types that shared two features. The first feature was their non-acceptance of the compliment and the second was their non-rejection. These response types in various ways deflected, questioned, or ignored the compliments. In using one of these types, the recipient maneuvered through the straits of Pomerantz's Scylla and Charybdis, avoiding both self-praise and other-disagreement. Mitigating responses accounted for 45 per cent of the US corpus.

a. *Deflecting Informative Comment.* This type was the most common of the mitigating responses. In this category, Speaker$_2$ provided additional information about the attribute praised, and by doing so, impersonalized 'the complimentary force by giving . . . impersonal details' (Herbert 1988: 13).

(6) F: I like your jacket.
     M: I bought it at REI. (A47)

(7) F_1: You look great. I mean it. You look wonderful.
     F_2: I can hardly believe I'm going to be 54. It sounds very old. I can actually remember when I was going to be 30. (A85)

Herbert (1988: 14) noted that occasionally, in the informative comments that followed the compliment, the recipient ignored 'the praise aspect of the compliment and instead treat[ed] the previous utterances as a mechanism for introducing a topic'. This phenomenon occurred in the example below.

(8) **F₁**: That's really a good quality.

   F₂: Well, I read about it in developmental psychology. I can tell what people are up to and then I usually give them my motivation speech. I mean, like most teachers, I don't like people who don't do work, who, at least, don't read the material. (A4)

At times, these qualifying comments functioned in a manner that downgrades the compliment, a strategy, as noted by Wolfson (1989a), that further avoids self-praise.

(9) **F**: Nice sweater.

   M: It's one of my oldest. (A50)

(10) **F₁**: It was very sweet of you.

   F₂: It seemed kinda silly. I don't know. Yeah. Well, but anyway. (A18)

This category accounted for 32 per cent of the American compliment responses in this study, a frequency similar to Chen's (1993). Chen's category, Deflection, comprised 29 per cent of his corpus.

b. *Reassurance or Repetition Request*. At times, Speaker₂ requested additional reassurance that the compliment was genuine. Such responses were ambiguous. It was difficult to discern the recipients' intentions in asking the questions. Did they want an expansion or repetition of the original compliment or were they questioning the sincerity of the sender?

(11) **F₁**: I like your dress.

   F₂: You don't think it's too bright? (A62)

(12) **F₁**: Nice shoes.

   F₂: Do you really like them? (A54)

Reassurance or Repetition Requests accounted for 13 per cent of the compliment responses.

6.1.3 Rejections

a. *Disagreeing Utterance*. Disagreeing Utterances occurred when Speaker₂ disagreed with Speaker₁'s assertion. This compliment response type occurred infrequently within the present corpus, in 3 interchanges or approximately 3 per cent of the sample.

(13) **M₁**: How did you get to be so organized?

   M₂: I'm not organized.

   M₁: I mean neat. You are very neat.

   M₂: I am not. (A11)

(14) **F₁**: You look so good and healthy.

   F₂: I feel fat. (A12)

The infrequency of this response type in the United States is consistent with the work of other researchers (Herbert 1988; Chen 1993). By using this response type, Speaker₂ clearly and directly disagrees with the judgment of Speaker₁, thus violating both Pomerantz' (1978) Principle I: Agree with and/or accept compliment and Leech's (1983) Agreement Principle. Americans' preference for *not* using this response type suggests that, out of all the response types, it may be the most damaging to the solidarity of the relationship between Speaker₁ and Speaker₂, more damaging, for example, than agreeing with Speaker₁ and thus praising oneself, a response type that made up 14 per cent of this sample.

6.2 Compliment responses: gender of US recipients

American males ($n = 40$) and females ($n = 47$) employed each of the compliment types, and no compliment response type was used predominantly by one gender. Eleven females and 14 males used Appreciation Tokens, 6 females and 6 males used Agreeing Utterances, and 4 females and 2 males used Compliment Returns. Sixteen females and 12 males employed Deflecting Comments and 7 females and 4 males employed Reassurance or Repetition Requests. Two females and one male disagreed with the compliment. Two recipients did not respond verbally to the compliment they received.

6.3 Compliment response types: Syrian Arabic data

Using the categories described above, this section presents the classification of the Arabic data. The Arabic compliment responses fell into two of the three categories. Recipients either accepted or mitigated the compliments they received. There were no rejections. However, within these categories, the Arabic compliment responses differed from the English responses in several ways. The Arabic compliment responses are summarized in Table D5.2.

6.3.1 Acceptances

Sixty-seven per cent of the Syrian compliment responses were coded as Acceptances.

a. *Appreciation Token.* Only 1 of the Arabic compliment responses was coded as an Appreciation Token, a common American response type.

(15)   **F₁**: *yikhzi l-ʿeen ʿala ha-sh-shaʿr! yaaʿeeni, mitl Sundrella.*
         (May the [evil] eye be thwarted for this hair! My eye, [you look] like Cinderella!)
       F₂: *shukran!*
         (Thank you.) (S47)

In this interaction, Speaker₁ used the expression *yikhzi l-ʿeen* ('may the evil eye be thwarted') to protect the recipient from the evil eye. In many parts of the world, it is believed that the evil eye can bring harm to people by drawing the attention of evil to them (Maloney 1976).[3] By merely praising a person, Speaker₁ might cause harm to come to that person. To counteract this effect, the expression *yikhzi*

Table D5.2 Frequency distribution of Syrian Arabic compliment response types

	Number	Percentage
A. Accept		
1. Appreciation Token	1	02
(e.g. *shukran* [thank you])		
2. Agreeing Utterance	6	12
(e.g. *kill taSaamiimi naajHa*		
[All my designs are successful])		
3. Compliment Return	7	13
(e.g. *w-inti heek yaa Sawsan*		
[And you are the same, Susan])		
4. Acceptance + Formula	21	40
(e.g. *m'addame*		
[it is presented to you])		
Subtotal	35	67
B. Mitigate		
1. Deflecting or Qualifying Comment	13	25
(e.g. M_1: Your body has filled out.		
M_2: I used to work out a long time ago.		
2. Reassurance or Repetition Request	4	08
(e.g. Is that really me?)		
Subtotal	17	33
C. Reject	0	0
Total	52	100

n = 52

l-ʿeen ('may the evil eye be thwarted') is used in many countries in the eastern part of the Arab world (e.g. Jordan, Syria, Palestine, and Lebanon).

b. *Agreeing Utterance.* In the Syrian data, this response type was slightly less frequent than in the US data. Six (12 per cent) of the Syrian interactions were classified as Agreeing Utterances. All six are between males.

(16) M_1: *fiʿlan taSmiimak bi-dillʿala khibirtak w-ʿala zaw'ak ir-rafiiʿ.*
           (Truly, your design points to your experience and to your exquisite taste.)
      M_2: *kill taSaamiimi naajHa.*
           (All my designs are successful.) (S43)

(17) M_1: *jismak halla'Saar mniH w-khaaSSatanʿaDalaat ktaafak.*
           (Your body now has become fit, especially your shoulder muscles.)

M₂: *ana halla'aHsan waaHid bi-n-naadii.*
(I'm now the best one in the club.) (S31)

This response strategy violates Pomerantz' (1978) principle of avoiding self-praise and the social solidarity principle (Herbert 1988; Herbert and Straight 1989; Wolfson 1989a). It may be that in Syria agreeing with Speaker₁ (and thus praising oneself) is not the kind of egregious error that results in 'a gossip item, an unfavorable character assessment', the kinds of negative behaviors that Pomerantz predicts may result from agreement responses (Pomerantz 1978: 89).

c. *Compliment Return.* The frequency of Compliment Returns in the Syrian corpus was 13 per cent, slightly higher than the frequency of Compliment Returns in the American data (7 per cent). Examples of Compliment Returns included the following:

(18) **F**₁: *inti mhandse naajHa, daayman bi-t'addmi shii jdiid w-bi-tkhalli n-naas tiHtirmik, w-khaluu'qa w-shakhSiyytik ʿawiyye, yaʿni mitl z-zibdiyye S-Siini, mneen ma rannaytiiha bi-trinn.*
(You are a successful engineer; you always present something new and you make people respect you, and [you are] well-mannered and have a strong personality; in other words you are like a china bowl; from whichever side you hit it, it resonates.)

    F₂: *w-inti heek yaa Sawsan bass muu Haase b-Haalik.*
(And you are the same, Susan, but you do not know it.) (S2)

(19) **F**: *inta nashiiT w-shughlak nDiif w-mustaqiim bi-ʿamalak, maa fii daaʿi la-Hada yraajiʿ shughlak waraak, zaki w-SariiH w-Habbaab.*
(You are dynamic and your work is well-done and you are straightforward in your work; there is no need for anyone to go over what you do, [you are] smart and honest and amiable.)

    M: *shukran, w-inti nafs sh-shii.*
(Thank you, and you are the same.) (S9)

In contrast to Agreeing Utterances, Compliment Returns affirmed the interpersonal connections between the interlocutors; they served to bond the relationship together.

Although the focus of this study is on responses to compliments, the compliments in exchanges 18 and 19 are of interest in that they closely resemble the Egyptian compliments in Nelson *et al.* (1993); they contain more words than US compliments and exchange 18 contains a metaphor. The length of these compliments is related to features of Arabic discourse: (1) repetition of almost the same idea with only a minor change in words, and (2) the use of several adjectives in a series (Shouby 1951). In exchange 18, the person giving the compliment compares the recipient to 'a china bowl; from whichever side you hit it, it resonates'.

d. *Agreement + Formula.* The most common response type in the Syrian sample was Agreement + Formula; it was employed in 40 per cent of the corpus. Responses were coded as Agreement + Formula if they included a particular utterance or saying that is commonly used in Arabic when responding to a particular kind of compliment. These expressions are automatic and often ritualistic. They fulfill a particular social function and should not be interpreted primarily at the semantic level. As far as we know, this response type does not appear in any other language group studied.

One common ritualistic compliment response was *m'addam* ('[It is] presented [to you]'). With this response, Speaker₂ offered the object of the compliment to Speaker₁. Syrian speakers, in uttering *m'addam* seldom intend for Speaker₁ to accept the object. The expression is formulaic, an expected polite response to particular compliments. In the interactions below, the recipients used *m'addam* when complimented on a necklace and a blouse.

(20) F₁: *'a'dik ktiir Hilu, Ha-yaakul min ra'btik sha'fe.*
(Your necklace is very beautiful; it will eat a piece of your neck.)
F₂: *shukran ruuHii! m'addam, maa b-yighla 'aleeki shii.*
(Thank you my dear! [It is] presented [to you], nothing can be too precious for you.)
F₁: *shukran! 'ala SaaHibtu aHlaa.*
(Thank you! It looks much nicer on its owner.) (S20)

(21) F₁: *Mabruuk! shu shaarye bluuze jdiide?*
(Congratulations! Have you bought a new blouse'?)
F₂: *ee waLLa, Marreet bi-S-SaalHiyye w-shifta 'ala l-waajha fa-'ajabitni ktiir, shtareeta, m'addame!*
(Yes, by God. I was passing through SaalHiyye [district of Damascus] and I saw it in the display window and I liked it very much, so I decided to buy it. [It is] presented [to you].)
F₁: *Tithanni fiiha. InshaaLLaah tihriiha bi-l-hana.*
(May you enjoy it. May you, God willing, wear it out in happiness.)
F₂: *ALLaah yiHfazik!*
(May God keep you safe.)[4] (S24)

In both of these interactions, the recipients uttered the formulaic expression *m'addame* ('[It is] presented [to you]'), but in neither case did Speaker₁ accept the object offered. In exchange 20, Speaker₁ countered with *shukran! 'ala SaaHibtu aHlaa* ('Thank you! It looks much nicer on its owner.') With this utterance, Speaker₁ not only politely rejected the offer of the necklace, but also praised Speaker₂ again ('It looks much nicer on its owner'). In exchange 21, Speaker₂ rejected the offer with the utterance: *Tithanni fiiha. InshaaLLaah tihriiha bi-l-hanaa* ('May you enjoy it. May you, God willing, wear it out in happiness.')

Three formulaic expressions are illustrated in the interaction below. When complimented on his success, Speaker₂ used the following expressions: *t-tawfii' min aLLa* ('success is from God'), *min riDa L-Laah w-riDa L-waaldeen* ('this success] [comes] from God's satisfaction and my parents' satisfaction with me'), *li-kuli mujtahidin naSiib* ('He who works hard will have a share [of success]').

(22) **M₁**: *waLLa inta dayman mwaffa' b-tijaartak yaa abu mHammad.*
(By God Abu Muhammad [father of Mohammad], you are always successful in your trade.)

M₂: *waLLaahi t-tawfii' min aLLa, haada min riDa L-Laah w-riDa l-waaldeen yaa abu SubHii, wi-ba' deen yaa siidi li-kuli mujtahidin naSiib.*
([I swear] by God, success comes from God, this [success] [comes] from God's satisfaction and my parents' satisfaction [with me], and after all my friend He who works hard will have a share [of success].)

M₁: *waLLaahi haada Ha', aLLa y'allii maraatbak kamaan w-kamaan.*
([I swear] by God this is true, May God raise your stature more and more.) (S4)

In exchanges 20, 21, and 22, the compliment/compliment response sequence continued after Speaker₂ had responded to Speaker₁. The response of Speaker₂ did not signal the end of the compliment/compliment response interaction; it was but part of the repartee, the dialogue, that continued between the two speakers.

In the interaction below, Speaker₁ praised Speaker₂ on her beauty. Speaker₂ responded with the formulaic expression, *inshaaLLa b-tiHla iyyaamik* ('May your days be more beautiful').

(23) **F₁**: *wishshik Daawi w-mnawwar yaa imm ayman, yimkin la'innik mirtaaHa l-yuum fa-Hilyaane.*
(Your face is shining today, Um Ayman (mother of Ayman); [this is] perhaps because you are relaxed today, so you look beautiful.)

F₂: *inshaaLLa b-tiHla iyyaamik, haada nuur l-'iimaan yimkin.*
(May your days be beautiful, this is perhaps the light of faith.) (S14)

As illustrated below, the expression *haada b-'yuunik bass* ('this is only in your eyes') was also used in response to a compliment on personal beauty.

(24) **F**: *shuu Halyaan lak Ghayyaath, shuu 'aamil b-Haalak?*
(How handsome you have become, Ghayyath, what have you done to yourself?)

M: *waLLaahi? haada b-'yuunik bass.*
(Really? This is only in your eyes.) (S13)

6.3.2 Mitigating Responses
The general category of Mitigating Responses accounted for 33 per cent of the Syrian data.

a. *Deflecting or Qualifying Comment*: Thirteen speakers or 25 per cent of the sample employed this response type; it was used by 32 per cent of the Americans.

(25) **F**: *inta insaan naajiH la-innu shughlak mniiH w-shakhSiyytak 'awiyye maa bi-tkhalli Hada yiHki 'aleek w-bi-lwa't nafsuu maHbuub w-waasiq min nafsak.*
(You are a successful person because you do your job well and [because] your personality is strong, you do not allow anyone to say anything

negative about you and at the same time [you are] amiable and self-confident.)

M: *Yaa sitti shukran, hiyye ashya ʿandiyye laazim kull insaan ykuun heek biduun takabbur.*
(Thank you madam, these are simple things; no one should be conceited.) (S6)

(26) **F₁**: *Bass inti Hilyaane ktiir l-yuum.*
(But you look very beautiful today.)

F₂: *laa, muu kill hal'add, maʿ inni taʿbaane l-yuum.*
(No, not to this extent, [this is] despite the fact I am tired today). (S15)

These Deflecting or Qualifying Comments provide cross-cultural support for Pomerantz's (1978) notion that compliment responses are solution types to the dilemma of avoiding self-praise without disagreeing with Speaker₁.

b. *Reassurance or Repetition Request.* This response type accounted for 4 (8 per cent) of the compliment responses, a frequency slightly lower than in the US corpus (13 per cent).

(27) **M**: *ana Habeetik la-innik unsaa bi-kill maʿna l-kalime w-ʿindik shakhSiyye mu'assira.*
(I have come to like you because you are a woman in the full sense of the word and because you have an impressive personality.)

F: *haada kullu ana?*
(Is that all me?) (S3)

(28) **F**: *shuu! shu ha-Taʿm l-Hilu haad, taariik mizwi'ya Saamir!*
(Wow! What a beautiful suit. You have good taste Saamir.)

M: *leesh? Aajabik ?*
(Why? Do you like it?) (S22)

6.3.3 Rejection: Disagreeing Utterance

None of the Syrian data was coded as rejections. If, as has been assumed, compliments function as 'social lubricants' and 'increase or consolidate the solidarity between the speaker and the addressee' (Holmes 1988: 486), it may be that, among Syrians, rejecting compliments decreases that solidarity to such a degree that it is seldom used.

6.4 Compliment responses: gender of Syrian recipients

Both Syrian males (*n* = 27) and females (*n* = 25) employed most of the compliment types; one compliment response type, Agreeing Utterances, was used predominantly by one gender. Six males and no females used Agreeing Utterances, one female used an Appreciation Token, 4 females and 3 males used Compliment Returns, and 12 females and 9 males used Acceptance + Formula. Six females and 7 males employed Deflecting Comments, and 2 females and 2 males employed Reassurance or Repetition Requests.

7. LIMITATIONS OF THE STUDY

Data for this study was obtained from one strata of the larger population of Syria and the US. The Syrian compliment responses were uttered by middle class people from an urban area (i.e. Damascus) and most of the American compliment responses were given by Caucasian university graduate students. One cannot assume that these findings generalize to other groups within Syria or the US or to other Arabic-speaking or English-speaking countries. Further research is needed to know how generalizable these findings are.

8. FOCUS ON SECOND LANGUAGE LEARNERS

In order for students to become communicatively competent in a second language, they need both grammatical and pragmatic competence (Thomas 1983). However, achieving pragmatic competence may, at times, be complicated due to pragmatic transfer – using the rules governing speech events from one's L1 speech community when interacting with members of an L2 speech community. Pragmatic transfer can lead to pragmatic failure, to not understanding the illocutionary force of an utterance, to not understanding what is meant by what is said (Thomas 1983). Such situations can result in cross-cultural misunderstandings and communication breakdowns. Cross-cultural studies such as this one contribute to our knowledge of appropriate compliment/compliment response competence in Syrian Arabic and American English and also to our understanding of pragmatic transfer as a possible cause for pragmatic failure.

The results of this study suggest similarities and differences in Syrian Arabic and American English compliment responses. Similarities include the overall manner of responding – both Syrians and Americans are much more likely to either accept or mitigate the force of the compliment than to reject it outright. In addition, members of both groups use some similar response types (e.g. Agreeing Utterances, Compliment Returns, Deflecting or Qualifying Comments, and Reassurance or Repetition Requests). Finally, males and females in both groups employ most of the response types. An exception is Agreeing Utterances; Syrian females did not use this response. Students of English and Arabic can use these similarities between Arabic and English compliment responses to their advantage by learning the responses that are similar in both languages. As Kasper and Blum-Kulka (1993) point out, behaviors that are consistent across L1 and L2 usually result in communicative success. However, Hurley (1992) warns that the similarity of an L2 form to a form in the learner's L1 can also be a pragmalinguistic problem. The danger is that the L2 learner may overgeneralize the form to inappropriate settings.

Although the two groups share similarities in compliment responses, they also differ in important ways. In responding to compliments, US recipients are much more likely than Syrians to use Appreciation Tokens (e.g. thanks). The infrequency of this response in the Arabic data suggests that the utterance *Shukran* ('thank you') by itself is not usually a sufficient response to an Arabic compliment and needs to be supplemented by additional words. By itself, it may sound flat and awkward because it appears to signal the end of the conversation. As illustrated at the beginning of this article, American students of Arabic may respond to a compliment given by a native-speaker of Arabic by saying *Shukran*. If the intent of the American, drawing from his or her L1 strategies, is to respond in an appropriately polite manner and if the native Arabic speaker interprets the force of the utterance differently (e.g. that Speaker$_2$ wants to end the conversation), pragmalinguistic failure has occurred. To avoid this type of misunderstanding, it is important that Arabic as a second language students learn the more extended kinds of Arabic responses illustrated in this study.

ESL students are often taught that an appropriate response to most compliments in American English is 'thank you' (see Levine, Baxter, and McNulty 1987). Wolfson (1989b) points out, however, that the use of 'thank you' in English depends on the status and social distance of the interlocutors. Even though these social variables influence the use of 'thank you' in English, Wolfson (1989a) believes that 'thank you' remains an appropriate response for many compliment situations. ESL teachers of Arabic-speaking students can teach 'thank you' as an appropriate compliment response, but they should be aware that although 'thank you' appears to be a simple and easy response strategy to learn, such plain utterances may be difficult for Arabic speakers because they seem inadequate; they may not appropriately express what the speaker wants to convey.

Another major difference in compliment response strategies is the Syrians' frequent use of formulaic expressions in accepting a compliment; Americans do not use this type of response. One formulaic expression that is particularly troublesome to non-native Arabic speakers is *m'addam* ('[it is] presented [to you]'). For non-native Arabic speakers, the illocutionary force of the utterance is ambiguous; (does Speaker$_2$ want Speaker$_1$ to take the object or not?). However, for native Arabic speakers in most contexts, *m'addam* is a polite ritualistic expression, *not* a genuine offer of the object. In response to *m'addam* Speaker$_1$ needs to respond with an appropriate expression (e.g. *ʿala SaaHibtu aHlaa* ['It looks much nicer on its owner']). To achieve pragmatic competence in Arabic, American students of Arabic need to learn the specific formulas used in responding to compliments on particular attributes. Additional studies are needed to learn more of these formulaic expressions and more about the particular contexts in which they are used.

A final difference between American and Syrian compliment/compliment response sequences is length. A cursory glance at the English and Arabic data reveals that the Arabic sequences are much longer than the English; they contain more words and are more likely to continue beyond the initial compliment and corresponding response. This interaction between speakers relates to the sincerity of the compliment and the compliment response; the longer the interaction, the greater the sincerity. The length also relates to the value Arabic speakers place on eloquence. As Nydell (1987: 103) notes, 'the ability to speak eloquently is a sign of education and refinement' and 'how you say something is as important as what you have to say'. If Arabic-speaking ESL/EFL students, in an attempt to make compliment responses sound sincere to their own ears, use more words than a native English speaker, 'pragmatic failure might result from overindulgence in words', causing native speakers to sense a lack of appropriateness (Blum-Kulka and Olshtain

1986: 175). English-speaking students of Arabic, on the other hand, may have difficulty with the number of words in Arabic compliment/compliment response sequences, particularly with the formulaic expressions expected in response to certain compliments. If the length of the sequence results in their feeling phony and insincere, they may fall back on their L1 strategies. In this case, pragmatic failure may result not from too many words, but from too few.

(Revised version received October 1995)

Acknowledgements
Funding was made possible by an internal grant provided by the Research Office of Georgia State University. We would like to thank Andrew Cohen and the three anonymous reviewers for their helpful comments on this manuscript.

Notes
[1] The remaining 30 per cent were categorized as Comment History, Reassignment, Return, or Praise Upgrade.
[2] The M or F in front of the utterances refers to male and female speakers. The (A) or (S) following the interchange refers to American or Syrian.
[3] We also have the evil eye phenomenon in the US and Great Britain when we say 'Knock on wood' and 'Touch wood' to maintain good luck.
[4] The Syrian interlocutors frequently used religious expressions, whereas none of the Americans did so.

References
Barninnd, D. and S. Araki. 1985. 'Intercultural encounters: The management of compliments by Japanese and Americans.' *Journal of Cross-cultural Psychology* 16: 9–26.
Beebe, L. and T. Takahashi. 1989. 'Sociolinguistic variation in face-threatening speech acts' in M. R. Eisenstein (ed.) 1989: *The Dynamic Interlanguage Empirical Studies in Speech Variation*. New York: Plenum Press.
Beebe, L., T. Takahashi, and R. Uliss-Weltz. 1990. 'Pragmatic transfer in ESL refusals' in R. Scarcella, E. Andersen, and S. Krashen (eds.) 1990: *On the Development of Communicative Competence in a Second Language*. New York: Newbury House.
Blum-Kulka, S. 1982. 'Learning how to say what you mean in a second language: A study of speech act performance of learners of Hebrew as a second language.' *Applied Linguistics* 3: 29–59.
Blum-Kulka, S. 1983. 'Interpreting and performing speech acts in a second language. A cross-cultural study of Hebrew and English' in N. Wolfson and E. Judd (eds.) 1983: *Sociolinguistics and Language Acquisition*. Rowley, MA: Newbury House.
Blum-Kulka, S., J. House, and G. Kasper. 1989. 'Investigating cross-cultural pragmatics: An introductory overview' in S. Blum-Kulka, J. House and G. Kasper (eds.) 1989: *Cross-cultural Pragmatics: Requests and Apologies*. Norwood, NJ: Ablex.
Blum-Kulka, S. and E. Olshtain. 1986. 'Too many words: Length of utterance and pragmatic failure.' *Studies in Second Language Acquisition* 8: 165–79.
Canale, M. and M. Swain. 1980. 'Theoretical bases of communicative approaches to second language teaching and testing.' *Applied Linguistics* 1: 1–47.
Chen, R. 1993. 'Responding to compliments: A contrastive study of politeness strategies between American English and Chinese speakers.' *Journal of Pragmatics* 20: 49–75.
Edmonson, W., J. House, G. Kasper, and B. Stemmer. 1984. 'Learning the pragmatics of discourse.' *Applied Linguistics* 5: 113–25.

Eisenstein, M. and J. Bodman. 1986. 'I very appreciate: Expressions of gratitude by native and nonnative speakers of American English.' *Applied Linguistics* 7: 167–85.

Garcia, C. 1989. 'Apologizing in English: Politeness strategies used by native and nonnative speakers.' *Multilingua* 8: 3–20.

Habermas, J. 1970. 'Introductory remarks to a theory of communicative competence.' Inquiry 13: 3. Reprinted in H. P. Dreitzel (ed.) 1970: *Recent Sociology*. London: Macmillan.

Herbert, R. K. 1988. 'The ethnography of English compliments and compliment responses: A contrastive sketch' in W. Oleksy (ed.) 1988: *Contrastive Pragmatics*. Philadelphia: John Benjamins.

Herbert, R. K. and S. Straight. 1989. 'Compliment-rejection versus compliment-avoidance: Listener-based versus speaker-based pragmatic strategies.' *Language and Communication* 9: 35–47.

Holmes, J. 1988. 'Compliments and compliment responses in New Zealand English.' *Anthropological Linguistics* 28: 485–507.

Holmes, J. and D. F. Brown. 1987. 'Teachers and students learning about compliments.' *TESOL Quarterly* 21: 523–46.

Holsti, O. R. 1969. *Content Analysis for the Social Sciences and Humanities*. Reading, MA: Addison-Wesley.

Hurley, D. S. 1992. 'Issues in teaching pragmatics, prosody, and non-verbal communication.' *Applied Linguistics* 13: 259–81.

Hymes, D. 1971. 'Competence and performance in linguistic theory' in R. Huxley and E. Ingram (eds.) 1971: *Language Acquisition: Models and Methods*. London: Academic Press.

Hymes, D. 1972. 'On communicative competence' in J. B. Pride and J. Holmes (eds.) 1972: *Sociolinguistics*. Harmondsworth: Penguin.

Hymes, D. 1974. *Foundations in Sociolinguistics: An Ethnographic Approach*. Philadelphia: University of Pennsylvania Press.

Johnson, D. 1979. *Entertaining and Etiquette for Today*. Washington, DC: Acropolis Books.

Kasper, G. and S. Blum-Kulka. 1993. 'Interlanguage pragmatics: An introduction' in G. Kasper and S. Blum-Kulka (eds.) 1993: *Interlanguage Pragmatics*. New York: Oxford University Press.

Knapp, M. L., R. Hopper, and R. A. Bell. 1984. 'Compliments: A descriptive taxonomy.' *Journal of Communication* 34: 19–3 I.

Krippendorf, K. 1980. *Content Analysis: An Introduction to its Methodology*. Beverly Hills: Sage.

Leech, G. 1983. *Principles of Pragmatics*. London: Longman.

Levine, D. R., J. Baxter, and P. McNulty. 1987. *The Culture Puzzle*. Englewood Cliffs, NJ: Prentice Hall.

Maloney, C. 1976. *The Evil Eye*. New York: Columbia University Press.

Manes, J. 1983. 'Compliments: A mirror of cultural values' in N. Wolfson and E. Judd (eds.) *Sociolinguistics and Language Acquisition*. Rowley, MA: Newbury House.

Nelson, G. L., W. El Bakary, and M. Al-Batal. 1993. 'Egyptian and American compliments: A cross-cultural study.' *International Journal of Intercultural Relations* 17: 293–313.

Nydell, M. K. 1987. *Understanding Arabs: A Guide for Westerners*. Yarmouth, ME: Intercultural Press.

Olshtain, E. 1983. 'Sociocultural competence and language transfer: The case of apology' in S. Gass and L. Selinker (eds.) 1983: *Language Transfer in Language Learning*. Rowley, MA: Newbury House.

Olshtain, E. and A. Cohen. 1983. 'Apology: A speech act set' in N. Wolfson and E. Judd (eds.) 1983: *Sociolinguistics and Language Acquisition*. Rowley, MA: Newbury House.

Pomerantz, A. 1978. 'Compliment responses: Notes in the cooperation of multiple constraints' in J. Schenkein (ed.) 1978: *Studies in the Organization of Conversational Interaction*. New York: Academic Press.

Rose, K. R. 1994. 'On the validity of discourse completion tests in non-Western contexts.' *Applied Linguistics* 15: 1–14.

Schegloff, E. and H. Sacks. 1973. 'Opening up closings.' *Semiotica* 8: 289–327.

Shouby, E. 1951. 'The influence of the Arabic language on the psychology of the Arabs.' *Middle East Journal* 5: 284–302.

Takahashi, T. and L. M. Beebe. 1993. 'Cross-linguistic influence in the speech act of correction' in G. Kasper and S. Blum-Kulka (eds.) 1993: *Interlanguage Pragmatics*. New York: Oxford University Press.

Thomas, J. 1983. 'Cross-cultural pragmatic failure.' *Applied Linguistics* 4/2: 92–112.

Thomas, J. 1984. 'Cross-cultural discourse as "inequal encounter": Toward a pragmatic analysis.' *Applied Linguistics* 5: 226–35.

Wolfson, N. 1981. 'Compliments in cross-cultural perspective.' *TESOL Quarterly* 15: 117–24.

Wolfson, N. 1983. 'An empirically based analysis of compliments in American English' in N. Wolfson and E. Judd (eds.) 1983: *Sociolinguistics and Language Acquisition*. Rowley, MA: Newbury House.

Wolfson, N. 1989a. *Perspectives: Sociolinguistics and TESOL*. New York: Newbury House/Harper and Row.

Wolfson, N. 1989b. 'The social dynamics of native and nonnative variation in complimenting behavior' in M. R. Eistenstein (ed.) 1989: *The Dynamic Interlanguage: Empirical Studies in Speech Variation*. New York: Plenum Press.

Wolfson, N. and J. Manes. 1980. 'The compliment as social strategy. Papers in Linguistics.' *International Journal of Human Communications* 13: 391–410.

Activities

❏ Summarise the Tannen excerpt in one short paragraph and give your opinion vis-à-vis her stance. Choose one particular aspect from these pages that you would like to test. Design a small investigation project to test it. When you have the results, compare them to Tannen's opinion. If they are different, say why that may be.

❏ Describe the project that Nelson, Al-Batal and Echols carried out, saying briefly:

i   what their hypothesis/theory was

ii what method they used

iii what their results were

iv how they interpreted the results

Carry out a similar project to compare the compliment responses of two groups. You may not necessarily want to look at two different nationalities or cultures. You could investigate how people of different genders, classes and ages respond to compliments.

❏ This is a project on indirectness and cultural variables:

i   Choose one of the social factors involved in power and indirectness: status, role, age, gender, education, class, occupation and ethnicity.

ii Think of a theory or hypothesis that you would like to test. Express it as a comparison, for example 'When seeking help, women use more indirectness than men', 'When there is a difference in status, the one in power uses indirectness more than the one in a less powerful position', 'Indirectness is used by middle-class people to working-class people, not by working-class to middle-class.'

iii Check how important the contextual constraints (the size of the imposition and the formality of the situation) are, compared with the social factor (status, role, age, gender, education, class, occupation, ethnicity) that you chose.

iv Think of a way that your findings could be of use in society. Who might be interested in your results or helped by them and why?

v Write up your project; describe your method of data collection and analysis in a way that would allow someone else to reproduce your study.

❏ Take any other aspect of the politeness strategies or politeness maxims that interests you, and think of a social or cultural variable that might influence how it is expressed. Form a theory. Carry out a project to test your theory.

❏ Think about everything that we have been looking at in this book:

i Do you think that in pragmatics, conversation analysis, speech acts, cooperative principle and politeness principle share a common core? Explain in detail your answer with examples.

ii How does your answer to (i) here, relate to the context outside the text, and the context within the text?

REFERENCES

Auden, W. H. (1958) *A Selection by the Author*, Harmondsworth Middlesex: Penguin.

Austin, J. (1962) *How To Do Things With Words*, Oxford: Clarendon Press.

Barker, P. (1991) *Regeneration*, London: Penguin.

BASE, (2000) The 'British Academic Spoken English' corpus, developed at the Universities of Warwick and Reading, with funding from Universities of Warwick and Reading, BALEAP, EURALEX and the British Academy.

Bellinger, D. and Gleason, J. B. (1982) 'Sex differences in parental directives to young children', *Sex Roles* 8: 1123–39.

Belloc, H. (1896) *The Bad Child's Book of Beasts*, London: Duckworth.

Blakemore, D. (1992) *Understanding Utterances*, Oxford: Blackwell.

Brodine, R. (1983) 'Referential cohesion in learner compositions', *Papers on Work in Progress* 10: 13–20.

Brown, G. and Yule, G. (1983) *Discourse Analysis*, Cambridge: Cambridge University Press.

Brown, P. and Levinson, S. (1987) *Politeness*, Cambridge: Cambridge University Press.

Catterick, D (2001) 'Mapping and managing cultural beliefs about language learning among Chinese EAP Learners', University of Dundee, unpublished paper, BALEAP 2001.

Conley, J. M., O'Barr, W. M. and Lind, E. A. (1979) 'The power of language: presentational style in the courtroom', *Duke Law Journal* 1978: 1375–99.

Cook, G. (1989) *Discourse*, Oxford: Oxford University Press.

Coulthard, M. (1986) *An Introduction To Discourse Analysis*, London: Longman.

Coupland, J. (2000) *Small Talk*, Harlow: Pearson Education Limited.

Cruse, A. (2000) *Meaning in Language: An Introduction to Semantics and Pragmatics*, Oxford: Oxford University Press.

Cutting, J. (1998) 'Opening lines from the floor', *Language at Work* 13: 123–6, Clevedon: Multilingual Matters.

—— (1999) *Papers from Seminar of the British Association of Applied Linguistics*, 'The grammar of spoken English and its application to English for academic purposes', Sunderland: Sunderland University Press.

—— (2000) *Analysing the Language of Discourse Communities*, Oxford: Elsevier Science.

de Beaugrande, R. and Dressler, W. (1981) *Introduction To Text Linguistics*, London: Longman.

Eggins, S. and Slade, D. (1997) *Analysing Casual Conversation*, London: Cassell.

Elmore, L. (1989) *Hombre*, London: Chivers Press.

Fairclough, N. (1989) *Language and Power*, Harlow: Longman.

Fillmore, C. (1976) 'The need for a frame semantics in linguistics', in *Statistical Methods in Linguistics*, Stockholm: Skriptor.

Garfinkel, H. (1967) *Studies in Ethnomethodology*, Engelwood Cliffs, NJ: Prentice Hall.

—— (1967) *Studies In Ethnomethodology*, Englewood Cliffs, NJ: Prentice Hall.

Goffman, E. (1981) *Forms of Talk*, Philadelphia: University of Pennsylvania Press.

Golding, W. (1954) *Lord of the Flies*, London: Faber and Faber.

Greene, G. (1978) *The Human Factor*, London: Penguin.

Grice, H. P. (1957) 'Meaning', *Philosophical Review* 66: 377–88.

—— (1975) 'Logic and Conversation', in P. Cole and J. Morgan (eds) *Pragmatics (Syntax and Semantics)* vol. 9, New York: Academic Press.

Grundy, P. (2000) *Doing Pragmatics*, London: Edward Arnold.

Gumperz, J. J. (1982) *Discourse Strategies*, Cambridge: Cambridge University Press.

Halliday, M. A. K. and Hasan, R. (1976) *Cohesion In English*, London: Longman.

— (1989) *Language, Context, And Text: Aspects Of Language In A Social-semiotic Perspective*, Oxford: Oxford University Press.

Hatch, E. (1992) *Discourse And Language Education*, Cambridge: Cambridge University Press.

Heller, J. (1962) *Catch 22*, London: Corgi.

Helm, J. (1967) *Essays on the Verbal and Visual Arts*, New York: Pergamon Press.

Hoey, M. (1991) *Patterns of Lexis in Text*, Oxford: Oxford University Press.

Holmes, J. (1992) *An Introduction to Sociolinguistics*, London: Longman.

—— (2000) 'Doing collegiality and keeping control at work: small talk in government departments', in J. Coupland (ed.) *Small Talk*, Harlow: Pearson Education Limited.

ICE-GB (1998) *International Corpus of English, Survey of English Usage*, London: University College London.

Keenan, E. (1974) 'Norm-makers, norm-breakers: uses of speech by men and women in Malagasy community', in R. Bauman and J. Sherzer (eds) *Explorations in the Ethnography of Speaking*, Cambridge: Cambridge University Press.

Kelly, T., Nesi, H. and Revell, R. (2000) *EASE Volume One: Listening to Lectures*, CELTE, Warwick: University of Warwick.

Kreckel, M. (1981) *Communicative Acts and Shared Knowledge in Natural Discourse*, London: Academic Press.

Labov, W. and Waletsky, J. (1967) 'Narrative analysis: oral versions of personal experience', in J. Helm (ed.) *Essays on the Verbal and Visual Arts*, New York: Pergamon Press.

Lakoff, R. (1975) *Language and Woman's Place*, New York: Harper and Row.

Larsen, S. (1983) 'Text processing and knowledge updating in memory for radio news', *Discourse Processes* 6: 21–38.

Lawrence, D. H. (1981) *Short Stories*, London: J. M. Dent and Sons Ltd.

Lederer, R. (1987) *More Anguished English*, London: Robson Books.

Leech, G. (1983) *Principles of Pragmatics*, Harlow: Longman.

Levinson, S. C. (1983) *Pragmatics*, Cambridge: Cambridge University Press.

Macaulay, R. (1967) *Crewe Train*, London: Collins.

McCarthy, M. and Carter, R. (1994) *Language as Discourse: Perspectives for Language Teaching*, London: Longman.

Mey, J. (1994) *Pragmatics: An Introduction*, Oxford: Blackwell.

Milne, A. A. (1994) *Winnie the Pooh. The Complete Collection of Stories*, London: Methuen Children's Books.

Mountain, J. (1987) 'An investigation of some textual properties of discursive compositions written by native speakers and L2 (Italian) advanced learners', unpublished MA project, University of Birmingham.

Nelson, G. L., Al-Batal, M. and Echols, E. (1996) 'Arabic and English compliment responses: potential for pragmatic failure', *Applied Linguistics* 18/3: 411–33.

Ochs, E., Schegloff, E. A. and Thompson, S. A. (1996) *Interaction and Grammar*, Cambridge: Cambridge University Press.

Paretsky, S. (1995) *A Taste of Life*, London: Penguin.

Rankin, I (1992) *Tooth and Nail*, London: Orion Books Ltd.

Rees, N. (1999) *The Cassell Dictionary of Anecdotes*, London: Cassell.

Reynolds, M. (1963) *Little Boxes*, New York: Schroder Music Co.

Rosten, L. (2000) *The Education of Hyman Kaplan*, London: Prion Books Limited.

Sacks, H. (1986) 'Some considerations of a story told in ordinary conversation', unpublished manuscript.

—— (1992a) *Lectures on Conversation*, vol. 1, Cambridge, MA: Blackwell.

—— (1992b) *Lectures on Conversation*, vol. 2, Cambridge, MA: Blackwell.

Sacks, H., Schegloff, E. A. and Jefferson, G. (1974) 'A simplest systematics for the organization of turn-taking for conversations', *Language* 50: 696–735.

Sawyer, (1992) *BB King*, London: Quartet Books Ltd.

Schiffrin, D. (1994) *Approaches To Discourse*, Oxford: Blackwell Publishers.

Searle, J. R. (1969) *Speech* Acts, Cambridge: Cambridge University Press.

Sherrin, N. (1995) *The Oxford Dictionary of Humorous Quotations*, Oxford: Oxford University Press.

Sinclair, J. McH. and Coulthard, R. M. (1975) *Towards an Analysis of Discourse*, Oxford: Oxford University Press.

Skuja, R. (1983) 'An analysis of the organisation features of argumentative compositions written by teachers and pupils in Singapore', unpublished MA project, University of Birmingham.

Smith, B. R. and Leinonen, E. (1992) *Clinical Pragmatics*, London: Chapman and Hall.

Sperber, D. and Wilson, D. (1982) 'Mutual knowledge and relevance theories of comprehension', in N. Smith (ed.) *Mutual Knowledge*, London: Academic Press.

—— (1987) 'Precis of Relevance', *Behavioural Sciences and Brain Sciences* 10: 697–754.

—— (1990) *Relevance*, Oxford: Basil Blackwell.

—— (1995) *Relevance*, Oxford: Blackwell.

Stenström, A. B. (1994) *An Introduction to Spoken Interaction*, London: Longman.

Stilwell Peccei, J. (1999) *Pragmatics*, London: Routledge.

Stotsky, S. (1983) 'Types of lexical cohesion in expository writing: implications for developing the vocabulary of academic discourse', *College Composition and Communication* 34/4: 430–46.

Stubbs, M. (1983) *Discourse Analysis*, Oxford: Basil Blackwell.

Swales, J. (1990) *Genre Analysis*, Cambridge: Cambridge University Press.

Tannen, D. (1981) 'Indirectness in discourse: ethnicity as conversational style', *Discourse Processes* 4 (3): 221–38.

—— (1984) *Conversational Style: Analyzing Talk Among Friends*, Norwood, NJ: Ablex Publishing Corporation.

—— (1986) *That's not What I Meant!: How Conversational Style Makes or Breaks Your Relations With Others*, New York: William Morrow.

—— (1994) *Gender and Discourse*, Oxford: Oxford University Press.

Thomas, J. (1995) *Meaning in Interaction*, London: Longman.

Thurber, J. (1963) *Vintage Thunder*, London: Hamish Hamilton.

Trask, R. L. (1999) *Key Concepts in Language and Linguistics*, London: Routledge.

Updike, J. (1970) *Bech: A Book*, Middlesex: Penguin Books.

van Dyk, T. A. (1993) *Elite Discourse and Racism*, London: Sage.

Verschueren, J. (1999) *Understanding Pragmatics*, London: Arnold.

Wardhaugh, R. (1985) *How Conversation Works*, Oxford: Basil Blackwell.

Warren, C. (1953) *ABC des Reporters. Einführung in den praktischen Journalismus*, München: Fink.

Williams, E. (1973) *George: An Early Autobiography*, London: Hamish Hamilton.

Wilson, D. and Murie, A. (1995) *Factors Affecting the Housing Satisfaction of Older People*, Birmingham: University of Birmingham.

Wodak, R. (1996) *Disorders of Discourse*, London: Longman.

Wodak, R. and Lutz, B. (1986) 'Ein Amerikaner in China. Nachrichten als Fortsetzungsroman', *Medien Journal* 4: 202–7.

Woolf, V. (1978) *Between the Acts*, London: Grafton.

Yule G. (1996) *Pragmatics*, Oxford: Oxford University Press.

GLOSSARIAL INDEX

Printed in the United Kingdom
by Lightning Source UK Ltd.
112351UKS00006B/1